AF871063

Aspen's Health Care Quality Review

AN ASPEN PUBLICATION®
Aspen Publishers, Inc.
Gaithersburg, Maryland
1999

Copyright ©1999 by Aspen Publishers, Inc.
Jane Garwood, Publisher
Jane Lowers, Editor
All rights reserved. No part of this book may be reproduced or used in any form without permission in writing from the publisher.

Printed in the United States of America
ISBN 0-8342-1607-8

Table of Contents

Introduction

Health care quality spans every segment of the industry, from cornerstone mission statements to the smallest change in a patient handbook. As quality directors strive to turn theory into practice, this book brings you both the research of industry leaders and the field-tested projects of front-line QI staff at hospitals and health systems.

We hope this book will challenge you – to consider the role of reengineering in your organization today, as outlined by health care consultant Russ Coile (page 9), or to consider what your hospital could be like with a patient- centered model of care used by Griffin Hospital, Bergan Mercy Hospital and others (page 61). We also hope it will stimulate you to try new ideas – consider adding health status assessment such as the SF-36 to primary care practice (page 123), or reduce confusion by using "visual controls," consultant Duke Rohe's time-saving tips for helping staff remember to how to use equipment, track patients and help patients find the right hospital locations (page 139).

Wherever possible, this book contains additional resources: contact information for sources quoted in the articles or bibliographies of references to help you pursue your QI project in greater depth.

Want to know more? These articles are drawn from nearly a dozen newsletters and journals produced by Aspen Publishers, Inc. In the back of this book you'll find descriptions of each of these publications and subscription information. You can also learn more about all of our products on the Web at www.aspenpublishers.com.

Aspen Publishers, Inc. is dedicated to providing the information resources you need to improve and strengthen patient care. Our editorial and research teams look forward to helping you make health care quality a greater part of your organization's culture.

Jane Lowers
Managing Editor
Healthcare Publications
January 1999

Part I
Organizational Quality

The Second Wave of Health Care Re-Engineering: New Focus on Processes and Growth

Hospitals, health systems, health maintenance organizations (HMOs) and large medical groups systematically have applied re-engineering to a variety of clinical and administrative functions. Many organizations have realized significant cost savings, but have experienced a backlash of unanticipated "human costs" to morale, leadership and innovation.

At the core of the criticism is the charge that re-engineering has become just another management fad like "zero-based budgeting" or "intrapreneurship," and has not produced lasting change.

Promoters of re-engineering argue that problems experienced in implementation are only part of the learning curve, and that in many cases, re-engineering was not allowed to go far enough to make fundamental changes in the processes and culture of the organization.

Today, re-engineering is being refocused on growth strategies, such as growing market share, developing new products and improving customer satisfaction and repeat business.

Hospitals and health systems are now using re-engineering of clinical pathways to grow services in ambulatory care, home health and the continuum of care (Greene, 1996).

From Panacea to Paranoia

At the start of the 1990s, excitement ran high among hospitals and health systems regarding the potential for re-engineering to slash labor costs, shorten length of stay and reduce support costs. The private sector experience had been very positive. Some companies had achieved 20% to 35% cost reductions and 40% to 50% improvement in process time.

Michael Hammer's 1990 management best seller, *Reengineering the Corporation*, was a primer for a business revolution. The targets for process re-engineering were bloated bureaucracies of under-worked middle managers and high-paid vice presidents while labor toiled away using tools and systems that often harkened back to Henry Ford's production lines of the 1920s.

Health care, with labor costs historically consuming more than 50% of the expense budget, was a prime target for re-engineering. By 1995, some 56% of hospitals nationwide reported having implemented at least five cost reductions in the prior two years (Bebiak, 1995).

Most hospitals implemented job restructuring/work redesign, clinical pathways, non-clinical expense reductions and layoffs. But, the overall

From *Russ Coile's Health Trends*, Vol 9:8, 1997

results were disappointing. Most hospitals achieved less than a 4% reduction in their costs to show for all the re-engineering efforts.

Employing a broader combination of work redesign and clinical pathways yielded somewhat better results, but still less than restructuring. Worse yet, health care executives worried that re-engineering could lead to reductions in quality.

Re-engineering is a much more comprehensive approach than downsizing. It involves a fundamental reassessment of every major production and support process in the organization, and often generates radical prescriptions for change.

Re-engineering Reconsidered: The Second Wave

Today, re-engineering is being reintroduced in a "second wave" of health care projects, but this time the goals are capitation readiness, integrated care delivery and business growth. Managed care and the assumption of risk are the driving forces compelling health care organizations to build regional care networks that can manage the comprehensive health needs of large enrolled populations.

In order to survive and grow, integrated delivery systems must:

- structure a single enterprise with a clear strategic vision;
- involve a broad range of stakeholders in redesign and re-engineering;
- reconfigure the service continuum to match a population-based model;
- significantly reduce costs by re-engineering patient care and business processes;

EXHIBIT 1: STRATEGIC APPROACH TO RE-ENGINEERING PROCESSES

Assessment	Strategy	Design	Implementation	Evaluation
Clinical program and service inventory	Opportunities for improvement	Redesign clinical pathways	Implementation program rollout	Set benchmarks
Patient care/support program analysis	Priority matrix	Re-engineer processes	Implementation work teams	Performance measurement
Clinical services utilization review	Resource allocation to re-engineering effort	Options for substitution	Pilot projects	Feedback to teams
Information technology	Information systems plan	Redesign info	Install info system	Quantitative results
Management structure	Management audit	Restructuring	Organizational rollout	Reward/incentives

Source: Steven Gray, 1996, p. 3.

- redeploy capital, technical and human resources on a regional-market basis;
- achieve clinical integration and reduce clinical utilization where appropriate; and
- win commitment to the new patterns and processes from managers and caregivers.

When performed properly, re-engineering health care organizations can achieve results to shout about. In Birmingham, Ala., the Brookwood Medical Center has reduced its costs by $9 million in a six-year period (Herman, 1995). In the process, Brookwood brought together almost 100 work groups involving 700 employees and 100 members of the medical staff.

From the beginning, Brookwood CEO Gregory Burfitt built confidence from employees and managers by guaranteeing no layoffs. With strong management support, a wide number of re-engineering solutions were adopted. More than a third of the hospital's 2,400-person workforce – some 873 people – changed their jobs as a result of re-engineering.

RE-ENGINEERING FAILS WHEN PROJECTS:

- are too narrowly focused;
- lack a long-term perspective;
- suffer inadequate commitment or shifting priorities from top management;
- are subject to psychological and political disruptions; and
- fail to make extraordinary efforts to achieve potential gains.

Flawed Concept or Execution?

One ticket to disaster is a meeting in which the CEO calls together senior and middle managers and says:

"We are gathered here today to talk about reducing the budget of every department in this institution by 25%. I have no plan to present to you, no Ross Perot-style flip charts explaining what this means. That's because the plan hasn't been developed yet. You're the people who will do it." (Lumsdon, 1994)

Re-engineering fails when projects:

- are too narrowly focused;
- lack a long-term perspective;
- suffer inadequate commitment or shifting priorities from top management;
- are subject to psychological and political disruptions; and
- fail to make extraordinary efforts to achieve potential gains.

Re-engineering advocate Hammer believes that the key is process, a perspective that turns an organization "sideways" to look at the core functions that are performed everywhere across the enterprise.

A process perspective is holistic, as opposed to modern management's emphasis on tasks. This distinction between "part" and "whole" is fundamental to understanding how re-engineering should work and why it has failed when managers focused on familiar tasks instead of harder-to-understand core processes.

TEN STRATEGIES TO 'RE-ENGINEER RE-ENGINEERING"

It is clear that downsizing, which is often accompanied by restructuring and business process reengineering, can, if not properly managed, lead to little process improvement and unintended but all too common declines in organizational performance.

—**Seth Allcorn**
The Human Cost of a Management Failure
(Allcorn et al., 1996)

No pain, no gain, has been the slogan of many re-engineering programs. With almost 10 years of experience in the private sector and health care industry, there have been enough experiments in re-engineering to know what works, and the likely problems that must be overcome. To launch a new wave of re-engineering programs, it will be necessary to drastically change the processes and goals.

In one example, the Middlesex Hospital, Conn., set a stretch goal of 25% cost reductions and achieved 15% in the first year — a savings of more than $10 million. Defending his stretch goal, Middlesex CEO Robert Kiely says: "How many times can you freeze wages, leave positions unfilled or make draconian cuts?" (Lumsdon, 1994, p. 26).

Here are a set of 10 important strategies for improving the scope, depth and impact of re-engineering health care processes.

Strategy #1: Vision-driven

There must be a call to mission and vision — a set of higher purposes and priorities — to motivate managers and employees to undertake re-engineering. If the goal is simply to improve the bottom line, only those senior managers whose bonuses are tied to profitability are likely to enthusiastically embrace re-engineering. Goals like quality, reinvestment in new facilities or equipment, patient-centered care, and expanding community services can be compelling arguments for making re-engineering work.

Strategy #2: "Stretch" Goals

Setting high goals for re-engineering will have a galvanizing, empowering impact on the organization. Michael Hammer cautions that "being timid in redesign" is one of the easiest ways to shortchange re-engineering's potential (Hammer, 1995, p. 24). Setting stretch goals — also known as "big, hairy, audacious goals" — creates a climate for clean-slate innovative solutions in an uncritical idea-generating process.

Strategy #3: Clinical and Cost Focus

It is imperative that clinicians and financial managers cooperate in planning and implementing re-engineering projects (Meyer & Feingold, 1995). If the projects are to be evaluated comprehensively, developing clinical paths must include "costing" the resources. Many clinical pathways lack sufficient detail to complete a thorough financial analysis. Costs must be addressed explicitly, not implicitly, as is often done.

Strategy #4: Strategic Plan

In the face of many possible re-engineering targets, many hospitals have been tempted to "let a thousand flowers bloom," as the Chinese saying goes. This misses the opportunity to align re-engineering with organizational strategies, financial priorities and critical changes in the market. Strategic plans for re-engineering lay out the objectives, methods, implementation steps, staff responsibilities and benchmark indicators for evaluation.

One mid-Atlantic hospital, Jersey Shore Medical Center, developed 60 redesign plans that covered the hospital's many departments, satellite operations, and teaching activities, and reached a 14% cost reduction on the way toward a stretch goal of 25% (Lumsdon, 1995).

Strategy #5: Benchmarking

Re-engineering in the health field is more complex than simply making comparisons with other service industries. Because approximately 75% to 85% of all in-hospital costs are related to patient care, the focus should be on clinical re-engineering.

Thousands of clinical pathways have been developed in the past 10 years across America's hospitals and leading health systems, and a growing body of outcomes research now is available concerning the impact of clinical improvement programs. To assist this analysis, benchmarks of clinical performance can be identified from competitive markets and "best-of-breed" organizations.

Strategy #6: Information Technology

No one will ever know if re-engineering works without detailed performance assessment. Substantial investments in information technology are needed before many hospitals and health systems can calculate whether re-engineering is meeting their goals.

The most difficult aspect of measuring re-engineering's impact will be to link clinical events with cost data. The process used to develop clinical pathways must develop a financial model — a charge/cost model — that captures and integrates the data for performance analysis (Meyer & Feingold, 1995, p. 36).

TEN STRATEGIES TO 'RE-ENGINEER RE-ENGINEERING" (Cont.)

Strategy #7: Trust

In order for re-engineering to gain acceptance and whole-hearted cooperation, there must be trust between management and the rank-and-file. This means no surprises, candid communication and an "open book" policy regarding results (Bebiak, 1995, p. 9).

Strategy #8: No layoffs

Assuming trust to be a critical success factor, then a strong no-layoffs human resources policy must be clear from the outset of the re-engineering program. This dramatically reduces paranoia and resistance, and shifts the incentive structure to reward process innovation. With a management guarantee of retraining and alternative employment for any displaced workers, middle management and frontline employees can apply themselves freely to radical redesign concepts.

Strategy #9: Incentives

To achieve and sustain performance improvement, it is essential to support the change initiatives with "new pay" programs that are aligned with the business strategies and work process improvements. A national compensation survey by the Hay Co. found that a third of hospitals are restructuring their pay systems to incentivize performance and teamwork (Farrell & Pagoaga, 1995).

Incentives can include merit pay, non-cash recognition, spot-cash awards, and predetermined incentives. Although merit pay programs still cover some 60% of hospitals, more than 40% of health care institutions were rewarding workers and managers with recognition and bonuses.

Strategy #10: Shared Values

Re-engineering is a process of consensus-building around new organizational goals and the best methods to achieve them. All key stakeholders — board, medical staff, administration and employees — must recognize the need for change. ■

Frontline workers often were given new, broader responsibilities, but little training and no change in authority. Re-engineering threw out the old organization chart, but no one was in charge of implementation — it was not part of anyone's job description, and it was seldom rewarded by the organization's compensation system.

One-shot improvements, even if dramatic, are of little lasting value (Hammer, 1996). A number of hospitals and health systems that set performance benchmarks and downsized to meet them then ran into a wall when asked to meet next year's benchmarks. They had used their best ideas in the first year and had little left to cut in the second year without seriously compromising quality or service.

These limited-scope applications of re-engineering demonstrate the need for re-engineering and benchmarking to focus not just on best indicators (Greeson & Lowenhaupt, 1996). A process-centered organization must continuously experiment to achieve ongoing performance improvement, not once a year, but seeking and rewarding innovation on an everyday basis.

Hammer says the single most important part of re-engineering is the customer. The customer does not see or care about the company's organization chart or policy manual. To the customer, the company is defined by the way in which it delivers services or products to the customer.

Health care organizations that design their core processes around the customer may take many nontraditional approaches to patient services such as scheduling, admitting, food service, surgery or nursing care.

Re-engineering the Corporate Culture

Corporate culture — "the way things are done around here" — may be the most difficult barrier to successful re-engineering. Workers and managers must change the way in which they think and behave.

A new process needs "new people" who think and behave in new ways. Resistance can be expected. Workers feel threatened. So do managers, who fear loss of authority and responsibility. In too many organizations, "re-engineering" is a code word for downsizing and layoffs.

Top management has the ability to change the corporate culture, with sustained support and incentives to reinforce the new direction. But lack of management commitment can be fatal to re-engineering's acceptance by the organization.

Re-engineering work processes cannot ultimately succeed unless the core values and vision are also reengineered. Many health care organizations have followed the practice of summarizing their corporate values on small plastic-coated pocket cards. By themselves, however, the cards cannot really effect new attitudes or behavior. Changing the corporate culture requires actions such as:

- putting top priority on the desired changes;
- communicating new values in a fresh, distinctive way;
- reconstructing the budget to support new processes;
- providing high-visibility monitoring of performance;
- creating a new performance reward system that is aligned with the re-engineering goals;
- making top managers "walk the talk" in personal dedicated commitment;
- continuously improving the process and never being satisfied with performance; and
- sustaining long-term commitment to the new behaviors and processes.

This Noisy Process Is Far From Over

Re-engineering health care has been a noisy process that often has pitted nurses and physician caregivers against managers and financial officers. At issue are fundamental priorities. Should the organization put patients first, and spend whatever it takes to meet their needs? Or should the organization recognize the realities of managed care controls and government discounts and cut costs to the bone? These extreme positions often have framed the debate over the suitability of re-engineering to improve the efficiency of health care services.

Love it or hate it, there is no question that re-engineering is necessary. Everyone needs to understand that today's health care organization is a "burning platform" whose structural costs are being systematically reduced by government health care cuts, managed care and capitation (Greeson & Lowenhaupt, 1996, p. 10).

REFERENCES

Allcorn, S. et al. (1996). "The human cost of a management failure: Organizational downsizing at General Hospital. Westport, Conn.: Quorum Books.

Bebiak, J. (1995). "Process design and discipline are critical to cost-reduction success." *Strategies for Healthcare Excellence*, 8 (7), pp. 8-11.

Dentzer, S. (1996, March 11). "The fallout from dumping workers." *U.S. News & World Report*, p. 58.

Gray, S. (1996). Reengineering for integrated delivery systems, Ann Arbor, Mich: Chi Systems, Inc., pp. 1-6.

Greene, J. (1996). "Retooling without layoffs." *Modern Healthcare*, 26(9), pp. 76-82.

Greeson, D., & Lowenhaupt, M. (1996). "A benchmark strategy." *Physician Executive*, 22(10), pp. 10-15.

Hall, G., Rosenthal, J., Wade, J. (1993, November/December). "How to make reengineering really work." *Harvard Business Review*, pp. 119-131.

Hammer, M. (1990). *Reengineering the corporation*, New York: HarperBusiness.

Hammer, M. (1995) *The reengineering revolution.* New York: HarperBusiness.

The concept of re-engineering is sound, and its application is needed in health care. But, how can health care organizations avoid the mistakes of the past and use the tools of re-engineering to build sustainable organizations?

Here are some preliminary answers and new directions:

- **Reduce variation:** Physicians and nurses have argued that patient care must be customized to every patient. But, re-engineering is demonstrating that yes, it can "mass" customize by using clinical pathways and standardized care plans. A reduction of 10% in variation of length of stay, for example, may yield cost savings of 20% to 25% by eliminating costly outliers.
- **Benchmark with the best-of-breed:** Prepare for a managed care world by using indicators from advanced markets and successful health care organizations. Benchmark standards are now available from consulting firms, actuaries, professional associations, and group purchasing organizations such as VHA and Premier.
- **Innovate continuously**: The road to organizational improvement begins with creating a "comfort zone" for experimentation. Senior management must encourage innovations in service delivery and support processes. A truly innovative organization supports a culture of risk-taking, industry-setting practices and testing new models.
- **Use incentives:** To change behavior, performance rewards must be substantial and symbolic. To achieve real changes in behavior, incentives must equal at least 15% of compensation. Rewards can be symbolic (non-cash) as well as financial, sending a message that the organization appreciates its "pioneers" and "early adopters."
- **Leave money on the table:** Too often, change in health care organizations is delayed while management waits for the market to shift. That is not the way to become an industry or market leader. Many hospitals and health systems are beginning to organize for capitation, but hesitate to treat every patient as if he or she was capitated.

Once a market reaches 15% HMO penetration, the future is clear, and when it reaches 25% penetration, the war is over. Starting now may mean "leaving money on the table," but the organization will be fully prepared for capitation and the new market when it arrives. Don't wait for the future. It's here.

Steven Gray is president of Chi Systems, Inc., a national health care consulting firm based in Ann Arbor, Mich. Chi Systems has worked with 25 health care clients in re-engineering projects on a national basis.

REFERENCES, cont.

Hammer, M. (1996). *Beyond reengineering: How the process-centered organization is changing our work and our lives.* New York: HarperBusiness.

Herman, J. (1995). "Restructuring the health care delivery system," Health Systems Review, 28(2), pp. 18-29.

Lumsdon, K. (1994). "Want to save millions?" Hospitals & Health Networks, 68(21), pp. 24-32.

Moskal, B. S. (1996, February 16). "Reengineering without downsizing." Business Week, pp. 23-24, 28.

Effect of System Restructuring on Quality Leadership

When John King became chief executive officer of Legacy Health System in 1991, he was dedicated to using quality as a transformational strategy. But he and Legacy faced challenges that confront leaders of many health systems today. Legacy planned to restructure itself from a multihospital base to a fully integrated delivery system managing covered lives. Quality efforts, however, focused on acute care at the system's five hospitals in the Portland area. Improvement approaches differed among the hospitals, and continuous quality improvement was perceived as each hospital's responsibility, not an embedded part of the system's culture. Separate boards and managers oversaw CQI and quality assurance at each facility, but no one looked much at quality across the continuum of care.

Seven years later, as King prepares to depart, quality is a cornerstone of Legacy's system-building strategy. At the leadership level, a system board approves quality priorities and monitors key aspects of systemwide performance, while a core executive team coordinates systemwide improvement initiatives.

Legacy Health System Acts as a System From the Outset

Legacy Health System, formed in 1989, now includes two suburban hospitals; two tertiary care hospitals in downtown Portland, Ore., merged from two separate hospitals; a large home care company; four primary care clinics and several smaller entities responsible for such services as intermediate care, occupational medicine and skilled nursing care. It also owns a 75% interest in Managed Healthcare Northwest, which offers several managed care plans, and is a 50% owner of Caremark Behavioral Health Services. Legacy has a long-term partnership with Regence Blue Cross Blue Shield of Oregon, and with Legacy physician groups has formed the Northwest Physicians Alliance.

Before Mr. King agreed to serve as CEO, he explicitly asked senior management and the Legacy governing board to commit to a unified, systemwide approach to CQI, and this approach has been a hallmark of his leadership style. "We didn't pilot our CQI effort unit by unit; our approach was to 'hold hands and go out the gate together,'" says Rhoda L. Ryba, formerly vice president of quality improvement and organizational development at Legacy, and today senior associate at Breakthrough Learning Inc. "Mr. King said we needed a common language to unite these diverse entities that used to be competitors."

In Legacy's system-building strategy, the system board sets broad quality priorities and receives reports on a systemwide dashboard of indicators, system process improvement reengineering efforts, highlights of operating unit quality issues, system accreditation status and annual CQI assessment

From *The Quality Letter for Healthcare Leaders*, Vol 8:5, 1996

results. Since restructuring, the board has taken a much more active role in quality; reports and discussions on quality-related issues are included at every board meeting.

"The dashboard of indicators and systemwide process improvement are the most significant issues for the board," says Ms. Ryba. "The board actively promotes CQI culture and processes throughout the organization. Several board members are business leaders who use CQI in their own industries, and they know what it means, in terms of resource allocation, for a corporation to take on a major, systemwide reengineering effort."

After the merger, Legacy launched a systemwide CQI effort and selected one corporate leader for CQI and quality issues. While each operating unit still has a quality director, a systemwide council now puts together a yearly strategic plan for quality and manages the organizational infrastructure for quality. "We shifted to this system five years ago, and it dramatically changed how quality was managed throughout the organization," Ms. Ryba said in 1996. The presidents of the operating units serve together on the system quality board, and yearly quality plans are based on a systemwide dashboard of indicators. The performance of top executives of each unit is judged primarily on the basis of systemwide performance, so they have no incentive to maximize their unit's performance at the expense of other parts of the system.

Legacy's corporate QI department currently consists of three system QI directors and a manager responsible for clinical outcomes measurement. Organizational development (and CQI training) is centralized, with a director and five full-time employees. "We use the same improvement tools and techniques for medical quality initiatives and studies that we do for redesigning administrative processes."

BEST-PRACTICE STRATEGIES FOR RESTRUCTURING QUALITY LEADERSHIP

At the Board Level

- ✓ Include quality in the system board's responsibilities.
- ✓ Form a quality committee of the system board and/or include quality as a regular system board agenda item.
- ✓ Develop systemwide measures of quality across the continuum of care.
- ✓ Focus on the continuum of care, including disease management, home care, rehabilitation and ambulatory/physicians' offices, not just acute care.
- ✓ Focus on the improvement of community and population health, not just the delivery of care.
- ✓ Discuss and approve systemwide quality policies, plans, and strategic priorities at the board level.
- ✓ Hold management accountable for achieving quality goals.

At the Management Level

- ✓ Adopt a single CQI approach and language.
- ✓ Name a senior executive to lead systemwide quality efforts.
- ✓ Form a systemwide quality council with strong clinical involvement to charter and support systemwide improvement initiatives.
- ✓ Use CQI principles and tools to redesign the care process and to assist in the cultural transformation to an integrated delivery system focused on maintaining and improving health.
- ✓ Keep corporate staff lean and focused on systemwide initiatives.
- ✓ Give individual facilities flexibility to implement quality initiatives locally.
- ✓ Develop clinical pathways, a case management program and similar projects designed to standardize care throughout the system based on best practices.

A number of Legacy's clinical programs, such as heart, oncology, laboratory, rehabilitation, pediatrics and women's services, are managed on an integrated systemwide basis, including all hospital sites and home care services.

The most important lesson Legacy has learned, Ms. Ryba says, is to act as a unified system from the very beginning. "In our system, people all speak the same language; from one hospital to the next, the quality functions and reports all use the same terms." One reason this is so important, she says, is that since many patients use several different parts of the system, variation in clinical processes would generate confusion among patients. Second, if quality methods were introduced one unit at a time, this might have tended to promote internal competition and a "silo mentality," working against system integration.

LEGACY HEALTH SYSTEM

1 tertiary care hospital, downtown Portland

2 suburban hospitals

1 home healthcare company

Providers of intermediate care, occupational medicine and skilled nursing

Allina Health System

Respect Past Organizational Cultures

Allina Health System, based in the upper Midwest, includes 19 hospitals (12 owned and seven managed), seven nursing homes, 65 clinics and 9,000 physicians and contracted providers; its health plan has 950,000 members. It was formed in 1994 with the merger of HealthSpan Health System, then the fifth largest not-for-profit secular healthcare system in the country, and Medica. The new system needed a new name. "We made up the word Allina because we're trying to align the interests of healthcare providers with the financing and purchasing of care," says Executive Officer Gordon Sprenger.

ALLINA HEALTH SYSTEM

19 hospitals
7 nursing homes
65 clinics
9,000 physicians and contracted providers
980,000 health plan members

The system board's first task was to develop a clear vision for the future. It set a strategic focus of using quality principles for decisionmaking, resource allocation and self-evaluation. The strategic plan identifies five key clinical areas — cardiovascular, cancer, pregnancy, diabetes and asthma — in which Allina will establish "best practice" standards throughout the entire system. At the time Allina was formed, the health plan used quality standards established by its medical directors; each hospital had its own, independent quality standards. "We brought all those together to create a single process, the clinical care model for establishing the best practice of care across the continuum," Mr. Sprenger says. "That may seem obvious, but it was a major event," he adds.

How can the governing board of such a large organization effectively manage and improve quality of care? The key, says Bryan Bushick, M.D., Allina's system vice president for performance measurement and improvement, is to use general indicators to report at the board level and more detailed, specific indicators on the same themes deeper within the organization. For example, the system board may use a single measure, such as the pediatric inpatient hospitalization rate, as a proxy for care of asthma patients. Each hospital, in turn, would track additional asthma-related measures, such as the number of patients treated in the emergency department for acute asthma attacks, while the health plan might monitor measures of primary care, such as the percentage of patients who have received peak flow meters and been trained to use them.

A newly formed healthcare system must focus on a systemwide approach to quality management, says Jan Ophoven, M.D., Allina's vice president for medical policy. Before the merger, the health plan had a complex infrastructure of advisory committees to deal with clinical quality and establish clinical guidelines, and the care delivery component had both a centralized quality council and a facility-specific infrastructure dealing with regulatory compliance and clinical quality. "The hospitals used a very different vocabulary from the health plan," Dr. Ophoven recalls.

Allina is now developing a clinical care model that will include all dimensions of care. "We are focusing on the entire continuum of care, starting with an at-risk population, looking at prevention, detection, risk assessment, early diagnosis and disease management, through to long-term care. We have created a vehicle for a mixed group of voices to come together and discuss strategic priorities, key requirements and outcomes," Dr. Ophoven says.

Unlike Legacy, Allina does not believe in having all parts of the system pursue the same initiative at the same time. "Various parts of this integrated organization are working on multiple strategies simultaneously. What we have developed is a strategy for provider communication and involvement and a linkage between managed care and the traditional care delivery model," Dr. Ophoven says.

The role of Allina's corporate quality department is to coordinate measurement, clinical quality and improvement and to "act as a catalyst to accelerate improvements and transfer knowledge," says Julianne Morath, Allina's system vice president for quality. The corporate quality function includes responsibility for identifying and analyzing improvement opportunities with the greatest leverage to create value. "We look at processes that run through the whole organization," she says.

"We started out with strong traditions and success in quality from different parts of the organization, and that became a barrier to our ability to learn from each other."

Julianne Morath
Allina Health System

For example, many Allina units have worked to improve internal processes for scheduling patient appointments, but that is not enough, Ms. Morath says. "We want our customers to be able to schedule an appointment anywhere within the system, from any access point. They should be able to schedule diagnostic tests, procedures or other services from their primary care site. When a patient is hospitalized, it should be easy to schedule home care or other required follow-up services and gain access to information."

Although it has a key role to play in coordinating quality management and improvement and ensuring that expert resources are available to operating units, the corporate quality function is tightly staffed. "We do not want a large central quality department because that creates the expectation that they are responsible for quality," Mr. Sprenger says. "Quality is not department or project focused. Quality is an intrinsic business strategy of Allina and a responsibility of all its members," states Ms. Morath.

What has Allina learned at this point in the process of system integration? "Honor predecessor cultures," Ms. Morath says. "For example, we started out with strong traditions and success in quality from different parts of the organization, and that became a barrier to our ability to learn from each other." In response, Allina brought together a group to identify "best practice" in this area. The group designed a change management tool kit using common methodologies and an agreed-upon eclectic approach. "This is an example of respecting previous organizational cultures but at the same time intentionally building a new one that will be effective systemwide," Ms. Morath says.

HealthSystem Minnesota

Focus on the Constants, but Don't Delay the Hard Stuff

While HealthSystem Minnesota does not include a health plan or insurance function, it does care for about 17% of greater Minneapolis' population. The system consists of Methodist Hospital, 500 physician employees in Park Nicollet Clinic and a 40-physician Primary Physician Network, as well as 30 clinical offices, a philanthropic foundation and a research and education institute. The hospital/medical group merger took effect in July 1993. After functioning for a year with two co-presidents, the system chose a single chief executive in July 1994.

Once the new chief executive was in place, one of the first challenges was to consolidate quality management and develop new management roles and reporting relationships. In 1991, when the two organizations first resolved to merge, they decided to develop an operational blueprint in five major areas, including quality. Senior leaders made a number of quality-related recommendations and defined a timeline, leadership responsibilities and indices of progress for each recommendation. Among the recommendations:

- Focus on root community needs;
- Use knowledge and experience in continuous improvement as one criterion in selecting new system board members;
- Establish a consistent format for reporting quality throughout the system;
- Develop specifications for best practices that integrate outpatient and inpatient aspects of treatment for a variety of high-cost, high-volume conditions;
- Learn and adopt a standard meeting process; and
- Strengthen internal collaboration within the system by changing performance evaluation methods to reduce competitive elements, visibly recognizing collaborative efforts and reporting total system financial data in run-chart or control-chart format.

The new operational plan created a system board quality committee, equal in stature to the finance committee. Quality personnel who served throughout the system were united into a coordinated department under the leadership of a system medical director. "The quality committee is the way the board performs quality oversight for the entire system, ranging from credentialing to quality assurance and quality improvement functions to utilization review," then-CEO James L. Reinertsen, M.D. said in 1996.

HEALTHSYSTEM MINNESOTA

1 acute care hospital

2 cancer treatment centers

30 clinical offices

1 philanthropic foundation

1 research and education unit

Reinertsen has since been replaced by David Wessner, M.D.

Community health is a top priority for the system board. It regularly reviews a panel of 16 dashboard indicators related to five areas — relationships with patients, care, service, internal joy and pride in professional work, and stewardship (financial performance).

Currently the board tracks member renewal rates, the satisfaction/delight index, time to obtain an appointment, time to answer phones, employee turnover rate, and a range of outcome measures including bypass survival rate, myocardial infarction survival rate, pediatric immunization rate and cesarean birth rate. The board monitors quality management throughout the system by tracking the number of fully implemented clinical guidelines and pathways performing at benchmark levels. To measure the vigor of clinical care improvement activities in the system, the board tracks "key process or system improvements" that have enhanced the quality of care.

"Change is dizzying, and people's nerves get frazzled. Remind them about the constants, the reasons we're here. The constants will be different in each organization, but find them and say, 'Look, we're still committed to this, and we're still doing it."

Dr. James L. Reinertsen
former CEO, HealthSystem Minnesota

Both Methodist Hospital and Park Nicollet Clinic had a strong tradition in quality improvement and training development activities. "When you have two strong traditions, there often is some disruption in bringing them together," Dr. Reinertsen observes. The two organizations used to have two dozen people at the level of vice president or above; the merged system has half that number. "When people worry about whether they still have a job, it inevitably deflects their attention from the task at hand," Dr. Reinertsen notes.

The most important lesson Dr. Reinertsen has learned is to keep staff focused on systemwide issues during the transitional period. "Don't delay the hard stuff," he says.

"It's also very important for the organization to communicate during this period about what hasn't changed," he says. "Change is dizzying, and people's nerves get frazzled. Remind them about the constants, the reasons we're here. The constants will be different in each organization, but find them and say, 'Look, we're still committed to this, and we're still doing it.'"

"By the way," Dr. Reinertsen adds, "during this transitional period we continued to improve quality. Our myocardial infarction survival rates went from 92% to 98%, for example. We haven't lost momentum. You have to keep people's eyes on the ball throughout this period — and that's not easy. It's like telling an orchestra, 'There's a war going on, but you still need to play good music.'"

Fairview Hospital and Healthcare Services

Restructure to Facilitate Quality Improvement

Fairview Hospital and Healthcare Services consists of seven hospitals, 180 primary care physicians in 27 clinics, home care, and four long-term care facilities through an affiliation with the Ebenezer Society, a group serving the needs of the elderly. The organization recently merged two hospitals in northwest Minneapolis, creating one technologically modern facility, and it is planning a similar merger of three hospitals northeast of the city.

Fairview has developed a hybrid system of governance and quality leadership, with both systemwide and division-level quality initiatives. Its quality improvement program includes more than 200 quality improvement teams in progress at any one time. Many of the teams are institutionally based, with oversight delegated to the division board and outcomes reviewed by the system board.

The system board establishes a number of systemwide quality priorities each year, and divisions are asked to respond to those priorities in their operational planning. For example, the board has made wait times a systemwide priority. However, teams will address wait times in home care different from teams addressing wait times in clinics or hospital radiology departments. "The divisions are dealing with fundamentally different processes, and the solutions are going to be different," says Chief Executive Officer Richard Norling.

At the same time, Fairview is using "functional integration teams" to improve systemwide processes in nine key functional areas: nursing/Medicus Patient Classification System, medical records, imaging, medication, laboratory, rehabilitation, nutrition services, behavioral services and occupancy services. These teams report to the system chief operating officer, who reports to the CEO. "We saw quality improvement as a key facilitating mechanism for converting from a hospital-centered organization to an effective community-centered organization," says Mr. Norling. "Boards still exist on a division basis, but increasingly they understand that approximately 70% of their cost is related to the nine key functional processes. They are coming to understand that we're operating as a system."

For example, clinical laboratory services for all settings are under the direction of one administrative director. Reference labs have been standardized throughout the system, saving Fairview $850,000 annually. Lab testing and reporting processes also are being standardized across the system.

Mr. Norling sees restructuring as a key to governing an integrated system. "We started out with a focus on understanding customers and process improvement, which has led to an increasing understanding of the importance of structure and of redefining our structure to facilitate further improvement." Reorganizing a system must be process based, not institutionally based, he says. "We look at consistent processes across the system and improve them."

In addition to reviewing the panel of system performance each month, the board also reviews and approves annual objectives associated with Fairview's 10-year quality transformation plan. It then reviews managerial performance in accomplishing those objectives. "If management has not performed sufficiently well against those quality objectives, managers receive no incentive payouts, regardless of how well we may have performed in terms of market share and financial return. If the board thinks we have sacrificed our investment in continued organization building for

FAIRVIEW HOSPITAL AND HEALTHCARE SERVICES

7 hospitals

27 clinics

1 home care service

4 long-term care facilities

short-term profits, it has the ability to say, 'You've made a mistake.'"

Health Systems Share Common Goals

As recently formed healthcare systems work through the process of becoming fully integrated, they are developing new ways to manage quality, each unique to their organization. The four systems profiled here do suggest, however, that two emphases are emerging as common elements of restructured health systems. One is a focus on community and population health improvement, not just on the delivery of care. "Allina's vision statement says we want to be recognized as an innovator in community health," notes Mr. Sprenger. "That's a major paradigm shift for us, in terms of shifting resources further upstream — closer to the underlying source of many healthcare problems — and preventing rather than treating disease."

The second point many systems emphasize is a seamless integration of continuous quality improvement into every aspect of the organization. When healthcare providers first began to focus on quality improvement several years ago, they often thought of it as a new project — something done at a certain time, during a given meeting, at a specific management retreat.

The large, fully integrated systems on the cutting edge of healthcare today no longer envision quality as a project or program to be worked on at a specific time. They do quality all the time; continuous improvement is the way they think. At HealthSystem Minnesota, "we don't even talk about CQI anymore," Dr. Reinertsen says. "We don't use the word. It's part of what we do — every report, every committee, every management group and management-supervisor relationship. We no longer have a CQI department — this is everybody's work."

"If management has not performed sufficiently well against those quality objectives, managers receive no incentive payouts, regardless of how well we may have performed in terms of market share and financial return."

Richard Norling
Fairview Healthcare Services

Effect of System Restructuring on Quality Leadership, Part 2

When four Denver hospitals consolidated under a single board and management, they prepared to face the tough tasks of streamlining into a single health system. That meant drafting new bylaws, integrating medical staffs and developing a unified credentialing system. "In late 1993, when we started serious work on integration, there were very few models available for us to emulate," recalls Robert Gillesby, M.D., vice president for medical affairs for Columbia-HealthONE.

In fact, the process of dealing with medical staff restructuring is so new, there are no proven paths to success," says Linda Haddad, J.D., a partner at Horty, Springer & Mattern, a Pittsburgh law firm specializing in healthcare law, who has been a consultant for several restructured health systems. "I don't think we've done two the same way," she says. "As yet, there is just no standard model."

Healthcare consultant Hugh Greeley, chairman of The Greeley Co., Marblehead, Mass., agrees. "At the present time, there is some confusion in the field regarding a system's ability to consolidate medical staffs. Hospitals must consult state licensure laws and regulations on this issue to determine how much consolidation is possible. In some states, there may be a rationale for maintaining separate medical staffs. At the same time, systems that have merged hospitals often attempt to merge the activities of previously separate medical staffs into one systemwide medical staff operating through facility-specific divisions. For example, while each division may have an operating committee for medical activities, the integrated medical staff may have one medical executive committee."

Resistance to Change

Medical staffs often resist a full merger of functions, Ms. Haddad says. "They find it threatening. When several facilities serve one geographic area, and the medical staffs overlapped somewhat before restructuring, almost invariably one medical staff believes itself superior to the other." When the setting or population served varies, integration can be a problem.

"Medical staffs often see the advantage of coordinating functions," Ms. Haddad says. "They often cooperate on issues that don't matter too much, such as cutting the number of committees or having fewer meetings. But when it gets down to the nitty-gritty of medical staff leadership, debates on whether to have one medical executive committee or more are intense."

Physicians often fear that increased centralization may lead to a loss of power and control, she says. "If you talk to physicians one-on-one, they will usually acknowledge that certain decisions have always been relegated to the board or to management. At the same time, physicians believe they

From *The Quality Letter for Healthcare Leaders*, Vol 8:6, 1996

had more influence on those decisions when they were made within a smaller arena."

The role of the vice president for medical affairs also undergoes substantial change. "As a system consolidates, VPMAs go through great trepidation and concern," says Mr. Greeley. "Eventually the system will probably have one vice president for corporate medical affairs, who may have other physicians reporting to him or her, responsible perhaps for certain activities. We also see some systems where one person becomes the corporate vice president for medical affairs and the larger facilities also retain a VPMA for some period of time, until the medical staffs are fully integrated and performance review is centralized."

BEST-PRACTICE STRATEGIES FOR RESTRUCTURING QUALITY LEADERSHIP

In Medical Staff Leadership:

- Merge medical staffs, maintaining sensitivity to specific local circumstances.
- Communicate with physicians at every step. Use social activities to increase integration of the system; use meetings and continuing discussions to publicize changes and invite physician input.
- Have a single systemwide vice president for medical affairs. If larger facilities continue to have VPMAs, increase their systemwide responsibilities.
- Start with nonthreatening changes, then move on to more highly charged areas.

In Credentialing:

- Start by centralizing administrative processing of applicants and reapplicants.
- Centralize analysis of information.
- Centralize decisionmaking.

Mr. Greeley, who specializes in consulting on medical staff issues, views the medical staff as having two responsibilities related to quality — to monitor it and to help improve it. "The physicians who head these systems should be working to consolidate quality improvement activities so they are beneficial across the system," he says.

Making the Transition

Mr. Greeley offers his recommendations to aid the transition to a more integrated medical staff:

- Recognize that you can't force physician integration. Instead, design a series of activities and structures that permit and facilitate physician integration. For example, hold a quarterly series of medical staff socials — so physicians start to meet their opposite number and discover they don't have horns.
- Form a council of chiefs to meet on a regular basis to discuss systemwide medical staff issues, such as duplication in committees and credentialing.
- Begin a dialogue on consolidating the various medical staffs into one systemwide medical staff operating throughout all divisions.

Mr. Greeley advises systems to start by consolidating the functions that are nonpolitical and nonthreatening, then move on to the more highly charged functions.

Credentialing is a medical staff issue that offers both nonthreatening and threatening consolidation opportunities, according to Mr. Greeley. He identifies three different phases of credentialing:

- Phase 1, administrative processing: collecting, verifying, storing and summarizing information concerning applicants and reapplicants.
- Phase 2, analysis of collected information: generally done by a combination of department chairs, credentials committees or medical executive committees.

- Phase 3, decisionmaking.

Centralizing the decision making function — phase 3 — can be very threatening, because of perceptions of loss of control; administrative functions — phases 1 and 2 — are nonthreatening and therefore relatively easy to combine.

"Within any system it makes infinite sense to centralize phase 1, so administrative processing is done by one office in a standardized manner," Mr. Greeley says. "I expect major integrated systems will shortly centralize phase 2, because it makes so much sense to do so. Probably within five years they will have centralized phase 3 to the extent it is lawfully possible to do so."

In some integrated systems, components of the system are separate legal entities, and therefore it is impossible to completely centralize decisionmaking. For example, a physician hospital organization associated with an integrated system may not delegate decisionmaking under standards set by the National Committee for Quality Assurance and under most state laws.

> **"It was extremely difficult to establish medical staff policy."**
>
> John P. Cossa, M.D.
> West Jersey Health System

How Four Systems Tackled Restructuring

As healthcare organizations today merge into larger systems, they face many challenges in redefining appropriate roles and processes for quality leadership. The changing role of medical staff leaders and the vice president for medical affairs within an integrated system and support functions such as physician credentialing can be approached in a number of ways.

West Jersey Health System

The West Jersey Health System includes four acute care hospitals, an ambulatory surgery center, a very large home healthcare service, a school of nursing, a medical staff of 1,145 physicians, and a total of 729 hospital beds. It is one of the few health systems that has developed fully integrated medical staff leadership.

The system is one of the largest not-for-profit systems in New Jersey, serving a three-county area. In 1982, when a fourth hospital was acquired, the facility was allowed to keep its separate medical staff and function as a separate division. A single set of bylaws theoretically governed both staffs, but in actuality each had its own policies. "How patients were treated and how quality was evaluated and measured were very different in the two divisions," recalls John P. Cossa, M.D., senior vice president for medical affairs and medical director of the system.

For example, patients with chest pain needing emergency care were seen by a cardiologist in one division and by a general internist in the other, and there were significant differences in policies related to management of these patients. Quality assessment and performance improvement programs were completely separate; the hospitals had no way to share information to improve performance overall. There were two medical executive committees, each chaired by the division's chief of staff. "It was extremely difficult to establish medical staff policy," Dr. Cossa says, "because approval by one committee tended to lead to disapproval by the other."

Two years ago the system decided to focus on medical staff integration, motivated in part by an upcoming survey by the Joint Commission on Accreditation of Healthcare Organizations. Dr. Cossa brought in consultant Hugh Greeley, who "painted a very bleak picture for our board," Dr. Cossa says. The board mandated that the system would have a single medical staff, and it set a strict nine-month deadline for completion. Dr. Cossa convened a task force that met weekly, defined a clear time line and made regular progress reports to the board. "Resistance was significant," Dr. Cossa says. "Without strong board support, we would still be arguing about this issue. But the board essentially said that if the medical staff did not unite themselves, the board was going to do it for them."

"Without strong board support, we would still be arguing about this issue. But the board essentially said that if the medical staff did not unite themselves, the board was going to do it for them."

John P. Cossa, M.D.

New bylaws to support the consolidation process took effect in January 1995. The number of clinical departments was cut in half, 45 specialty sections were cut to 26, and 37 medical staff committees were cut to 25 (and have now been reduced to 12). The system now has a single standard for credentialing physicians, a single chief of staff and a single medical executive committee. In addition, West Jersey Health System has saved approximately $1 million per year by cutting the amount of physician time required for medical staff committee meetings, Dr. Cossa says.

Today this sort of full, systemwide integration of the medical staff is rare. What does it take to make it happen? Strong board support was obviously a factor in the West Jersey Health System story. In addition, some medical staff must strongly support the process. "There were people who had been here for many years," Dr. Cossa says. "They were frustrated because it was virtually impossible for them to function effectively. Those people saw this change as an opportunity."

West Jersey Health System did have its JCAHO survey about a year after the unification of the medical staff. "We came through it without a hitch," Dr. Cossa reports. "The reviewers were delighted to see how our medical staff is organized and credentialed and how the medical executive committee functions."

His advice for other organizations: "Once hospitals merge, full integration should not be delayed. The longer separate structures are allowed to retain the status quo, the more difficult it is to make changes. The medical staff issue, which is always a very tough one, should be addressed early on."

HealthSystem Minnesota

HealthSystem Minnesota, which primarily is made up of Methodist Hospital and Park Nicollet clinic, consolidated its corporate management in September 1995, reducing the number of top managers by one-half. Although management for the hospital and the clinic used to be separate, it is now systemwide.

"We recognized that the boundaries between a separate hospital and clinic had an adverse impact on patient care delivery processes and the quality of care," says Richard Migliori, M.D., the system's chief operating officer and senior vice president. "For example, the most common reason for operating room delays was the fact that patients didn't have appropriate preoperative evaluation, history and consent forms. All those processes take place in the ambulatory office setting, yet its impact was only witnessed at the hospital. Traditional hospital/clinic distinctions tend to deepen these interface problems, preventing effective management solutions."

At the same time, the hospital and clinic have, and will probably continue to have, separate medical staff structures. About 30% of the hospital's business comes from independent physicians; Park Nicollet does about 30% of its business with contracted hospitals. "We've kept the two structures separate because we don't want to disenfranchise our independent physicians, who hold about half the hospital's leadership positions," Dr. Migliori explains.

"Our credentialing system must be malleable because payers require multiple credentialing functions from us, and they often have differing standards about requirements a physician has to meet to fill certain roles."

Richard Migliori, M.D.

Systemwide management empowers and facilitates front-line quality improvement efforts, Dr. Migliori says. Over the past few years the myocardial infarction survival rate increased from 92% to 98%. "This happened because some cardiologists decided they wanted to standardize processes of care. To be effective, they had to reach out across the next interface. Team planning among pharmacists, cardiologists, emergency room doctors and primary care physicians changed the care process. Management's role in this planning process is to provide a structure that facilitates direct interaction among different parts of the system. The previous structure created a subtle inhibition; sometimes people were saying, 'Stop. Before you cross that interface, you will have to get approval from management.'"

HealthSystem Minnesota is currently consolidating all administrative credentialing functions and has made a strategic decision to apply the same credentialing and privileging standards throughout the system. The standards apply to every employed or independent physician who practices at the hospital. "Our credentialing system must be malleable because payers require multiple credentialing functions from us, and they often have differing standards about requirements a physician has to meet to fill certain roles," Dr. Migliori says.

Fairview Hospital and Healthcare Services

Minneapolis-based Fairview Hospital and Healthcare Services, a vertically integrated system of 11 hospitals, 740 affiliated physicians, 31 specialty clinics, 39 primary care clinics and 24 nursing homes, is in a transitional stage, still working to develop an integrated structure. Medical Director Gordon Alexander, M.D., is responsible for integrating medical staff and clinical care functions.

"One aspect of my job is to facilitate the transition toward appropriate standardization and rationalization of our activities," he says. At present, the largest hospital in the Fairview system and many of the clinics also have their own medical directors to deal with local issues at a local level. Over time, Dr. Alexander predicts, the system is likely to give these 31 site-based medical directors increasing systemwide responsibilities rather than move to more full-time system directors. These site directors

“I’m not convinced that managing local issues from afar is going to work.”

Gordon Alexandrer, M.D.
Fairview Hospital

are currently involved in central scheduling, nurse triage, credentialing and an expanding list of other activities.

Fairview has standardized and centralized what Mr. Greeley calls phase 1 of credentialing — the support function. “We are now working with our medical staff to understand how much of the remainder can be combined across the system,” Dr. Alexander says. “We will credential people centrally but leave the establishment of privileges to be defined by individual needs of the local community within system norms. We’re going through an evolutionary process right now, trying to decide how far along that continuum we want to go.”

When it comes to medical staff structure, a mix of attitudes and opinions prevails within the Fairview system. Some of the specialists in particular would like to be involved in long-term planning on a systemwide basis. Major payers, too, have a greater understanding of ways to improve quality through coordinated care and would welcome increased integration. Some departments, such as cardiovascular services, are now fully integrated, while others “don’t seem to have a strong feeling of the need for systemness,” Dr. Alexander says. One reason for this disparity may be that Fairview already is involved in an integrated cardiac care network (sponsored by Blue Cross Blue Shield of Minnesota), and cardiac specialists sense the advantages of systemwide management of care. In contrast, the scope of practice for other specialties currently varies at the different hospitals in the system, posing additional challenges to full integration of these departments.

The way Fairview deals with its pharmacy and therapeutics committees is indicative of its current stage of development. It feels some decisions should be site specific, while others should be made systemwide; therefore the P&T committees at present meet as a system committee every other month and as site-based committees on alternating months.

“We’re not trying to force any model upon them. I’m not convinced that managing local issues from afar is going to work,” Dr. Alexander says. “We’ll see what evolves from this. What the P&T committees are doing may turn out to be a wonderful model for other functions. At the same time, our bias is that it makes more sense to have one formulary for the city as opposed to one for each hospital. That’s where we’re heading, but we’re not there now.”

Columbia-HealthONE

Columbia-HealthONE, a Colorado-based joint venture between not-for-profit HealthONE and for-profit Columbia/HCA, demonstrates the anomalies that can arise when mergers and restructuring proceed at a rapid pace. Formed in October 1995, the system includes 10 Colorado hospitals and nearly 70 clinics.

“Our brief history has been one of continued interruptions and realignments,” says Robert Gillesby, M.D., system vice president for medical affairs. “We describe ourselves as ‘a system in evolution.’”

In fall 1993, three Denver hospitals and Bethesda PsycHealth, a mental health services provider, merged to form HealthONE. About six months later they merged their medical staffs into a single medical staff, united under a basic set of bylaws.

How do you go about merging medical staffs? "The first step is massive amounts of communication," Dr. Gillesby says. "You just have to communicate, communicate and communicate. Get the leadership together. We held meetings at 6:30 in the morning. When the stakeholders had reached an impasse over relatively minor differences in their bylaws, we brought in a consultant for a one-day meeting with all the medical staff officers, opinion leaders and administrative doctors; we had a simple agreement by the end of the day."

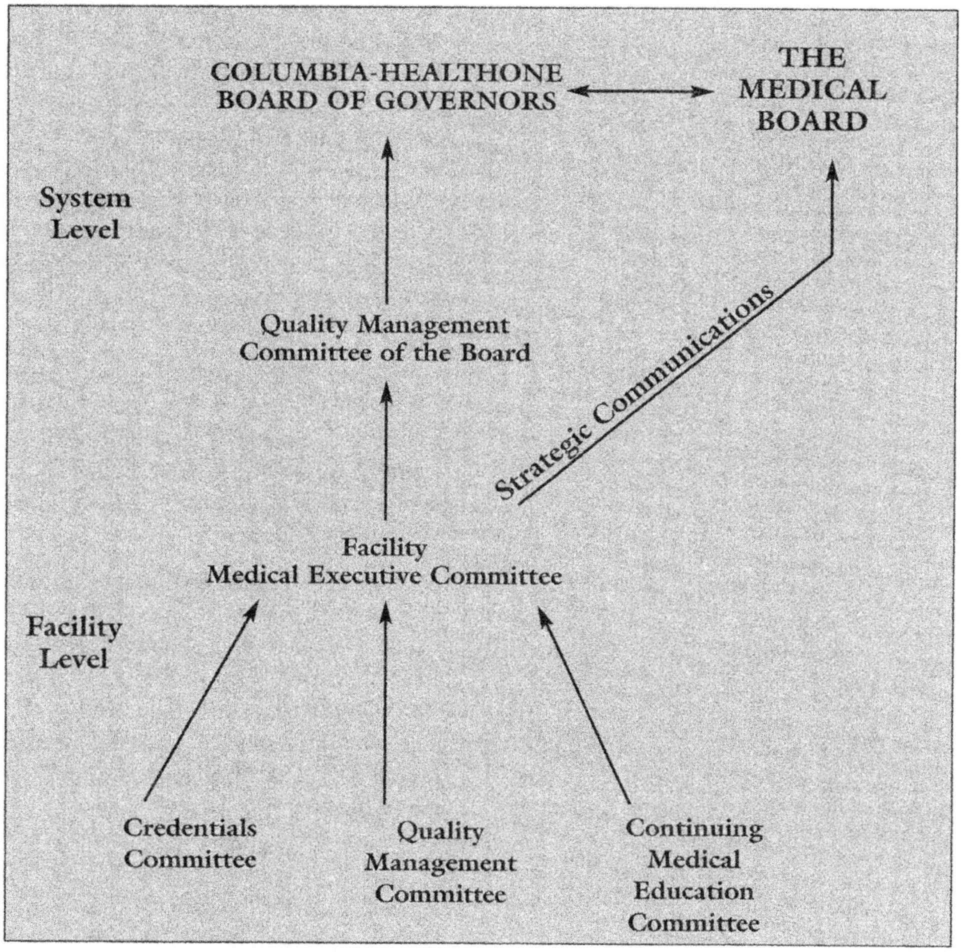

HealthONE's strategy was to agree on a streamlined set of bylaws, one set of rules and regulations and a single hearing and appeals manual. Then each acute care facility formed a separate division of the medical staff, with an individual organization and function manual defining how that division should be run. "If our downtown facility, which is a 700-bed tertiary care facility, wants to have 12 medical departments, and our suburban facility, which is somewhat smaller, wants to have four departments, that's fine. They each describe that structure in their organization and function manual," Dr. Gillesby says.

Each division of the medical staff has its own staff president, chairs of various departments and a medical executive committee with subcommittees on credentials and quality improvement. In addition, the presidents and presidents-elect of each division form the medical board, which meets monthly with the CEO, VPMA and chairman of the board of Columbia-HealthONE for strategic planning and high-level communication.

Almost all credentialing for the HealthONE medical staff is done by a central verification office. "Given a single medical staff bylaws, we are working toward the development of uniform credentials and privileges throughout the system," Dr. Gillesby says. "We do centralized credentialing; nobody really minds because it's very detailed and tedious and they are just as happy to give that up. It is extremely important, however, to find someone with the necessary expertise to head up this process. Otherwise your credibility will be destroyed."

As HealthONE moved toward centralized credentialing, a number of difficult issues emerged. Physicians were grandfathered throughout the system at the highest level of privileges they had formerly achieved in any part of the system. In a few cases, this led to controversy. For example, in one case a physician's privileges had formerly been restricted at one institution, and after the merger those restrictions were lifted when the doctor was grandfathered through a second hospital. In another case, a physician whose privileges had been removed at one institution was able to get them restored easily at a different facility. "We had to make a rule that individuals whose privileges were removed at one institution had to reapply at the same location to get them back," Dr. Gillesby recalls. "It was a minor issue, but it is an example of the sort of problem that can develop."

Just two years after the merger that formed HealthONE, its joint venture with Columbia/HCA added three more acute care hospitals as well as additional psychiatric and rehabilitation facilities to the system. At present, Columbia-HealthONE includes four facilities with a united medical staff and five facilities with individual medical staffs all organized under one Board of Governors.

Centralized credentialing is proceeding for 3,000 physicians and 1,100 allied health practitioners. "There is a great deal of enthusiasm here for a unified medical staff throughout the entire system," Dr. Gillesby says. "However, we have put this on hold right now. We expect a JCAHO survey of all facilities this fall, and we're not sure that we could develop the 'one standard of care' that the Joint Commission requires in time. So we have further integration on hold at present, but we think it will be only a short delay."

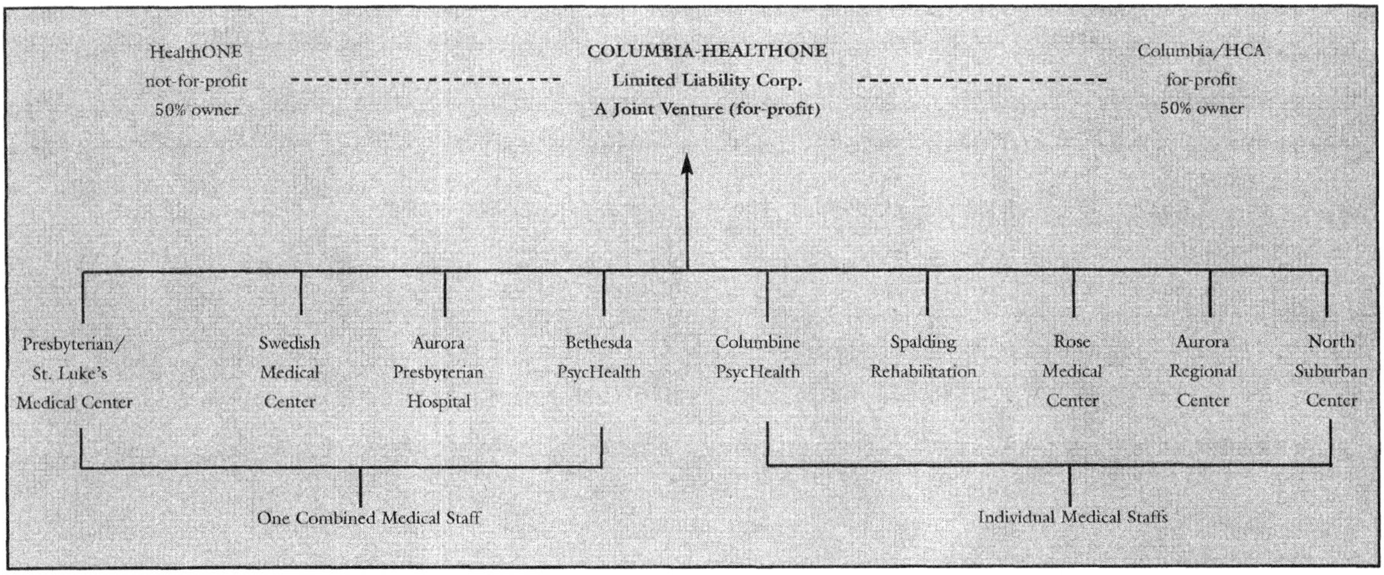

Publicize Process and Involve Physicians

As healthcare organizations grow and strive to integrate former competitors within a single system, they must develop a new way of looking at essential functions within the organization. Highly competent organizational leaders may find their traditional roles changing, as the system repositions itself to offer community-based preventive services and maintain the health of a population.

Ms. Haddad, who has observed and worked with organizations striving to integrate quality leadership throughout a large, restructured healthcare system, has the following advice to offer:

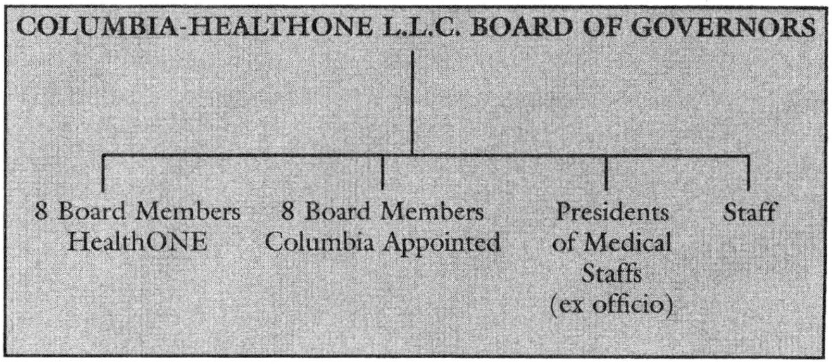

- Get physician leaders involved in the corporate discussions early. Physicians resent it when they learn about major decisions just before they hit the newspaper. "By physician leaders I don't mean just the president of the medical staff," she adds. "This is more personality-specific. I mean the physicians whose opinions are respected, who have the ability to work well with others and who are truly committed to the organization."
- Develop joint objectives, so physicians and medical leaders understand the reasons for increased integration. "These are threatening times for physicians, and when they don't buy into the big picture, it's hard for them to appreciate the advantages of increased coordination of functions," Ms. Haddad says.
- When the organization is ready to deal with medical staff leadership issues, form a task force of believers, Ms. Haddad suggests. Traditionally, many organizations form a broad-based task force representing a wide range of opinions. "They expect they will co-opt naysayers by having them involved in all the discussions, but in my opinion that slows the process down, dramatically. Instead, you need to form a task force of believers who are also salespeople."

It is equally vital, she says, for "the work of the consolidation task force to be public within the medical staffs. Publicize the process through newsletters or e-mail so any physician who wants to keep up with what is happening can easily do so. When the task force prepares a draft of the proposed new departmental structure, 20 copies should be available in the medical staff lounge." Physicians should be invited to make comments or suggestions in writing, she adds.

* * * *

Mr. Greeley predicts that by the turn of the century, many integrated healthcare systems will be taking a systemwide approach to quality management — they will have a single director of oncology systemwide, rather than several chairs of several oncology departments.

"In the past there was very little true physician leadership in the area of quality," Mr. Greeley says, "because the physicians who participated in quality management and improvement programs most often were volunteers. They were not compensated, they had no job descriptions and they filled their roles only for the short term — then someone else was elected to run the department or head up the quality improvement committee.

"I believe what we are seeing now is the professionalization of the physician's role in quality improvement. Physicians are beginning to be compensated for their participation in this activity and compensated for job performance that meets systemwide performance objectives. Across the country, people are starting to recognize that we have to pay serious attention to issues of quality improvement — and if you want a serious job done well in the United States, you don't do it with volunteers."

Creating an Integrated Credentialing System

As healthcare organizations merge into larger restructured systems, the systems typically look for ways to limit duplication and streamline systemwide processes. One candidate for consolidation is credentialing. There are clear advantages to be gained by standardizing the forms used in credentialing and centralizing the paperwork in one office.However, developing a fully integrated credentialing process, in which key decisions are handled the same way throughout the system, is a delicate matter that may be negotiated over years.

Sentara Health System in Virginia and West Jersey Health System in New Jersey have both moved relatively rapidly to create an integrated credentialing system. Their innovations include consolidated application forms and an expedited credentialing process for many physicians.

Sentara — Consolidated Forms

Sentara includes a regional tertiary hospital and three acute care community hospitals, totaling approximately 1,400 beds, nine skilled nursing and assisted living centers, and several managed care plans with more than 230,000 covered lives.

During the 1980s, as the system grew, it had one holding company board and six subsidiary boards. "In the 1990s we began to realize we needed to integrate more as a healthcare system and provide a seamless continuum of care. Having seven boards of directors and seven different management staffs was an obstacle to this process," recalls David L. Bernd, Sentara's chief executive officer.

In 1994, the system consolidated all its boards into one governing board and went from 38 directors to approximately 15. At the same time it started work on a unified credentialing process. "In the past, when doctors arrived in town, they'd have to fill out five separate forms just to get privileges within our system — three forms for our four hospitals, one for the managed care division and a fifth for our medical groups," says Mr. Bernd. "That meant we had to conduct five separate checks of the national practitioner data bank. The process was cumbersome, requiring each hospital board to make a credentialing decision, and many physicians had overlapping memberships on two or three medical staffs."

"You can imagine what happened when a medical school received five letters asking for records, all of them on Sentara stationery," adds Roger M. Eitelman, the vice president most closely responsible for credentialing issues. "They assumed it was a bureaucratic error; one letter was answered and four were thrown in the trash."

Today a physician applying for privileges in any part of the Sentara system fills out a single form and simply places a check mark next to each hospital or other subsidiary organization where he is applying for privileges. Credentialing recommendations are made by the medical staffs or by the IPA; final decisions are made by the medical affairs com-

"We cut the number of staff needed to process applications by 20%."

Roger M. Eitelman
Sentara Health System

From *The Quality Letter for Healthcare Leaders*, Vol 8:6, 1996

mittee of the board of directors. The full board receives a monthly report of credentialing decisions.

At this point, Sentara has centralized its application and administrative processes, substantially reducing the number of people needed to deal with administrative paperwork related to credentialing. However, the system still does not have a single physician credentialing committee. Because each facility developed as an independent entity, there are still three sets of medical staff bylaws. Each month the presidents of the three medical staffs plus the physician leaders of the other divisions come to the medical affairs committee with any issues related to credentialing, discipline, bylaws and the like.

"We are moving toward a unified credentialing process," says Mr. Eitelman. "Now that we have a single administrative process, we're asking the three medical staffs to look at differences in credentialing and see if they can be standardized into one set of requirements."

Mr. Eitelman predicts that broad issues such as whether physicians need to be board certified and malpractice insurance requirements will be standardized relatively quickly — within the next three to six months. He points out, however, that some institutions have different standards concerning some sensitive, highly specific issues, and these will take longer to resolve.

For example, at one hospital, any surgeon who is certified in general surgery would qualify for vascular surgery privileges, while at another the surgeon would have to have a subspecialty certificate in vascular surgery. A third hospital says the physician should have the certificate, but the board does have the power to make an exception.

Application for Medical Staff Privileges
Sentara Health System

Note: This application is not intended for Human Resources use.

Please place a check mark next to each division for which you are requesting privileges. The information provided can be used only by the entities checked below.

____ **Sentara Alternative Delivery Systems (SADS)**

____ **Sentara Bayside Hospital (SBH)**

____ **Sentara CarePlex (CarePlex)**

____ **Sentara Hampton General Hospital (SHGH)**

____ **Sentara Hospitals-Norfolk (Leigh and Norfolk General) (SH-N)**

1. *All information should be typed or printed legibly in black ink.*
2. *If more space is needed, attach additional sheets and make reference to the question being answered.*
3. *Complete the application in full. Merely attaching a curriculum vitae is unacceptable. Some questions may not apply to you, however note "Not Applicable" in the space. DO NOT LEAVE BLANKS.*

NAME IN FULL:______________________________

Have you ever been known by any other name (including maiden and previous married names)?

If so, what names?______________________________

Social Security No.____________________

Medicaid I.D. # ____________________

UPIN #: ____________________

I. CLINICAL AFFILIATION BEING APPLIED FOR

	SADS*	SBH	CarePlex	SHGH	SH-N (SNGH/SLH)
Specialty					
Subspecialty					
Subspecialty					

*ADS Provider Applicants Only - Based on recruiter's instructions.

"At this point, we don't have a complete list of all the sensitive issues, although the credentials committee chairmen typically have a pretty good idea of the more obvious ones," Mr. Eitelman says. "We'll standardize as fast as the medical staffs are comfortable with it; we'll take these issues one at a time."

Since credentialing is a highly technical area, Mr. Eitelman recommends drawing on a legal firm with specific expertise in credentialing. He does believe integrated systems should move in the direction of a standardized process. "First, it is clear that efficiencies can be gained. We cut the number of staff needed to process applications by 20%. Second, where there are different standards, it is my sense that the organization will tend to rise to the highest standard. As we start to improve, there will be increased willingness to have broader horizons and to be measured by national benchmark standards for best practice in credentialing."

West Jersey — Streamlined Processing

West Jersey Health System, with more than 1,000 physicians on staff, is usually processing 70 to 80 applications at any one time. It found it could effectively streamline the application and credentialing process by making key distinctions among the different types of applicants. At West Jersey a physician who has just completed a residency program and has a clean track record based on approved criteria is eligible for "accelerated track credentialing." Up to 50% of applicants could fall into this category.

The same detailed information must still be gathered for each applicant, but once all the data are in and the department chair, section chief and chair of the credentials committee have recommended that the physician should be appointed with certain privileges, the chairs of the medical executive committee, credentials committee and professional affairs committee of the board are authorized by policy to approve those appointments without waiting for the full committees to meet. In effect, this reduces the application process by approximately three months (see chart, page 18). These applicants' credentials profiles are subsequently presented to the credentials committee, medical executive committee and professional affairs committee for confirmation at their next meeting. The professional affairs committee of the board has the final authority to confirm, reject or question the application.

Like Sentara, as West Jersey Health System moved toward a fully integrated credentialing process, it found a great deal of variation throughout the system in criteria for appointing people and for actually providing privileges. Many departments and sections had their own criteria on specialty privileges. For example, ground rules varied on who was qualified to perform certain surgical and invasive procedures.

"As we explored the issue in more detail, we began to uncover not only differing formal rules but also unwritten rules or policies that were just based on a gentlemen's agreement within hospital sections," recalls John Cossa, senior vice president for medical affairs and medical director. These gentlemen's agreements were addressed by gradual development of board-approved criteria. "Once the criteria were in place, we were able to do away with the gentlemen's agreements," says Dr. Cossa. "It could have created nightmarish credentialing issues, but it didn't."

SENTARA HEALTH SYSTEM'S STEPS FOR ESTABLISHING UNIFORM APPLICATIONS PROCESSING AND CREDENTIALING

- ✔ Designate one committee as the credentialing body for all divisions of the healthcare system.
- ✔ Develop a standardized format for submitting credentialing information. This can reveal that each department is collecting different information. If that happens, seek agreement on a standardized set of information to be collected.
- ✔ Develop uniform forms for initial appointments and reappointments.
- ✔ Combine credentials files for the entire system at a centralized location.
- ✔ Establish appropriate uniform credentialing standards to be used throughout the system.

Source: Sentara Health System

WEST JERSEY HEALTH SYSTEM CREDENTIALING PROCESS

1. Request for application received by healthcare system.
2. Preapplication form sent to applicant.
3. Preapplication received by Department of Medical Affairs.
4. Application and enclosures forwarded to applicant.
5. Application and supporting documentation reviewed by Department of Medical Affairs for completeness.
6. Verification of information provided by applicant with primary sources. (Process can take three months or longer depending on the circumstances.)
7. All responses reviewed, with follow-up where necessary.
8. Application forwarded to department chair and section chief (where applicable) for interview with applicant.
9. Interview evaluations returned to Department of Medical Affairs.

TRADITIONAL PROCESS

Minimum of 30 days each step

10. Application forwarded to the next scheduled Credentials Committee meeting for review and recommendation.
11. Application forwarded to the next scheduled Medical Executive Committee meeting for review and recommendation.
12. Application forwarded to the next scheduled meeting of the Professional Affairs Committee of the Board for review and action.

ACCELERATED TRACK

As few as 5 days each step

10. Application forwarded to Credentials Committee chair for review and recommendation.
11. Application forwarded to Medical Executive Committee chair for review and recommendation.
12. Application forwarded to chair of the Professional Affairs Committee of the Board for review and approval.
13. Action taken by the chair of the PAC of the Board confirmed at the next meeting.

Criteria for Physicians on the Accelerated Track

—Applicant has consecutively completed all training within three years of submitting application in a program approved by the Accrediting Council on Graduate Medical Education or the American Osteopathic Association.

—Applicant has no more than one other hospital affiliation.

—Applicant has requested privileges consistent with the core privileges as defined for that specialty.

—There are no suggestions in the verified materials of potential problems, no prior malpractice or disciplinary actions or licensure restrictions or any type of investigations.

12 Ways To Get Physician Buy-in to Practice Guidelines

Although guidelines spell out best practices in treating many common diseases, variation in physician care of patients abounds. Following are 12 ways that have proven successful in overcoming barriers to physician use of guidelines.

Without doubt, the rapid proliferation of clinical practice guidelines during the past few years has generated an enormous amount of reading material for physicians. What's less certain is the extent to which physicians are putting these guidelines into practice, where they can affect patient outcomes. The degree of variability in patient care reported in the Dartmouth Atlas of Health Care and by researchers suggests that although all physicians are using some guidelines, many others are still underused by physicians.

"We're trying to figure out ways to approach physicians so that they will really want to use guidelines," explains Robert M. MacInnes, M.D., director of quality improvement for Blue Shield of California. His quandary with guidelines is probably familiar to quality improvement managers in many markets where physicians have contractual arrangements with multiple plans. Dr. MacInnes notes that the National Committee for Quality Assurance requires plans seeking its seal of approval to produce guidelines for their physicians and to somehow measure implementation. But in California, where IPA-model plans dominate the market, "physicians tell us that they get guidelines from all these different health plans, so they throw them all out in the waste paper basket," Dr. MacInnes laments.

His dilemma illustrates a problem that many health systems, plans, hospitals and practices are having difficulty addressing: getting physicians to put guidelines into action. Barriers to guideline implementation are numerous and sometimes difficult to identify. They include issues of credibility, autonomy and control, as well as more down-to-earth impediments that have to do with time, resources and lack of support.

"Implementation is a heck of a lot harder than development," says Thomas H. Stipp, health system manager at Cedars-Sinai Health System in Los Angeles.

Gordon Mosser, M.D., executive director of the Institute for Clinical System Improvement, a medical group association in Bloomington, Minn., that develops and implements practice guidelines, agrees but adds: "Implementation is not the hard part; it's the only part."

"Don't get carried away with development until you've got a plan for implementation," Mr. Stipp advises. "There are libraries of clinical pathways out there that aren't necessarily getting used."

From *The Quality Letter for Healthcare Leaders*, Vol 10:3, 1998

Range of Steps for Success

How exactly can a healthcare organization convince its physicians that following a particular guideline is the right thing to do — and then get them to do it? "There's no single thing anyone can do that will guarantee compliance, but probably a whole list of approaches that could be taken," says Donald E. Pathman, M.D., M.P.H., research director, assistant professor of family medicine and research fellow at the Cecil G. Sheps Center for Health Services Research, University of North Carolina at Chapel Hill. First and foremost, he and others interviewed for this article say, organizations need to recognize that most physicians want to provide the best care possible for their patients, but they need to be convinced that treatment changes suggested by guidelines accomplish that goal, and they often need various types of support to make those changes.

12 TIPS FOR GETTING PHYSICIAN BUY-IN TO GUIDELINES

1. Identify guidelines that address areas of clinical importance to physicians.
2. Establish guideline credibility.
3. Customize guidelines with physician involvement.
4. Break guidelines down into their simplest and most important components; key in on decision points.
5. Target the audience, to reach only those people necessary to put a guideline in practice.
6. Enlist physician champions to promote your guidelines.
7. Make it easy for physicians to follow guidelines.
8. Allocate the resources necessary to support guideline recommendations.
9. Make quality — not compliance — the basis for physician accountability.
10. Measure improvement, and share the data.
11. Keep guidelines relevant by updating them.
12. Align financial incentives with quality improvement goals.

A number of guidelines advocates offer advice on techniques they've found effective in winning converts to guideline use.

1. Identify guidelines that address areas of clinical importance to physicians.

Physicians are in business to take care of patients, not to reduce healthcare costs or make managers' lives easier. "You need to make sure that cost, administrative issues and public relations are not perceived as the motivation" behind a guideline, says Dr. Mosser. "If physicians think those issues are driving the [effort], they're not going to come to the table — or they'll come to the table in bad faith."

He suggests focusing on issues of controversy to pique physicians' interest, such as the management of stage 1 or 2 breast cancer, or on clinical problems that are common in everyday practice, such as acute low back pain or type II diabetes. These types of topics appeal to physicians' professionalism and can make a difference in their work.

2. Establish guideline credibility.

"Evidence" is the operative word here. Beware of guidelines based solely on "expert opinion." At Cedars-Sinai, guidelines are reviewed and rated according to the scientific evidence on which they are based, Mr. Stipp says. For example, randomized clinical trials get the highest grades, and studies that involve samples of more than 200 patients are valued more highly than those with patient samples of less than 200. "We do allow for expert opinion in tandem with best evidence," Mr. Stipp adds.

Source credibility is another important factor, as Dr. Pathman discovered from focus groups he conducted with pediatricians and family physicians on pediatric immunization recommendations developed by different organizations. He found that pediatricians were more likely to follow guidelines developed by their specialty society; likewise with family physicians.

Many pediatricians, he noted, weren't even aware that the American Academy of Family Physicians had developed immunization guidelines.

In addition, Dr. Pathman notes, many physicians saw little relevance to their own practices in guidelines by the U.S. Centers for Disease Control and Prevention. They believed the CDC's guidelines were designed specifically to care for poor populations, which might account for some portion of their own practices but not necessarily a large portion, Dr. Pathman says. Those findings, he adds, demonstrate the importance of creating public health guidelines that take physicians' interests and perspectives into account.

3. Customize guidelines with physician involvement.

Guidelines from on high don't go over well with most physicians. It's important to engage physicians in the entire process of evaluating, analyzing and tailoring guidelines. That's not to say that you need to reinvent the wheel: Most proponents of guidelines interviewed for this article claim it's perfectly acceptable — even desirable — to "steal" nationally developed guidelines. But those guidelines must be adapted to fit the needs of the delivery system, and that can't be done without physician involvement.

Physicians from relevant specialties must be included on guideline work teams. "They may not revise the guideline a whole lot," Dr. Mosser notes. "What's important is that they work it through and become very knowledgeable and familiar with it."

4. Break guidelines down into their simplest and most important components.

Scott Weingarten, M.D., director of health services research at Cedars-Sinai, advocates a "streamlined" approach to guideline implementation. Instead of expecting physicians to memorize long, complicated treatment guidelines, identify four or five key aspects of care that make a difference in patient outcomes. For example, says Mr. Stipp, for total hip replacement, the most important elements of outcome-focused care are administering the preoperative antibiotic, getting the patient into physical therapy, converting intravenous medication to an oral dosage form and preparing for discharge in three to five days.

Dr. MacInnes explains that he sits down with a small group of clinicians who are involved in the management of a particular procedure or condition. "We go through and I try to get a clear picture of how [the clinicians are] managing patients, and we [draw a flow chart of the processes]," he says. During those discussions, he identifies what he calls "leverage points," events in the care processes that either are points of variation in management or that have an impact on patient management. These leverage points, he says, "will usually tell you the answers to the questions regarding variation in treatment management." Typically, Dr. MacInnes says, he designs a one-page flow chart that includes the leverage points for each guideline that physicians can refer to easily in order to reach consensus on best management.

It's important, Dr. MacInnes says, to listen carefully to clinicians and clarify gray areas of treatment. For example, he says, in questioning physicians about management of patients with pneumonia, he was told that

It helps to develop a "brand identity" by using a standard format for all your guidelines, says Eric L. Book, M.D., senior vice president and chief medical officer of Wellmark Inc., Des Moines, Iowa. "Any organization can create graphics and package it so that one guideline has the feel of another," he says. "For a delivery system, it's nice to promote ownership." But, he adds, "the nicest-looking guideline in the world will not be implemented unless there's been some type of customized effort to support its implementation."

some patients require respiratory therapy as part of their treatment and some don't. He followed up by asking physicians how they determine whether respiratory therapy treatment is needed. The physicians said they check to see whether patients are wheezing and how well they can breathe. That reply, Dr. MacInnes says, translated into "reactive or obstructive airways disease getting in the way of managing pneumonia," a leverage point for the decision concerning respiratory therapy treatment.

5. Target your audience.

The fewer people you need to rely on to put a guideline into practice, the better its chances for being used, Dr. Weingarten asserts. For example, hospitalists — acute care specialists — are a good audience for hospital-based guidelines. "That's really a focused approach to hospital care, and you can concentrate your educational efforts as well," he says. In the clinic setting, physician extenders may be used in conjunction with primary care physicians to co-manage certain patients. For example, at one Cedars-Sinai clinic, pharmacists carry part of the responsibility for implementing hypertension management guidelines, Dr. Weingarten says.

Computerized medical reminder systems are effective support tools that provide important information to physicians at the time they need it, several guidelines advocates say. But Dr. Book notes that high technology is not always necessary: A pocket-size summary or flow chart of care processes can be just as useful.

6. Enlist physician champions to promote your guidelines.

Physicians listen to other physicians more than anyone else. Identify those physicians — there might be only a few — who support what you're doing, and recruit them to do presentations at quality improvement and staff meetings. This can be difficult when physicians are aligned with multiple hospitals, systems and plans. Physicians with loose ties to an organization may lack motivation for investing the time and energy needed to promote a guideline. "We look for the physicians who are aligned with us or are trying to align more closely," says Jim Bartelsmeyer, M.D., chairman of the Women and Infants' Quality Enhancement Team at BJC Health System, St. Louis.

7. Make it easy for physicians to follow guidelines.

"You can't just ask people to work harder to do the right thing," Dr. Bartelsmeyer asserts. His efforts to lower cesarean birth rates at BJC were initially very successful; overall C-section rates dropped by more than 10 percentage points, he says. But over time, those rates have begun to climb back up. "In retrospect, what we were trying to do was say, 'This is the right thing to do, and this is why you should do it.' It worked to a certain extent, but what we didn't do was make it the easy thing to do." Among the factors that BJC is examining to help bring about a permanent change: modifying the role of patient preference in C-section decisions and standardizing processes of care involving nurses in the labor delivery units.

David J. Abelson, M.D., associate medical director for HealthSystem Minnesota, says simplification is the crux of guideline implementation — not education or motivation. "Most guidelines reflect what physicians want to do," he asserts. "The key is to build processes to support doing the right thing." At HealthSystem Minnesota:

- Preprinted orders were designed to ensure proper early management of patients with myocardial infarction, saving time and minimizing errors. Dr. Abelson says that using these forms, physicians can check off boxes to order aspirin or beta blockers and make notes for each case.

- The process for handling phone calls regarding symptoms of urinary tract infection, a condition that commonly affects women, was redesigned to save clinicians time and make care more convenient for patients. A nurse records the woman's symptoms over the phone; if they fit the criteria for UTI, the nurse suggests the woman come in for a urinalysis. Later, an antibiotic can be prescribed over the phone.
- "Visit planning" was implemented. As explained by Dr. Abelson, every primary care encounter is viewed as an opportunity for preventive care as well. Before each visit, a nurse checks the patient's record to determine her last mammogram, flu shot, etc. Based on that information, she writes preventive care orders that are administered while the patient waits to see the physician in the exam room. Records on preventive care services are kept together in one section of the medical file. This approach has dramatically improved the system's use of preventive care services, Dr. Abelson says.

These examples all illustrate that "the best way is the easiest way," says Dr. Abelson.

8. Allocate the resources necessary to support guideline recommendations.

Cost can be a significant barrier to guideline implementation, and organizations serious about using guidelines have to consider costs during planning. For example, Michael Ralston, M.D., director of quality demonstration for Kaiser Permanente's Northern California Region says that when the health system committed to sigmoidoscopy over fecal occult blood testing as the preferred screening method for colon cancer, it dedicated a portion of its budget to purchasing necessary equipment — approximately $1.6 million in initial capital outlay — and training physician assistants and nurse practitioners in the procedure. Staffing, including physician and nonphysician support, came to approximately $5 million annually, although that figure has fallen slightly as the program has been implemented.

"We felt the investment would be borne out in the clinical results," Dr. Ralston says. "There was a willful decision to apply more resources to this." The use of sigmoidoscopy has increased dramatically, he says, adding that plan officials hope to be able to demonstrate improvements in five-year survival and reductions in colon cancer mortality.

Time is a resource too. At Allina Health System's River Valley Clinic in Hastings, Minn., patient staff educator Sharon Mathews, R.N., C.D.E., notes that members of a newly formed diabetes management team knew at the outset that they would need management's blessing to allocate several hours a week for their work on diabetes guidelines. Without that support, she says, the project could not have succeeded.

9. Make quality — not compliance — the basis for physician accountability.

Guidelines should not be regarded as edicts. Instead, they should be

Dr. Book notes that it's important to measure how guidelines are being used. In some cases it's possible to establish an appropriate level of compliance that won't be 100%. For example, in the management of uncomplicated sinusitis, a first-line antibiotic such as amoxycillin is considered appropriate for approximately 80% of patients.

"Not everyone can take it," Dr. Book says. "Ten percent of the population is allergic to it, and there may be some other reasons why physicians will not want to use a first-line antibiotic," he says. So if the data show that physicians are using a first-line antibiotic 100% of the time, "you know you are having a problem," he says. "You want to see reasonable compliance, but you also want physicians to use their judgment. Guidelines are never meant to replace the thought processes of physicians."

viewed as decision support tools for physicians. "We strongly send a message to physicians that they're not being held accountable for compliance with guidelines," says Dr. Ralston. "The accountability of the physician is to deliver the best care possible." Because guideline compliance is not tied to job performance evaluation, compensation or bonuses, the physicians "see no downside" to the guidelines program, he says.

10. Measure improvement, and share the data.

Demonstrating the effects of change is persuasive to physicians. Cedars-Sinai measures a variety of outcomes for each of its guidelines — including mortality, complications, length of stay and cost per case — at the product line level and at the individual physician level. "It cannot be done in a punitive way," Mr. Stipp notes. "Clinical judgment must supersede structured guidelines on a patient-by-patient basis. Trend analysis and risk adjustment are important factors to include in displaying variations in practice to physicians."

The diabetes team at River Valley Clinic used guidelines from the American Diabetes Association to identify three outcomes measures: glucose control, rate of annual diabetic retinal eye exams and rate of annual micro albumin exams for kidney function. The idea, Ms. Mathews says, was to keep outcomes reporting simple and concise; at the same time the team would provide physicians with evidence that it was helping them manage their patients better. A computer software program enabled the team to produce graphs that track patient outcomes; those reports are generated every six to eight months.

Dr. MacInnes suggests finding good benchmarks from other, similar organizations to show physicians for comparison. "If you bring that information back to physicians, they're very accepting of it," he says.

11. Keep guidelines relevant by updating them.

"You have to revisit your guidelines over time and update them as evidence and priorities change," Dr. Ralston asserts. "The guideline process is very dynamic. You can't just create a guideline and put it out there." Dr. Mosser says that under ICSI's program, guidelines are reviewed for revision every year. Usually those revisions are minor, he notes, and some work groups can simply do the job over the phone.

12. Align incentives.

Dr. Bartelsmeyer says failure to align financial incentives with goals for improving quality of care has limited the success of BJC's C-section program. "You don't have to pay doctors not to do C-sections, but underlying all this is their need to make their business financially successful," he notes. "Most physicians are in a small business environment, and they have to incorporate that consideration into their everyday practices. If you're doing something with financial disincentives or that is financially neutral, you're going to have difficulty." Dr. Book agrees. He recommends coupling financial incentives with good outcomes reporting, so that physicians can see for themselves the links between compliance, treatment outcomes, costs and economic rewards.

Dr. Bartelsmeyer says that BJC wants to explore other kinds of incentives as well. For example, the healthcare system is considering working with physician groups to promote guideline acceptance by offering to install computerized links between physician offices and BJC that include an electronic medical record. This feature makes it easier for physicians to manage their patients and document their medical histories. That, he says, is another approach to "making it more economically attractive for physicians to be part of our change process."

Start Small and Build

Organizations that are just testing the waters of guideline development should start with simple goals that focus on relatively few aspects of care but that can make a demonstrable difference in patient outcomes, these experts advise. In addition, don't expect to convert everybody at once. "You've got to go for the low-hanging fruit," Dr. Bartelsmeyer observes. "I'm looking for the middle 40% of people who think that what we're doing is probably a good idea but a little bit too hard to do ... It's that middle group I really want to engage."

Dr. Mosser agrees. "Start small with the receptive people," he says. "Then with success, the thing starts to take on a life of its own."

At the River Valley Clinic, not all physicians choose to refer their diabetic patients to the diabetes care team, Ms. Mathews notes. Yet even among those reluctant physicians, she's found, overall management of patients with diabetes has improved, even in aspects of care that the team has not been measuring, such as foot care. "It's made the whole awareness better," Ms. Mathews says of the team's work. Her conclusion? "Enthusiasm, she says, "is caught, not taught."

For more information ...

David Abelson, M.D.
HealthSystem Minnesota
Phone: (612)993-2036
E-mail: abelsd@park.hsmnet.com

Jim Bartelsmeyer, M.D.
BJC Health System
Phone: (314)966-6077
E-mail: jbartelsmeyer @
BJCmail.Carenet.org

Eric L. Book, M.D.
Wellmark Inc.
Phone: (515)235-4325
E-mail: bookel@wellmark.com

Robert MacInnes, M.D.
Blue Shield of California
Phone: (415)229-5441
E-mail: robert.macinnes
@blueshieldca.com

Sharon Mathews, R.N., C.D.E.
River Valley Clinic,
Allina Health System
Phone: (612)438-1815

Gordon Mosser, M.D.
Institute for Clinical System
Improvement
Phone: (612)883-7991

Thomas H. Stipp
Cedars-Sinai Health System
Phone: (310)855-5080
E-mail: stipp@csmc.edu

Donald Pathman, M.D., M.P.H.
University of North Carolina at
Chapel Hill
Phone: (919)966-4270
E-mail: don_pathman@unc.edu

Michael Ralston, M.D.
Kaiser Permanente,
Northern California
Phone: (510)987-3962
E-mail:
mike.ralston@ncal.kaiperm.org

Scott Weingarten, M.D.
Cedars-Sinai Health System
Phone: (310)724-6386
E-mail: weingarten@csmc.edu

Colorado Health Plans Collaborate on Single Set of Guidelines

To eliminate the deluge of similar but competing guidelines facing physicians, healthcare organizations in Colorado are teaming up to produce a single set of guidelines. The first two address pediatric immunizations and adult diabetes.

In 1996, Exempla Healthcare (then Primera Healthcare) released guidelines on low back pain at the same time that two other health plans in the Denver area sent similar guidelines to their physicians. Physicians threw out or ignored all the guidelines, according to Eric Book, M.D., former chief medical officer at Primera.

Not only will physicians not use guidelines if there are multiple versions for the same conditions, but variations in the format of the guidelines also are likely to convince physicians that it takes too much effort to search for the best practice, Book says. Besides, "physicians won't use things that interrupt their daily routine, like taking time to look things up on the shelf. They especially aren't going to look at different guidelines for different patients in different plans."

To solve the problem, Exempla proposed a collaboration among health plans in the Denver area to develop a single set of protocols.

"We were working from the premise that guidelines aren't proprietary, and that what's kept private at most institutions is actually very similar to what's available in the public domain," Book says. Given that each set of guidelines was developed from current research and demonstrated best practice, there's unlikely to be wild variation among the guidelines.

Reduced Redundancy Builds Buy-In

Fifteen of the state's 20 health plans opted to participate in the collaborative, representing the bulk of the managed care market statewide. Each health plan has two or three representatives involved in the collaborative, including the medical director. Each plan is required to take a leadership role in developing a set of guidelines and agrees to accept the collaborative's guidelines as its own.

"We may have a unique situation here in Colorado in that the very savvy medical and business communities realized that, to the extent that they can collaborate on quality improvement, it is of benefit to the plan, to purchasers and, most important, to the patients themselves," says Donna Marshall, director of the Colorado Business Group on Health.

Because the Colorado managed care market is advanced — with most physicians participating in multiple plans — the collaboration

From *Report on Medical Guidelines & Outcomes Research*, Vol 9:2, 1998 made sense from a medical viewpoint: Plan medical directors readily agreed that they could come up with a single standard of care that would be useful to all of their providers. In addition, the complexities of the healthcare market actually helped make the case for the collaborative at the executive level, according to Stewart Greisman, D.O., vice president and medical director of United Health Care of Colorado.

"At the plan level, it made sense to medical directors to get together and get physicians to do the right thing," he says. "If we can take the American Diabetes Association guidelines, get them reviewed by people we know and say 'Here's the way it's done in Colorado,' with a few minor changes, that makes sense."

Health plan executives bought into the collaborative when they realized its potential to decrease redundancy. Because the Colorado Medical Society is involved in the project and is collecting outcomes data for diabetes care, for example, every plan that participates in the collaborative should be able to get credit for a National Committee on Quality Assurance-qualified study while contributing far fewer resources than would be necessary for an internal project.

"The CEOs see it as a cost savings, the medical directors enjoy building consensus, the community benefits from a rational discussion of care among the health plans and medical societies, and the patients are the ultimate beneficiaries of enhanced care," Greisman says.

Setting a Single Standard

"This is one of the first efforts to deal with a major problem of healthcare: There can't be multiple best ways of doing things," says Diana Maier, M.P.H., Exempla director of research and epidemiology. "We're trying to show the most medically sound way of caring for patients."

Working teams of four to 10 physicians and other representatives compare each set of guidelines, reconcile the information to select the best composite, and develop a prototype according to a standard format. The proposed guidelines are reviewed by panels of 10 to 15 experts in the field, then finalized by the executive committee. The immunization guideline, in its final form, is a single, double-sided sheet that includes an immunization record sheet, a summary guide for age-appropriate immunizations through adolescence, other considerations for immunization and a set of references. The diabetes guideline includes a flow sheet to remind physicians of when different screening tests are needed and includes space to record the results of those tests.

"We expect that [outside] organizations will get involved in distributing guidelines that are of interest to them," Maier says. Guidelines will be distributed to plans' member physicians through the collaborative, rather than through each health plan, to ensure that physicians aren't once again receiving multiple copies. Guidelines also will be available on a Web site and through specialty newsletters. At least annually, or whenever significant advances in the field occur, the collaborative

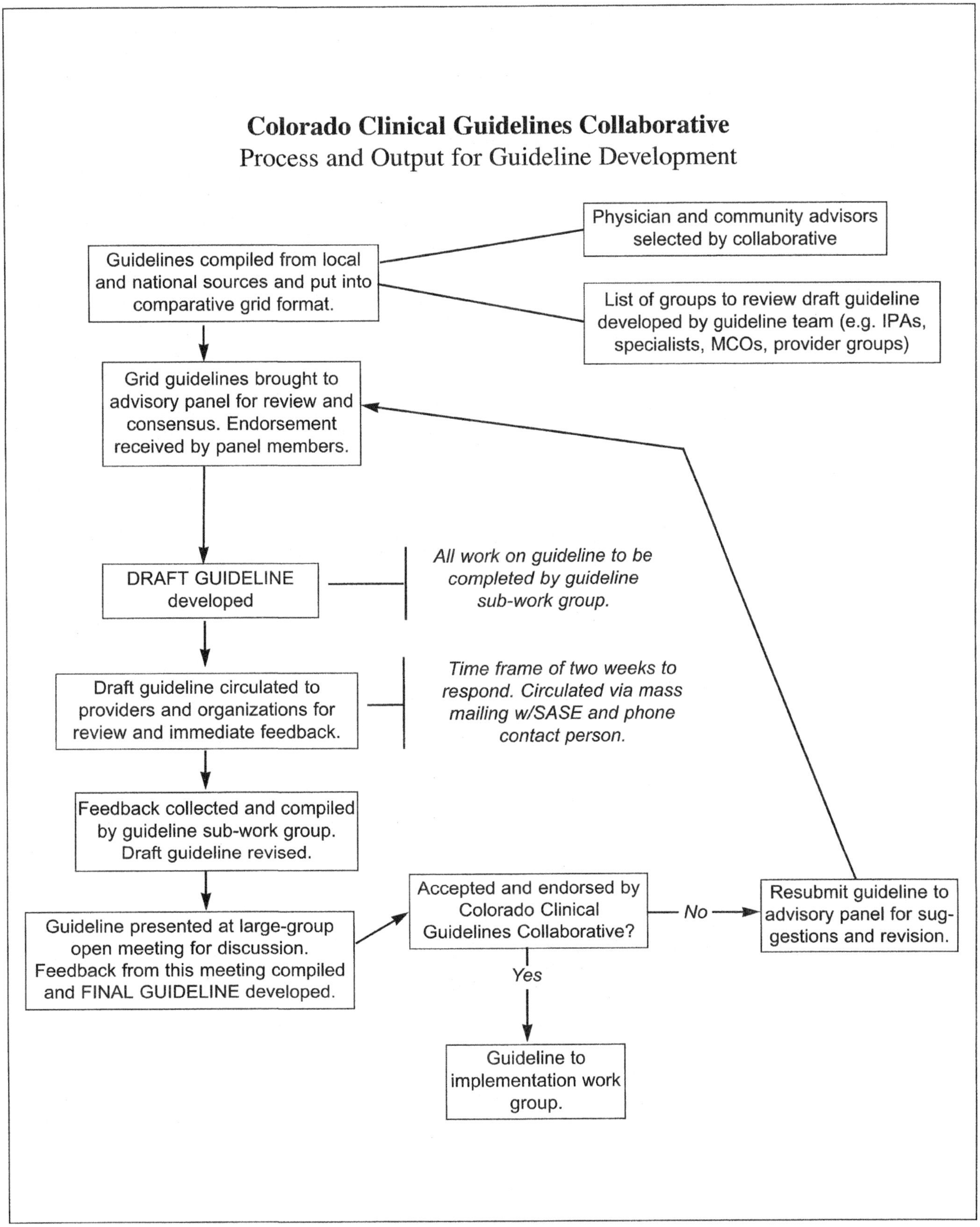
Colorado Clinical Guidelines Collaborative
Process and Output for Guideline Development
Physician and community advisors selected by collaborative
Guidelines compiled from local and national sources and put into comparative grid format.
List of groups to review draft guideline developed by guideline team (e.g. IPAs, specialists, MCOs, provider groups)
Grid guidelines brought to advisory panel for review and consensus. Endorsement received by panel members.
DRAFT GUIDELINE developed
All work on guideline to be completed by guideline sub-work group.
Draft guideline circulated to providers and organizations for review and immediate feedback.
Time frame of two weeks to respond. Circulated via mass mailing w/SASE and phone contact person.
Feedback collected and compiled by guideline sub-work group. Draft guideline revised.
Guideline presented at large-group open meeting for discussion. Feedback from this meeting compiled and FINAL GUIDELINE developed.
Accepted and endorsed by Colorado Clinical Guidelines Collaborative?
No
Resubmit guideline to advisory panel for suggestions and revision.
Yes
Guideline to implementation work group.

> ***For more information***
>
> Colorado Guidelines Collaborative
> 600 Grant St., Suite 700
> Denver, CO 80203-3525.

will update the guidelines. The Colorado Business Group on Health will be involved in developing complementary information for employers and consumers.

Still Room for Best Implementation Strategies

The project is being underwritten by unrestricted education grants from pharmaceutical companies, with a set fee for contributing health plans and a sliding scale for not-for-profit organizations.

Upcoming guidelines projects include asthma, including standards for inhaled steroids; depression in the elderly, including early identification by physicians and patients; and colorectal screening. The collaborative also is considering prenatal care, sleep apnea, smoking cessation and low back pain.

Once the first guidelines are implemented, the collaborative will begin collecting data to determine their effectiveness and the extent of their implementation. Eventually, the data collected could be used to influence providers through profiling.

"We all have common goals for how patient care is provided," Maier says. "If one plan can come up with a more successful way of implementing the guidelines, that's good, but hopefully we'll all learn from it."

Building Knowledge of Health Care as a System

It is currently fashionable to refer to large collections of health care providers and facilities as systems. Some of these collections have been gathered by trades, mergers, acquisitions, gifts or almost any other conceivable means. Usually some well-meaning people perceive an opportunity and begin to explore what that opportunity might mean for their own base of operations. Determinations of feasibility are usually done by financial analysts and lawyers. After feasibility has been determined, the entities decide to pursue further agreements and enter a period of due diligence and discovery, during which more is learned and revealed about each other. Public announcements are made. People previously thought to be "them" get tried on as "us." Some awkward and cautious meetings occur. "They" are not as bad as "they" once were thought to be. The discovery period ends. New top leaders are designated. Obligatory photographs are taken. Internal news about the promises of the new future is distributed.

After some time passes, the jobs of the top leaders become a bit more predictable. The internal work processes remain intractable. Anticipated savings do not materialize. The noisy external societal politics associated with the news of making the deal give way to the more immediate and seemingly never-ending internal organizational politics. Meanwhile, smaller, more loosely connected entities emerge from within the local environment. They seem able to compete on price and features for the immediate customers – the ones who have the purchasing power and authority. Health care leaders recognize these same prices and features as desirable but unreachable, given the preoccupation with accommodating, somewhat reluctantly, to their new systems. The apparently invulnerable larger systems suddenly seem so vulnerable. What happened? Are not systems superior to isolated entities trying to offer health care in this newly intensive market for health care? What do we mean by systems of health care anyway?

DEFINING A SYSTEM

A system is a functionally related group of interacting, interrelated, or interdependent elements forming a complex whole with a common aim. This article presents a 10-step exercise for building knowledge of the elements of an interdependent system of health care. Those who seek to improve the work of a system can use this exercise for designing and relating new improvement efforts to the general work of the organization.

It is in this context that we seek understanding of the phenomenon of system in health care in the United States today. Systems of things are complexes of things. It seems natural to refer to collections of health care elements that are complex as systems. After all, elements of the larger environment – hospitals, physicians, financing plans – have been brought together. But are they elements of the health system? How should we think of a system for creating/making health care today?

This article presents an exercise for building knowledge of the elements of an interdependent system of health care. Although the article is written for health care leaders, the method is applicable to many other human

From *Quality Management in Health Care*, Vol 5:3, 1997

service-giving settings and their leaders with minor editing. The 10-step exercise can help people develop an overview of the activities of their organization and allow them to see their work as a system.

Health Care as a System

The word system is currently used in ways that have at least three different definitions:

1. The prevailing social order; the establishment. Used with "the."

2. A set of objects or phenomena grouped together for classification or analysis.

3. A functionally related group of interacting, interrelated or interdependent elements forming a complex whole with a common aim.

It is in the difference between the latter two definitions that we can see the seeds of understanding that are critical to the system-leading task in health care today. What is the knowledge that will help them create an interdependent system? How can we understand the transition from a collection system to an interdependent system?

W. Edwards Deming defined a system for producing something as a group of interdependent people, items, processes, products and services that have a common aim. Figure 1 illustrates the relationships he defined. Over the next four decades, he continued to develop his thinking about work as a system, and it became part of a knowledge system that could guide the work of those seeking to lead the improvement of services or products. This general knowledge system and its application to health care and health care leadership have been described elsewhere.

> **DEFINING A SYSTEM**
>
> "No margin, no mission" is a frequent refrain among health care executives. While we have done a good job of tracking financial performance, few of us can measure other "softer" elements of our missions as readily. Even if we succeed in establishing performance measures for attributes such as quality, clinical outcomes or partnership, most of us continue to struggle to motivate employees to focus on organizational, rather than individual, performance.

In understanding a system that makes or creates a service or product and that is capable of continual improvement, we must consider how we make/create what we make, why we make/create what we make, and how we improve what we make as connected elements of one system. The knowledge that arises from the assembly of the entire construct can inform the work of the leader trying to foster the development of an interdependent system.

The Production of Health Care

It is possible to complete this exercise at several levels of specificity (e.g., an integrated health services delivery organization, a hospital, a free-standing clinic, a department within the clinic or a provider team within a department). The greatest personal insight generally comes when the leaders involved in a common level of work come together and focus on the production of their own service as a system. When completed for a particular service (e.g., childbirth care), attention should be given to understanding the impact on other services, lest the work on childbirth care invite optimizing that service at the cost of sub-optimizing the larger system of health care for the population.

Comments and tips to assist participants (leaders trying to build knowledge they can use) are included for each step. They represent the collective insights and ideas of many in numerous specific situations.

Step 1: Services or Products

The question is: What do you produce or make or create? Answering this question helps begin the knowledge building activity by focusing on what care, service or product is produced.

Tips:

List the important or highest-volume services or products first.

List services or products, not the activities necessary to produce them. For example, lab result reports are the product and laboratory testing is the process; organizational policy is the product and policy making is the process.

Remember health care workers commonly produce information, procedures, reports and recommendations, patient interventions, services, and a therapeutic environment among other outputs.

Note that some of what is produced is as a result of the main products. For example, jobs are produced as a result of producing services for patients, the primary work products.

Avoid the temptation to label what you make as your product when what you have identified is actually the result of a customers use of what you make. For example, patients may be able to make wiser, more knowledgeable decisions as a result of acquiring and integrating the information that you have produced for them. You make the information, not the decision.

Do not overlook the creation of an environment conducive to making what you make.

Step 2: Customers

The question is: Who uses or receives these services or products? The answer helps clarify the identity of those who benefit from what you make.

Tips:

List the direct beneficiaries of the services you most often encounter. Focus on the external customers, even though one professional or department may be thought of as a customer of another.

Be as specific as practical.

Remember that customers are those who need and/or benefit from the products and services you produce.

> **"Ask, What other services or products might meet that need? as a means of gaining further insight into the underlying need. Remember that the focus is on the need, not what you or anyone else may do to meet that need."**

Step 3: Community/Social Need

The question is: What is the underlying need that those beneficiaries or customers have for what you make? The answer helps you gain insight into the underlying need for what you do.

Tips:

Focus on the fundamental needs for your services: Why do people actually need what you make?

Ask, for each output that you make, What need am I meeting by providing ________? Think very specifically first, then look for any underlying concepts that tie these needs together.

Take each major customer and ask carefully about its need for what you make.

Do not worry at this stage about competitors – your brand versus another organization.

Work with the highest volume outputs and the most important customers rather than initially trying to address the needs of all customers for all services and products.

Ask, What other services or products might meet that need? as a means of gaining further insight into the underlying need. Remember that the focus is on the need, not what you or anyone else may do to meet that need.

Step 4: Customer Knowledge

The two questions here are: What measures or characteristics do customers use when they assess the quality of what you make? What about the customers might prompt their interest in assessing and judging quality that way? The answers to these questions help develop further insight into the ways you can improve based on what is important to your customers.

Tips:

Start with a single customer or recipient of your product, identify what you produce for this customer, and ask how that customer assesses quality for that product or service.

Focus on what might prompt each customer to assess quality that way. Connect those prompts to the measures of quality with an arrow from the prompt to the measure. These prompts can be thought of as drivers of the attributes of quality.

Step 5: Processes

The question here is: What steps do you use to make your product? The answers to this question reveal that there are several processes at work to generate what you produce. Some of them are more tightly linked to each other. Some of these linked processes form a core that represents the basic work of the organization. Other processes are linked in a supportive way to that main or core process.

Tips:

Begin by listing several processes, remembering that process names often end in -ing. (When working in a group, use 3x3 sticky notes, putting the name of one process on one note.)

Arrange the processes in a typical scenario that illustrates what usually happens when a patient moves through the care setting.

Those processes that come together to form the core process of what you do are made functional by the other processes that support that core. Both are important. Supportive processes are sub-optimized when they do not know the core process steps they support and do not know how they provide their services.

Remember that the core process of health care work is the work done in the care of the patient.

Arrange the steps in the core process to make it clear that the supportive processes help the core process.

Be sure you are describing the actual process not the one you hope exists. That is how you see the obvious areas for improvement.

Step 6: Inputs

The question is: What comes into your system and is changed by the regular actions of the core process to create the services or products? The answer builds knowledge of the needs, skills, materials or goods that regularly enter your system and form the beginning point for your work.

Tips:

List the human, financial, material and information inputs to your processes.

Remember that inputs come from internal as well as external sources.

Note that patient need is a general term for illness, anxiety and so forth. Physician skill is a general term for associative reasoning, listening, communicating, manual dexterity and memory. These examples represent common inputs to the core process of hospitals. You will be able to identify many others.

Step 7: Suppliers

The question is: Who or what specific people, departments or organizations provide the inputs? The answer identifies those who supply what you need to do what you do.

Tips:

List the supplier(s)for each input in step 6.

List suppliers of patients, goods and manpower.

List suppliers of patient need, physician skills and so on.

Note that sometimes the same person or department can be a supplier as well as a customer of the process. If so, the person or department usually supplies one thing and receives another. Presumably your process has added value to what they have supplied.

Step 8: Vision

The question is: Based on what you know about the need for your services and your knowledge of the customers, what is the aim for the future? A shared sense of the future is what workers need to align what they do and how they might improve in the future.

Tips:

Relate your aim to the underlying need in the community and society for what you produce and to your knowledge of your customers.

Place those social/community needs and customer knowledge side by side. This allows you to think about what it might take to better meet those needs in the future.

Note that your knowledge of what you do helps inform your understanding of what those processes can produce (process capability) in relation to the need and to your knowledge of the customer.

Be as specific as you can. If the picture of the future is clear, it is easier for people to understand and more likely to be realized.

Remember that your ability to state this aim clearly will improve as you keep working on it.

Ask the following question in terms of five years from now: What do we need to become that we are not now, based on our knowledge of need and of the customer?

Note that a vision of the future should permit your organization to be recognized as responsive and as discernible by those you intend to serve.

Step 9: Plan To Improve

The question is: Based on your aim for the future, on your knowledge of the need, on your knowledge of the customer, and on information from employees involved and knowledgeable about the daily work, what is strategically important to improve? The answers to this question provide the near-term focus (12 to 18 months) for work on the improvement of what you do. They integrate the improvement efforts of the hospital.

Tips:

Remember that you answer this type of question each time you build a capital or operating budget.

Limit the number of responses to one or two, certainly less than five.

Think of these as themes of improvement.

Think of these as the names of major gaps against which the next layer of the organization will be asked to plan.

Step 10: Design and Redesign

The question is: What specific process(es) will offer you the greatest leverage in securing the strategic improvements you seek? The answers offer greater precision for the immediate improvement plans and recognize that improvement will occur either by designing some new processes or by redesigning existing processes.

Tips:

Be as specific as you can, and be sure that you have actually named processes (i.e., what you must change to get the new results).

Limit the number of processes to between three and eight.

Identify some processes that simply need to be stabilized so that they are more predictable.

Discussion

Placing these answers in the configuration and connecting them using the arrows previously illustrated in Figure 2 can help you understand some of the important relations that exist among these elements. The following eight questions have been helpful to groups while using the exercise and after they have completed it:

1. What are the uses of the knowledge gained in this exercise?

2. What are the ways to continue to develop this knowledge?

3. What are the ways to share this information in the organization?

4. Are there others who might benefit from an exercise such as this?

5. Which sources of information and measures are currently helpful to you within your organization for these areas?

6. How might you validate or test your understanding of the need for what you produce?

7. How might you validate or test your knowledge of the customer definitions of quality? of the prompts that inform those definitions?

8. What will you do next to apply this knowledge?

When using this exercise, it is helpful to begin at the point that Ackoff describes as formulating the mess. For example, a group of faculty from various institutions explored the mess of building health professional capability for leading the continual improvement of health care within three disciplines: medicine, nursing and health administration. After building an awareness of the current reality, the focus then turns to how to design a different reality. The exercise described above gives participants that opportunity (i.e., the re-framing that occurs as participants complete the exercise illuminates what needs to occur to move from the current reality to the desired future system).

The challenge is to move from general insights about the interdependencies of the elements of a system to helpful information to guide efforts to change and improve health care. This process is made easier with a structured approach for depicting and actually drawing the system, its parts and some of their interactions. Once the system is drawn, it becomes possible for people who work within the system to examine the interrelationships. Health care that is organized as a system frees energies for meeting the needs of patients and communities. Health care organizations composed of parts that do not fit well with one another obligate organizational energies to achieve a sense of internal coherence and fit. This internal work takes away resources from meeting the customers' needs.

The arrows that emerge as the system diagram is completed help define the key relationships necessary for the production and improvement of work as a system. The arrows help describe the work of leadership and management. Connecting, establishing context, working on the whole system and its aim, and integrating the parts are the kinds of efforts top leaders must make. The arrows could be drawn in both directions. More arrows could be drawn. These arrows and the directions are intended to signal a pathway for planning and guiding the pathway for the identification of improvement work. Practicing the flows from one category to another is an exercise in integration that management must lead. The arrows are the work of management.

The benefits of Demings model of production viewed as a system include its widespread applicability for other types of organizations. This same exercise (with appropriate working changes) has been used by leaders of many different types of health service delivery organizations, churches, and repertory theaters, as well as by staff groups promoting knowledge and insight into quality and graduate health professional education. Use of the system diagram by senior leaders to relate the work of every worker to the organization as a whole helps enroll all workers in the work of the whole system. Those who would seek to improve the work of the system can also use this figure for chartering and relating new improvement efforts to the general work of the organization.

Building knowledge of interdependent systems is not easy. Using the language of production and making/creating something is awkward for service delivery professionals. If that awkwardness can be overcome, the new language invites the disclosure of new relationships and dimensions of the daily work.

It is in the interdependent system where the parts fit that best value and least waste related to aim occurs. It is this type of system that offers promise and advantage for the future development of health care.

References

Ackoff, R.L. The Democratic Corporation. New York: Oxford University Press, 1994.

Ackoff, R.L. Redesigning the Future. New York: John Wiley & Sons, 1974.

von Bertalanaffy, L. General System Theory. New York: George Braziller, 1968.

Churchman, C.W. The Design of Inquiring Systems: Basic Concepts of Systems and Organization. New York: Basic Books, 1971.

Checkland, P. Systems Thinking, Systems Practice. Chichester: John Wiley & Sons, 1981.

Mitroff, I.I., and Linstone, H.A. The Unbounded Mind. New York: Oxford University Press, 1993.

Deming, W.E. Out of the Crisis. Cambridge, MA: Massachusetts Institute of Technology Center for Advanced Engineering Study, 1986.

Deming, W.E. The New Economics. Cambridge, MA: Massachusetts Institute of Technology Center for Advanced Engineering Study, 1993.

Batalden, P.B., and Stoltz, P.K. A Framework for the Continual Improvement of Health Care: Building and Applying Professional and Improvement Knowledge To Test Changes in Daily Work. Joint Commission Journal on Quality Improvement 19, no. 1 (1993): 424-52.

Batalden, P.B., and Nolan, T. Knowledge for the Leadership of Continual Improvement of Health Care. In The AUPHA Manual of Health Services Management, edited by R.J. Taylor and S.B. Taylor. Gaithersburg, MD: Aspen Publishers, 1994.

Batalden, P.B., and Stoltz, P.K. QL Perspective Fostering the Leadership of a Continually Improving Healthcare Organization. The Quality Letter 6, no. 6 (1994): 9-15.

Ackoff, R. Creating the Corporate Future: Plan or be Planned. New York: John Wiley & Sons, 1981.

Gelmon, S., Wilson, W., and Norman, L. Formulating the Mess: Lessons of Organizing as a System. Quality Management in Health Care 5, no. 3 (1997): 13-17.

Vaill, P.B. Learning as a Way of Being. San Francisco: Jossey-Bass, 1996.

Batalden, P.B., Mohr, J., Strosberg, M., and Baker, G.R. Conceptual Framework for Learning Continual Improvement in Health Administration Programs. Journal of Health Administration and Education 13, no. 1 (1995): 67-9.

Designing for Patient-Centered Care — Making It Happen in Today's Marketplace

Healthcare organizations that have adopted Planetree, a more humanistic form of patient care, report better care outcomes and happier and more comfortable patients — at minimal cost.

A young woman sat alone peeling apples in the kitchen of an inpatient unit at Griffin Hospital, a 161-bed acute-care community hospital in Derby, Conn. She'd been there since about three o'clock in the morning, crying softly. Her mother was a patient in the hospital, terminally ill.

When the clinical director arrived that morning, a nurse who had been on duty the previous night suggested she go in and talk to her. The director entered the kitchen and gently asked the patient's daughter if everything was all right and if she could help in some way. The young woman explained that whenever she and her mom had faced a tough decision in the past, they used to sit in the kitchen and peel apples. Now she was faced with another tough decision, one she would have to make by herself—whether or not to sign a DNR ("do not resuscitate") order for her mother.

Admittedly, few hospitals would allow someone to walk in at three o'clock in the morning to peel apples. For the staff at Griffin Hospital, however, the young woman's request barely caused a stir. That's because Griffin Hospital is a participant in an innovative patient care program called Planetree that seeks to put respect for patients and their families at the center of medical care.

Planetree is the brainchild of Angelica Thieriot, a former hospital patient who found her routine medical treatment in the late 1970s so dehumanizing that she made it her mission to develop a new model of patient-centered care. The result was Planetree, a nonprofit organization dedicated to the creation of healthcare environments that support the physical, emotional and spiritual needs of patients.

Planetree was founded and incorporated in 1978. The first Planetree unit opened in 1985 in a 13-bed medical/surgical unit at Pacific Presbyterian Medical Center (now California Pacific Medical Center) in San Francisco. Today, the Planetree Alliance, as its group of 18 affiliated healthcare organizations is called, includes 23 hospitals in the United States and one in Europe and one community health center.

Demystifying the Medical System

"What Planetree is all about," says Laura Gilpin, M.F.A., R.N., director of the Planetree Alliance, "is demystifying the medical system for patients. It is about bringing a personal touch back to healthcare and rediscovering our human values, which I think we've tended to lose sight of in a healthcare paradigm that's become so focused on technology."

From *The Quality Letter for Healthcare Leaders*, Vol. 6:7, 1997

Tangibly, what Planetree means is hospital units where the smell of baking bread or fresh cookies might fill the air. Where volunteer massage therapists or musicians comfort patients with their healing touch or sounds. Where rooms and floor units are designed to enhance the patient's sense of relaxation and comfort. Where visitors are welcome around the clock and family and friends learn "care partner" skills formerly handled only by staff.

In essence, the Planetree philosophy is about addressing the needs of the whole person. And that means creating healthcare environments that not only nurture and heal but also empower and educate. Like most Planetree affiliates, Griffin Hospital provides patients with open access to their medical records; patients are even welcome to write comments in their charts. If they want to learn more about their particular illness, a resource center offers some 4,000 health-related books as well as audiotapes, journals and computer stations for their use.

Indeed, the hospital experience at Griffin, which in 1996 won the American Hospital Association's VISTA Award for an outstanding health facility, may be more comparable to entering a first-class hotel than the traditional hospital. The difference begins right in the hospital parking lot as classical music greets patients and visitors. Inside, more healing sounds are heard from the reception area's grand player piano. Walking through the carpeted and clutter-free hallways, a sense of quiet calm pervades. Entertainment lounges and activity rooms offer scheduled live music or games and movies. Patients and visitors can even prepare home-cooked meals in unit kitchens.

Images of "Club Med-style" healthcare often lead to assumptions of high-cost healthcare, but a sampling by THE QUALITY LETTER of select Planetree affiliates indicates that what makes Planetree effective does not entail extraordinary financial outlays. In fact, say supporters, the Planetree philosophy is in many ways especially appropriate to the cost-conscious concerns of today's managed care environment.

"Industry downsizing has created lots of problems in terms of staff morale," observes Ms. Gilpin. "We're all being forced to do more and more. What we're talking about in Planetree is reevaluating the way we view our role as healthcare professionals, moving away from a traditional task-oriented focus to a value-oriented focus. It's a different kind of paradigm, one that I believe makes it inherently easier to find satisfaction in our work."

For the nurses at Griffin Hospital, this shift toward a value-based focus began with redesign of their nursing model. "When we implemented Planetree," explains Lynn Werdal, R.N., M.S., Griffin's vice president for patient care services, "the nursing staff adopted a primary nursing model whereby a nurse is responsible for a small group of patients throughout their hospital stay, instead of only while they are in a particular unit." Admittedly, change is always a challenge, says Ms. Werdal, and the transition to a new nursing model was no exception. However, as she reports, the new system is now overwhelmingly favored among staff as a more personally rewarding and effective system of care.

The key factor in Griffin's success may be what Ms. Werdal calls their "secret ingredient" — regular retreats where nursing, support and ancillary staff gather for two days to learn more about the Planetree philosophy. The retreats feature various exercises designed to help staff better appreciate the hospital experience not only from the patient's perspective but also from that of other staff members and departments.

Griffin's emphasis on staff education extends to physicians, too. During the initial implementation of Planetree, the nursing staff developed an "adopt a doc" program whereby nurses were assigned to work one on one with select physicians to help acquaint them with the Planetree philosophy.

A Holistic Approach to Cost-Effective Care

According to Ms. Gilpin, Planetree's relevance in the current healthcare climate is further enhanced by its emphasis on volunteerism. "As hospitals face tighter budgets," she writes in the April 1997 issue of *PlaneTalk*, the newsletter of the Planetree Alliance, "volunteer programs can offer a range of services that are often beyond the time constraints of busy staff. Worries that volunteers could replace paid staff have given way to appreciation that help is available to provide simple comfort measures for patients and families."

The Volunteer Care Partner program in place at most Planetree affiliates trains volunteers to offer social support to patients who would otherwise be alone during their hospitalization. Griffin Hospital has developed a unique hand-holding program where volunteers comfort and hold hands with patients who must remain awake during eye surgery. The Planetree philosophy also strives to bring families more directly into the care process, instructing them in various aspects of care related to patient comfort.

"A lot of the literature talks about the high percentage of calls that are for patients' comfort needs," notes Carol Wahl, R.N., M.B.A., operations leader of patient care services and champion of Alegent Health system's Planetree program in the Omaha, Neb., area. "Families, if they sit by the bedside, want to be useful, to do something for their loved ones. So if you allow them to participate, they're usually very excited about it. We're not talking about them doing the work of nursing, but dealing with personal needs related to comfort that most patients would prefer to let the family do anyway. In the end, we find that it actually saves nursing time instead of creating more."

Ms. Gilpin adds that with shorter lengths of stay, family involvement has become even more important. "The average length of stay for a stroke patient, for example, is now four days, whereas 10 or 15 years ago it was more in the 10- to 14-day range. The family of a patient who has suffered a massive stroke needs to know how to feed someone on aspiration precautions or ambulate somebody with a deficit. In this sense, what Planetree has to offer lends itself well to the current healthcare climate."

In a sense, the volunteer concept extends to the patients themselves, who are encouraged to take more responsibility for their care. This includes learning basics of self-medication and proper nutrition or exercising the right to insert comments in their records.

Interestingly, physicians at Mid-Columbia Medical Center, a 44-bed Planetree affiliate in The Dalles, Ore., were initially concerned that if patients had more access to information, it would take more of their time to explain and interpret that information. "What we have found instead," says Jacque Scott, R.N., director of Planetree at Mid-Columbia and vice president of clinical services, "is that giving patients access to information — access to their records and charts — has actually made life easier and less costly in terms of time, because patients generally feel less confused and better able to deal with the issues. It has also made patients more of a liaison between specialists."

Commitment First, Capital Second

The 650-bed Bergan Mercy Medical Center in Omaha, Neb., became the 12th Planetree affiliate in November 1994. It is a member of Alegent Health System, which includes six acute care hospitals and more than 30 regional clinics and outpatient sites in Iowa and Nebraska. Currently, Planetree is in place in 15 units at Bergan Mercy and is being adopted throughout the Alegent system.

It was in Bergan Mercy's emergency department that Planetree principles were first implemented within the Alegent HealthSystem. Unlike some other Planetree affiliates, Alegent didn't consider renovation a necessary prerequisite to implementing the program. Initially, its goal was to engineer a series of easily implemented, "patient-friendly" redesigns to create a calmer, more comforting atmosphere.

Accordingly, some of the steps taken included no longer storing wheelchairs and crash carts in public view, adjusting the lighting to reduce glare, and installing erasable display boards in exam rooms where nurses could write their names or list scheduled tests for patients. The waiting room was also stocked with health-related pamphlets and touch-screen computers. And children's exam rooms were equipped with rocking chairs, TVs, VCRs and a supply of Walt Disney cartoons.

Another small but significant change was institution of the "100% callback" program, which requires that every ER patient receive a follow-up call within 24 hours after discharge. According to Ms. Wahl, simply having a nurse call to make sure patients are following postcare instructions or to answer any unanswered questions has notably reduced the percentage of return ER visits. Complaints against the department dropped from 37 in 1994 (before Planetree) to only two in the level 2 trauma center in 1995.

Whenever building renovation is on the agenda, Alegent does consider it an opportunity to incorporate Planetree architectural and environmental principles. Last year, with Bergan Mercy's ER targeted for a $1.3 million renovation, the hospital turned to research by Roger Ulrich, Ph.D., an environmental psychologist at Texas A&M University and an expert on healing environments, to determine ways to bring a nurturing influence into the building design. One idea was to add a lobby fountain, an aesthetically calming influence as well as an effective way to mask sound. In addition, ambulance arrivals now have a separate entrance, and locker areas have been expanded to better accommodate staff needs for a retreat from the noise and commotion.

Overall, Bergan Mercy reports that between 1994 and 1995, the average length of stay in the medical ICU declined from 3.2 to 2.5 days, in the surgical ICU from 2.7 to 2.1 days, and in the diabetes unit from 7.0 to 4.3 days. Of course, in today's healthcare economy, many factors influence the trend toward reduced lengths of stay. However, as Ms. Wahl notes, Bergan Mercy considers these trends indicative of a general improvement in the hospital's capacity to deliver high-quality care, which it believes has been enhanced by Planetree principles.

For Ms. Wahl, success with Planetree is a matter of leadership support combined with grassroots initiative and flexibility in implementation. "It's really not a matter of needing a lot of capital," she concludes. "You just need a lot of people who want to practice medicine this way."

A Hospital Without Walls

At Mid-Columbia Medical Center, which adopted the program hospital-wide in 1992, Planetree's emphasis on prevention and education has found its logical outgrowth in the hospital's current orientation toward community outreach. "Our strategy has truly become a community strategy," says Ms. Scott. "In a sense, we're trying to deemphasize the hospital and emphasize the community, to build a 'hospital without walls.' And that means improving and increasing our access points in the community."

Toward this end, Mid-Columbia has formed a regional network called Columbia Gorge Community Health Network with three other area hospitals. The network is currently coordinating or developing a series of community health programs that seek to address the health concerns of local residents, as identified in community- and state-sponsored surveys.

"One cultural consequence as a result of Planetree," notes Ms. Scott, "is that it has taught us not to feel like we're the experts in everything. In fact, often we are the ones who need to ask the questions, whether it is of the community, the children or other specialists, rather than trying to take the traditional role of the all-knowing, powerful institution."

"In the past, we weren't really used to asking patients what they needed," explains Ms. Scott. "In fact, we found a great deal of pleasure in anticipating people's needs. That was our golden rule — anticipate. But when we talk about empowering the patient, we're talking about asking them what they need rather than assuming we know what is best for them. I had a patient, for example, who was hesitant to walk in the corridor. Instead of just saying, 'You've just got to do it,' I asked her, 'What is the problem? Is there anything I can do?' And she said, 'Well, I hate my urine bag being out. My kids can see it. My husband can see it. My minister can see it. I just prefer not to walk around.' Then she suggested, 'Could you perhaps find a gift bag to use as a cover?' So a staff member went downtown and bought several different bags. Not only did it help her, but we found that about half of our patients wanted to use them."

"Before Planetree, despite our empathy, I think we would have been more inclined to dismiss these kinds of concerns," concludes Ms. Scott. "Now, we're more conscious of paying attention to these clues. The patients know we're more inclined to listen to them, so they're also more inclined to tell us what they need. And more often than not, they'll come up with a cost-effective solution."

Recently, Mid-Columbia has opened a Center for Mind/Body Medicine, modeled after a similar facility begun several years ago by Herbert Benson, M.D., at New England Deaconess Hospital in Boston. The center uses behavioral techniques that draw on the power and biology of belief to effect healing.

According to Ms. Scott, Mid-Columbia has a history of consistently high rates of patient satisfaction (95%), both before and after Planetree. However, as she notes, the personal stories patients and families tell are much more powerful now. In her estimation, Planetree has enabled Mid-Columbia to mature as an organization, rooting the facility more firmly in a patient/provider team approach, guided first and always by principles of prevention, education and empowerment. (Mid-Columbia's team approach is organized around a primary nursing model, assisted by volunteer staff, an arts coordinator, a care partner facilitator, a patient educator and a medical librarian.)

The Planetree Difference

Undoubtedly, patient-focused care has acquired a certain popularity of late in healthcare. Yet the term is often used to describe little more than an "efficiency experiment" — and an often short-lived one at that — as Patrick Charmel, senior vice president of operations for Griffin Hospital, recently commented in *Trustee* (November/ December 1996).

The Planetree difference, however, is that it is first of all committed to improving medical care from the patient's perspective. "It may be that initially people want to talk about cost-effectiveness and market differentiation as a way to win administrative buy-in," notes Lea Gamble, Planetree's chief operating officer. "But what Planetree is really about is changing the culture. I believe the people we are working with are really looking for something that has lasting value. They're looking for a better way to deliver care, and they feel Planetree is the right thing to do." She notes that most organizations that begin with one unit devoted to the Planetree program quickly move to make it institutionwide.

For Ms. Scott, it is the theme of respect for the individual that has proven most compelling. "I've found that it is often the small steps we take to demonstrate that respect that make all the difference in a person's hospital experience. Something as simple, for example, as providing gowns that cover people gives a message that you respect the patients, which is certainly what all of us want. It's important to begin with the 'little things' — those issues that may have bothered people for years — but which we as a profession have largely done nothing about."

Similarly, notes Ms. Wahl, the measure of Planetree's impact involves more than adding up the number of programs in place. "The Planetree philosophy is really about who we are and how we interact with people, including how we treat each other as healthcare professionals. It's about something as basic as paying attention to the language that we use. For example, at the end of visiting hours, we used to have an announcement over the speakers to the effect, 'Visiting hours are over. You are requested to leave the building quietly and promptly.' Now, we have a phrase that just says, 'Regular visiting hours are over, and we wish you a safe trip home.' And we leave open the option to stay overnight if the visitors wish."

Like any start-up venture or project, Planetree, of course, requires financial commitment, especially at the outset. A first-year affiliation, reports Ms. Gamble, costs $20,000; each subsequent year is $15,000; and there are other consulting and training costs. However, adds Ms. Gamble, "When you think about what healthcare organizations often pay consulting firms, we are not expensive." She cites Griffin Hospital as an organization that was struggling to maintain service areas when its leaders decided to redo the birthing center based on patients' wants and needs. They then decided to adopt Planetree principles throughout the hospital and "now they are thriving."

According to Ms. Gamble, Planetree has learned the value of a flexible approach toward implementation, recognizing that each organization presents unique needs and challenges. "Some hospitals may want to move faster than others," she says, "while others may want to spend less money or emphasize a specific component of the Planetree philosophy, such as integrating complementary therapies. Across the spectrum there are also differing cultural concerns. We try to be sensitive to each organization's priorities as we move through the core implementation."

Becoming a Planetree affiliate begins with an on-site visit and assessment by an organizational development specialist. A critical first goal is winning staff buy-in through staff retreats and "train the trainer" sessions. "Obviously, staff training is always an additional expense," says Ms. Gilpin. "But the money you invest in your staff comes back in the way of happier, more productive staff. We don't have any research on this, but I truly believe, for example, the climate of high medication errors in healthcare is primarily a result of staff stress. So anything you're doing to improve morale will certainly help in the long run."

The national office provides access to consultants with many different skills — from specialists in staff retraining to noise abatement specialists to interior decorators and lighting specialists — that will contribute to the homelike comfort conducive to healing.

"Basically, you can spend as much or as little as you want in implementing the concepts," concludes Ms. Gilpin. "Planetree itself is really a kind of cost-neutral proposition. I speak to many healthcare organizations, and I generally find that they like our emphasis on patient education, but the attitude typically is that it is very expensive to implement. In response, I often tell people an open-chart policy is free, kindness is free. There are a lot of things you can do that will add nothing to your budget."

In her view, although the number of Planetree affiliates has fluctuated over the years, their success or failure is largely inseparable from the broader financial health of the sponsoring organization. Overall, however, Planetree hospitals report improvements that they attribute in significant ways to adoption of Planetree principles. Mid-Columbia's length of stay, for example, has declined from 4.1 to 3.5 days, despite a higher acuity index, and turnover among nursing staff has gone down to less than 3% in the past five years.

According to its national office, five Planetree affiliates report no staff turnover as a result of job dissatisfaction since implementation, and seven hospitals have received more letters of praise and fewer complaints. Griffin Hospital reports an inpatient patient satisfaction level of 93% for the past two years (the national average is 84%). The Samuels Planetree Unit at Beth Israel Medical Center in New York City reports that patients rate staff as more attentive to their fears and more likely to involve family and friends than other units. At California Pacific Medical Center, the original Planetree model site in San Francisco, a 1988 study conducted by the University of Washington showed that the percentage of patients using the ER within six months after hospitalization was 8.2% on the Planetree unit and 14.9% for other units.

The real story of Planetree cannot be adequately captured in even the most impressive statistics. It is more in the intangible dynamics of human relationships — in the meaningful ways that healthcare professionals make their work an expression of their humanity — that the real measure of Planetree is revealed.

"We play the Brahms Lullaby whenever a new baby is born," says Ms. Wahl, "which we started as a celebration of life. It's a meaningful and moving moment for the families. But we've also found that the Brahms Lullaby provides a sense of closure when somebody dies. It's these small gestures, as so many people have told us, that often have a huge personal impact."

"What we like about Planetree," concludes Ms. Werdal, "is that its proponents aren't afraid to use the 'S' word, to talk about healing as a spiritual quest, which I don't necessarily mean in a religious sense. Our work is about trying to address what it is that gives human beings a purpose for living, offers joy or inspires hope." Angelica Thieriot believed that illness is a transformational experience. "Planetree is about trying to reach inside and touch the souls of other human beings, to make them as complete and whole as possible during the time they are in our care. In this sense, healing is very different from curing. A person can die healed, if by healing we mean that peace of mind that comes from within. If we can help our patients find this inner peace, then we have done our job."

Integrating Women's Healthcare — Serving the Whole Woman

"One-stop shopping" is the buzzword for advocates of health systems integrating women's care. But will women's health improve? Although evidence is short, systems integrating services say that they're responding to what women tell them they want — and early results suggest they're on the right track.

For decades, women's healthcare focused primarily on reproductive organs. The complex and unique healthcare needs of the "whole" woman — which cut across medical specialties and psychosocial disciplines — were largely overlooked. Now, in the last decade of the 20th century, society is finally awakening to the need to provide better care for women.

Key evidence that society is zeroing in on women's health needs is the creation of the Office of Research on Women's Health at the National Institutes of Health. This office was established in 1990 after the Congressional Caucus for Women's Issues asked why women were routinely left out of NIH-funded medical research — an exclusion that left many unanswered questions about the best ways to treat women. After a U.S. General Accounting Office investigation confirmed that most research dollars were going to studies of men only, ORWH was formed to remedy the problem. In addition to ensuring that clinical trials involve adequate numbers of women, ORWH is funding a 14-year study of 150,000 women at 45 medical centers across the country — the nation's largest study ever on the health of either men or women.

Another effort that illustrates the groundswell of interest in improving women's healthcare is the National Centers of Excellence in Women's Health program, launched in 1996 by the Public Health Service's Office on Women's Health under the leadership of Susan Blumenthal, M.D., deputy assistant secretary for women's health, Department of Health and Human Services. Through this initiative, academic institutions with strong programs in women's medicine receive funds from the PHS to help them develop effective models of medical care, research and training for other organizations to emulate.

Six centers across the country were awarded funds in 1996, and six more were selected this month. Each must already have the foundation for "one-stop shopping" centers that provide comprehensive care to address the needs of women at all stages of life, including:

- Preventive medicine and screening;
- Diagnosis and treatment of disorders that affect women (not just reproductive care);
- Emphasis on both physical and mental health; and
- Health education.

From *The Quality Letter for Healthcare Leaders*, Vol. 9:7, 1997

Having a full range of services easily available is important, HHS believes, so that women can take care of many medical needs — including preventive care — in as few visits as possible. Returning for multiple appointments is something that many women today — whose time is already spread too thin — are unable to do. The centers are also charged with setting research agendas on women's health issues, creating strategies to promote women's participation in clinical trials, forming alliances with businesses and community groups, developing a women's health curriculum for medical schools, and fostering the career development of women in academic medicine.

Not only government, but employers as well, are exhibiting increased interest in women's health — especially now that women make up nearly half the nation's work force and will constitute 63% of new employees by the year 2000. In 1995 the Washington Business Group on Health initiated its Corporate Leadership in Women's Health program to promote knowledge of women's healthcare services among large employers and to provide guidelines for developing high-quality, cost-effective programs.

The Case for Integrating Services

Both the CLWH and the PHS programs emphasize an important trend today: integration of women's health services. With integrated care, women's needs are tackled in a coordinated, comprehensive way. The goal is to avoid duplicating efforts within the institution, while at the same time ensuring that no aspect of a woman's healthcare is overlooked.

The push toward integration stems from "intense competition in healthcare delivery and the drive toward managed care, which has opened the eyes of providers to the need to collaborate," says Chip Caldwell, senior vice president of Premier Performance Services, the Marietta, Ga.-based decision support and consulting division for Premier's network of 1,400 hospitals. He notes that his firm and others involved in process redesign have seen demonstrated time and again that integration brings value in terms of both cost and quality improvements. "The best approach," he says, "is to address the continuum of care, from preventive services and health maintenance through primary, specialty, institutional and after care."

Integrated Care Is on the Upswing

Lack of research on women, the increasing numbers of women in the work force and the benefits of integrating services are important reasons why so much attention is being turned to women's health — but there are many others cited by women's health advocates:

Women control most healthcare dollars. They are the major users of the healthcare system and are the primary decisionmakers when it comes to healthcare for their families.

Overall, women must deal with a greater range of concerns, including reproductive health, menopause, psychosocial issues, chronic diseases and mental health. Some health problems are unique to women or affect women differently than they do men.

Women live longer, which means they will constitute a larger share of the future population. Also, as they age, they will be more susceptible to disease.

The philosophy toward women has changed in the American culture, so that today, equality and equal access are emphasized.

A 1993 survey by researchers at Johns Hopkins University identified 3,600 women's health centers in the United States serving about 14.5 million women — a little more than one-tenth of the female population. Only 12% of those offered primary care, while 71% focused on reproductive health, 4% on childbirth and 6% on breast cancer and care. Though more recent survey results are not available, industry watchers believe the number of institutions offering comprehensive, integrated care is on the upswing. Today, it is hard to find a stand-alone women's health center that hasn't affiliated or isn't in the process of affiliating with an integrated healthcare system.

Case studies and anecdotal reports suggest that integration of services will improve health outcomes for women, but solid evidence is lacking. "That kind of research has not been done," admits Carol Weisman, a health service researcher who led the Johns Hopkins survey. "It's a critical need." Currently, measures of the quality of women's health services are limited mostly to patient satisfaction surveys and analysis of screening rates.

Despite the scarcity of hard outcomes data, healthcare organizations across the country are moving toward integrating women's services. "We're all searching for those outcomes to support our efforts," says Debbi Linhart, vice president of ambulatory care and strategic development at Magee-Womens Hospital in Pittsburgh. "But right now, our intuitive feeling is that when you design a program around women's needs and they are partners in their healthcare, they are more likely to participate, which leads to better health. For example, if a new mother comes back for the first baby visit, then you can do follow-up family planning. If she comes in for family planning, you can evaluate her for pelvic inflammatory disease."

Magee-Womens Hospital is one of the nation's few women's hospitals, with approximately 9,000 births annually. It also has the largest breast care program in the country and 13 satellite Womancare Centers serving patients throughout western Pennsylvania.

Integrated Care Programs: Signs of Progress

The following overviews come from organizations that have made positive strides toward integration of women's health services.

UCSF — Developing New Clinical Paradigms

The University of California at San Francisco Medical Center is among the six 1996 winners of the PHS OWH Centers of Excellence grants. The UCSF National Center of Excellence in Women's Health is a large, multidisciplinary, multidepartmental model of care. UCSF applied for the PHS grant, says Nancy Milliken, M.D., the center's director, because it wants to share the successes of its women's health program with other institutions and help develop "new clinical paradigms" that will make a difference in women's health.

UCSF launched its first two comprehensive healthcare sites in 1994 and added a community-based practice in 1996. At each, primary care and ob/gyn providers work side by side and coordinate with other practitioners in the system for specialized care in such areas as mental health, incontinence, breast care, osteoporosis management and HIV services. Providers at each location share information primarily by interpersonal communication but also via computerized medical records. These limitations of the information technology are a challenge in efforts to integrate care across multiple sites.

UCSF is striving to improve women's health not only through providing broad clinical services but also by promoting research, leadership, education and community outreach. A key goal is to disseminate new research findings that could affect women's health to the practitioners and out to the public as soon as possible.

The impetus for UCSF's integration efforts came from focus groups and one-on-one interviews of women in the community. After feedback suggested that UCSF's fragmented approach was not meeting women's needs, a formal business plan for integrated services was developed and presented to the medical center. Clinical care services are now under the joint direction of Dr. Milliken, an ob/gyn, and Laurel Dawson, M.D., an internist. Several standing committees address site-specific operations, patient education, marketing and community outreach.

Among topics pertinent to women in which UCSF is conducting research are osteoporosis prevention, healthy eating for women and domestic violence. Other areas the institution has identified for further attention and services because of their high incidence among women are depression, cardiovascular disease, incontinence and breast cancer.

Within the first three years of launching the first two comprehensive care sites, 60% of the women who came in for services "had had no other contact with the university," Dr. Milliken notes. "This suggests we're attracting new patients — many by word of mouth and through our community education programs."

HealthPartners — Fulfilling Its Research Mission to Improve Care

HealthPartners, one of the largest healthcare organizations in Minnesota — the result of a merger between a staff-model HMO, a contracted-care-model managed care group and a hospital and clinic system — recently won an HERA Award from Wyeth-Ayerst for its quality improvement efforts in women's and children's health. One of its successes was reducing ectopic pregnancy rupture rates from 32% to 5% over five years.

Four of HealthPartners' 19 staff-model clinics have women's centers that offer comprehensive care and educational resources. The largest of these, the Como Clinic, opened in the fall of 1996. Cheri Rolnick, Ph.D., HealthPartners' unofficial "women's health guru," does not coordinate clinical services but links all areas together in a mission of conducting research for better overall care.

Integration has been an emphasis at HealthPartners since its inception, Dr. Rolnick notes, simply by virtue of its being a managed care organization. Her belief that integration of women's healthcare is beneficial is "intuitive," she says. "It just makes sense to minimize fragmented care and to see people as a whole. A comprehensive managed care approach allows efforts to focus on systems that can lead to improvements in preventive care and overall health."

All patients have a comprehensive medical record that can be accessed by providers throughout the system. Although each clinic puts great emphasis on education, the Como Clinic has a special resource area staffed by nurses, in which women can view videos, read print materials and use computers to obtain detailed information.

Supporting HealthPartners' women's health efforts is its Center for Health Promotion, which provides community education programs to improve health. The center sets specific targets it can measure, such as increasing the numbers of women receiving mammography or prenatal care and reducing the numbers of low-birth-weight babies. The Institute for Clinical Systems Integration, a separately incorporated entity, creates guidelines and protocols on the best ways to prevent and manage specific conditions, including many affecting women, such as breast cancer, cervical cancer, domestic violence and infertility.

Memorial Healthcare System — Responding to Demand

Memorial Healthcare System in Houston is an 11-hospital integrated healthcare delivery system that does 12,000 deliveries per year. Since the organization started expanding and integrating women's health services in 1991, volume has increased every year — in some hospitals as much as 10% to 20% over the past two years, says Vicki Lucas, Ph.D., director of women's and children's services.

Besides offering primary care, the Memorial Hospital Southwest site has inpatient and outpatient gynecology services, reproductive care, a breast center and a wide range of wellness and education services, including screenings, seminars and support groups. Other sites offer comprehensive care for women as well. A centralized computer system allows for easy access to medical records and lab data throughout the system.

Memorial initiated its integrated care efforts because "women are demanding them," Dr. Lucas says. "They're tired of being dissected into pieces — their uterus and reproductive organs, their breasts. Human females are complex organisms. We know that outcomes are better when women are treated as a whole and when the impact of physical illness on psychological, spiritual and sexual aspects is taken into account."

Memorial's integrated approach to women's and children's services was put in place after a year of focus groups, interviews, data analysis, staff meetings, strategic planning and budgeting. The most compelling evidence that Memorial needed to revamp its women's services was data showing declining patient volume and revenue. The factual data that Dr. Lucas presented to administrators — suggesting that expanding and integrating women's services would bring in new patients — is what sold the program, she says.

North Iowa Mercy Health Network — Treating the Whole Woman

North Iowa Mercy Health Network, based in Mason City, Iowa, comprises 42 primary care clinics and 14 hospitals in 16 counties. The comprehensive Women's Health Center Clinic, located at the North Iowa Mercy Health Center, is "a very interdisciplinary approach all in one place," says Maxine Brinkman, director of women's services. The center has family practice, internal medicine, reproductive care other than obstetrics, counseling, therapeutic massage, a breast center, a continence clinic, alternative care and education. "To the public, care appears seamless," Ms. Brinkman notes. "That was one of our goals; we recognize that women are busy and need nonduplicative, easily accessible services."

North Iowa Mercy's integration efforts got under way in 1995. To start the program, the clinic developed a strategic plan with input and approval from a multidisciplinary task force that included senior administrators and representatives from services that provide healthcare to women.

Integrating women's healthcare was sparked by Ms. Brinkman's belief — and that of others at North Iowa Mercy — that "outcomes can be optimized by treating the whole woman in relation to her environment, throughout her lifetime," she says. Supporting these convictions are studies by the Stone Center at Wellesley College and David Sobel, M.D., of Kaiser Permanente demonstrating that approaches promoting relationship building, trust and authenticity improve outcomes. The Stone Center found that women who are connected through relationships are mentally healthier — "an excellent justification for seamless, integrated care," Ms. Brinkman notes.

So far, evidence that the integrated approach is working is limited to patient satisfaction surveys, which show that women are "very satisfied," Ms. Brinkman says. A five-year study is under way to measure how many more early-stage breast cancers are being caught by promoting mammography. Early detection not only improves health outcomes, Ms. Brinkman points out, but also saves money, since a late-stage breast cancer can cost $40,000 or more to treat, as compared with $13,000 in the earliest stage.

Keys to Success

These women's healthcare advocates and other women's healthcare experts and providers offered a wealth of tips for other organizations interested in providing more comprehensive, integrated services.

- **Make sure your services are based on a true commitment to women's health and are not simply a marketing tactic.**

"So many organizations put a label on something in order to market it, and it's really no different from what they had before," says Ms. Linhart of Magee-Womens Hospital, which with UCSF was one of the first six National Centers of Excellence.

- **Be aware of the politics that sometimes affect efforts to establish women's health services in what has traditionally been a patriarchal system.** "Ask yourselves, 'Are we doing the right things for the right reasons?'" says Ms. Brinkman. The four institutions profiled here, for the most part, broadly support the concept of comprehensive care for women, but there is acknowledgment that some providers feel their turf is threatened. Getting those providers to buy in means providing hard facts about benefits to women and the institution.

- **Know the population you're serving and identify unmet needs.**

It's important to listen to women in the community talk about the services they want, what they feel is lacking and how existing programs can be improved. All the healthcare organizations profiled here held focus groups of local women, and some conducted surveys. Many also found it helpful to look at how other healthcare organizations are meeting women's needs. "But remember there is no cookie cutter," cautions Ms. Linhart. "Design the programs for your specific population."

Feedback that organizations received from their research underscored the importance of being sensitive to women's needs and the pressures they face. As a result, the centers try to offer convenient hours that are workable for busy women; to create a safe, comfortable and welcoming environment; and to make privacy, confidentiality and preserving women's dignity a priority.

Dr. Milliken notes that, at UCSF, their focus groups turned up an unexpected result: Women in the community wanted one women's health center that did not have a primary care physician on site, because some felt that sites with both primary care and ob/gyn limited their choices and interfered with confidentiality. UCSF's response was to set up one ob/gyn-only site and three offering comprehensive care.

Denise Ghostlaw, director of The Women's Health Center of The Kingston Hospital in New York, discovered from focus groups held during the center's planning phase that some women felt that physicians did not treat them sensitively or take them seriously. Others were unsure how to get referrals or how to get into the system in the first place. As a result, the center, launched in 1994, promotes a philosophy of respect and empowerment for women and offers a referral hotline that links women with services throughout the community. Also, because women said they wanted more education, the center offers support groups and community forums that not only teach women about diseases and treatment but also coach them in working as "empowered" partners with their physicians.

During the information-gathering and planning stage, examine what is already available in the healthcare system, what is succeeding and what is missing. Then design programs to address unmet needs and tie the programs together with coordinated marketing, education, research efforts and outreach. Dr. Milliken and her colleagues at UCSF believe in one-stop shopping. However, they discovered they could not optimally meet women's needs when offering mental health services at the women's health centers. "We'd find that either the schedule of the mental health provider didn't match the demand, or their specialty wasn't what every patient needed, or the location was not convenient for women who needed a series of appointments." Instead, women are now referred to a centrally located referral service that offers a range of mental health services.

As programs get going, conduct surveys to gauge customer satisfaction and address areas where performance is weak. For example, Memorial Healthcare System increased its mammography rates by 30% after opening breast centers separate from the radiology department. "Women don't want to think about cancer," says Dr. Lucas. "We discovered that if mammography is framed within a well-woman perspective, it's more comfortable and reassuring and women don't mind coming in."

Make sure that clinics, services and physicians across the system have the same brochures, resource lists and other materials so that women receive a unified message. "Patients who get a consistent message wherever they go in the system, whether it's an obstetrical visit, parent education class, or labor and delivery, are happier," Dr. Lucas notes. And make sure that all providers are informed about the full scope of woman-oriented services in the health system so they can refer patients efficiently.

- **Ensure that providers of women's health services have gender expertise.**

Gender expertise provides a background that influences the overall culture of the organization and how healthcare services are offered, advises Ms. Brinkman. She defines gender expertise as "providing information and care that is based on research on women and that involves all aspects of a woman's physical, psychosocial and spiritual health throughout her lifetime." Women expect, she adds, "that their providers will be knowledgeable in how diseases and treatments affect women."

Don't assume that female staffers automatically have gender expertise. Ms. Brinkman advises adopting the approach used at her institution: bringing in experts on gender, diversity and customer relations to educate the staff so everyone becomes a woman's health advocate. She admits that "it's a challenge" to create a culture in which women's unique health needs are recognized and validated. Now, because she and her colleagues have raised awareness across the system, "when women's health is discussed, we are always invited to the table."

Tied in with promoting gender expertise is getting physicians and other stakeholders on multidisciplinary teams to buy in to what you're trying to accomplish. Share data with them so they understand where things stand and what needs to be done for improvement. "Consensus is essential," says Ms. Ghostlaw. "You need a shared vision, and from there you should seek participation not only from providers and staff, but from other agencies and institutions so you complement each other's efforts."

When possible, have one person in charge of women's health services who understands the continuum of care and is comfortable with both clinical and administrative issues.

Dr. Lucas says coordinating the efforts of 300 women's healthcare staff members at Memorial Hospital Southwest has led to a smooth-running operation, a 6% decrease in cesarean deliveries over three years and a savings of $4.5 million through standardization of supplies and equipment. But it's harder to add efficiencies or make changes at other women's healthcare sites over which she has no authority, she notes. She believes even more could be done if there were a vice president for women's services with direct authority and accountability across the system.

Set outcomes targets.

When setting these targets, such as lowering rates of cesarean sections or reducing length of stay in the neonatal intensive care unit, set congruent performance standards so that staff are held accountable for outcomes. "For example," says Dr. Lucas, "70% of my employees' evaluations are tied to very specific group performance standards that have to do with the three C's: cost, clinical quality and customer service." She notes that in a managed care environment, physicians' incentives are more readily aligned with those of the hospital: All are motivated to lower cesarean delivery rates, for instance.

Have the proper technology in place so you can communicate easily across multiple sites.

This includes voice mail, electronic mail and a modern computer system that gives practitioners easy access to patient charts. Many providers mentioned the value of being able to send computerized reminders to women about screenings, immunizations and other preventive care services.

Identifying Needs, Being Responsive

Although it may sound complex, providing better healthcare to women "really isn't tricky," says Ms. Brinkman, who, in addition to her position at North Iowa Mercy Healthcare System, is president of the National Association of Women's Health Professionals. "The main piece is identifying women's needs and being responsive. Then you have to get people on board who are schooled in gender expertise."

What women crave most, she says, "is a relationship with a provider. They want to be listened to, validated and treated with respect." If you start by asking women in your community what they want, you've taken the first step toward integrated healthcare.

Utah Health System Focuses on Patient Needs to Redesign Surgical System

A nurse-led project to redesign services at Salt Lake City's LDS Hospital went beyond saving time and money to add such perks such as valet parking. If able, surgery patients are allowed to walk to the operating room instead of waiting to be wheeled in on a gurney. And, instead of the traditional hospital gowns, some patients wear underwear and pajama bottoms during minor outpatient surgeries.

When patients walk in the door, they typically meet with a nurse coordinator instead of a registration clerk. Unnecessary lab tests and repeat blood draws have been eliminated. For example, nurses draw blood when IVs are inserted, saving the patient a second needle stick. Other typically routine procedures, such as chest X-rays and EKGs, are only performed when specifically indicated.

"People want to know—in this world of mergers and acquisitions—that health care providers still remember health care is about people and that hospitals are taking measures to help patients maintain their dignity," says Diane Kelly, a former neonatal intensive-care nurse and principal facilitator for work redesign at LDS.

By reengineering outpatient surgery, LDS maintained its all-RN staff — in lieu of cross-trained employees — and reduced the average cost-per-case by 14%. The redesign has helped move patients through the system more efficiently while increasing peak capacity by 50%. Despite restructuring, staff levels remained consistent and overtime was reduced by 30%.

Cutting Through Problems in Surgery

In 1990, LDS and two other Intermountain Health Care Hospitals merged under a single administrative team. The Salt Lake Valley Surgical Services Line includes six outpatient surgery sites, each with several operating rooms. The surgery line is budgeted for 500 FTEs and, in 1997, handled as many as 2,600 outpatient surgeries a month. Prior to the redesign, LDS' same-day surgery sites began backing up when patient capacity neared 50. These days, the surgical line can take on more than 80 visits a day with virtually no backlogs.

The pivotal point of this project began when an administrative director was assigned to this area. A clear vision was established to provide patient/family-focused care while maintaining a very high level of clinical outcomes. "The beauty of the surgery piece is that the organization structure was based on communication and relationships instead of hierarchy and power," Kelly explains.

While the six sites were all part of the same corporation, they competed for patients. The outpatient surgery centers had been sending ques-

From *Reengineering the Hospital,* Vol. 5:1, 1998

tionnaires to patients a week after surgery. Each of the centers, however, used different types of surveys, and the hospitals didn't use any. The system decided to develop a standardized survey and compare the six facilities. And that is where it all began, says Joan Lelis, administrative director for surgical services.

The Beginning

In 1994, the quality coordinator from each of the six sites became part of the quality committee. One of its first tasks was to establish consistent patient satisfaction surveys across all six sites. A pre-op and a post-op nurse from each site identified best practices throughout the system. Later, this team of nurses focused on processes in need of improvement. A big difference between the hospitals and the surgical centers, the team discovered, was the protocol used for releasing patients.

"The outpatient surgery centers discharged patients based on a scoring system rather than using vital signs," recalls Cheryl Young-Metos, a staff nurse at Intermountain Surgical Center and chairperson of the quality committee. "Patients are scored on consciousness, color, movement, oxygenation level, etc. That was appealing to nurses who were locked into the old method of using vital signs and having to keep the patient for a set time."

EKGs, Blood Tests and X-rays

A problem common to each site was physicians ordering unnecessary tests. While developing a consensus for minimum labs was a two-year process, Lelis says it was well worth the effort. Some physicians, the team learned, simply ordered the same battery of tests for every patient because that's what they were trained to do. Many of the tests, such as blood work, EKGs and chest X-rays weren't necessary for all patients.

The nursing team presented its ideas for change to the executive committee, a group made up of surgical services managers, staff nurse leaders and representatives from other disciplines. From there they pleaded their case to the medical executive committee at each site (these groups include the chief of surgery and the chief of anesthesiology). A set of lab minimums were ultimately established. Physicians, however, were not restricted from ordering as many tests as they felt they needed to treat the patient.

"It's very difficult to change mentality. The chief of anesthesia and the chief of surgery at each site helped explain the reason behind minimum labs to the physicians," Lelis explains. "It took two years of going in front of the committee each month and explaining the progress that had been made. But it was absolutely worthwhile. It's wonderful and very patient-friendly. It makes sense and it has reduced our costs, as well as costs to the patient."

The Late Show

Bottlenecks in surgery were a common and significant problem at LDS. Backups that occurred throughout the day could often be traced back to the first surgery of the morning. One or two surgeons arriving late to a surgery scheduled for 7:30 a.m., for example, created a domino effect, obliterating schedules for the rest of the day. Late starts became even more of a problem as community population growth and gains in market share increased patient volume.

The team tracked scheduled and actual surgery start times for each physician. According to the data, tardy surgeons were the overwhelming cause of delays and subsequent bottlenecks in the OR. This information was given to the chief of surgery who shared it with colleagues.

Simply getting surgeons to the hospital on time was only part of the solution. Some staff members had grown accustomed to chronically late surgeons, and typically weren't ready for the first patient until well after the 7:30 start time.

"Sometimes it's a vicious cycle, so we were attentive to the hospital side of it and made sure the room and patient were always ready by the scheduled starting time," Kelly says.

Getting the physicians involved was a key element, and fostered physician ownership in the redesign process.

The key to success, Lelis says, was that every aspect of the redesign was done from the patients' perspective. Since implementing changes, patient satisfaction levels among LDS' same-day surgery patients have increased to the level touted by the system's free standing groups.

Getting on Board With Patients

Patient advisory boards help hospitals see through patients' eyes.

After a successful organ transplant at an East Coast hospital, the recovering patient craved a grilled cheese sandwich and made numerous requests. The patient's new organ had traveled cross-country to the operating room in a matter of hours; it took four days for a grilled cheese sandwich to get from the hospital's kitchen to the patient's room.

While receiving the wrong lunch is a minor problem when compared to successfully transplanting an organ, seemingly minor problems can have a significant impact on how patients perceive their care and the hospital, explains Katharine Luther, RN, MPM, case management director at a 500-bed, not-for-profit within the Texas Medical Center, Houston.

At another large metropolitan hospital, Luther helped establish an advisory board made up entirely of hospital patients and their family members. Not long ago, Luther says, people working at a hospital wouldn't be concerned about what their patients had to say. However, in the wake of managed care and increased competition, patients have become a very valuable resource for improving the quality of care.

The Need to Partner With Patients

People in health care pride themselves on care they provide to patients, notes Luther. However, patients have come to expect a high level of care from their health care providers. What patients and their family members found lacking was a more caring attitude.

The board Luther established consisted of about 15 people ranging in age from the mid-20s to the early 70s. It was important that the board be representative of the hospital's patient population. Some patients were chosen because they had complained about something at the hospital. Upon examining their complaints, Luther says she realized these people often had valid points. And if the hospital wasn't meeting their needs, what about the rest of the patient population? As board members, these former complainers were very willing to help and became excellent proxies for the hospital.

Giving Patients What They Want

The board's task was to help the hospital determine what's most important to patients and how to incorporate that into their care. "For some patients, a hot cup of coffee in the morning is very important to them. If they have that, they can handle anything else," says Luther. "So we need to know how to get them that cup of coffee. If they can't have a cup of coffee, we need to explain why. If you can explain why they can't have something, they're usually okay with that."

From *Reengineering the Hospital,* Vol. 4:10, 1998

For example, lunch time is the only time in the day many patients can get away from work to call the hospital, but several hospital departments close for an hour at midday. The departments were oblivious to the problem until it was brought to their attention by the advisory board. In some departments, lunch hours are now staggered to provide coverage.

Members of all hospital departments were encouraged to use the advisory board. Staff members occasionally came to the monthly meetings with specific questions. Other times questions were more broad: "We're having problems with x, y, z. Any ideas on what we could be doing differently?" Sometimes the board came up with a solution, other times a question needed more discussion.

Problems in the Billing Department

For most patients, hospital bills might as well be written in Latin. Part of the problem, Luther says, is that billing departments expect patients to understand their insurance and the hospital's billing statements. Patients, on the other hand, know little about their insurance and believe it's the role of the billing department to educate them.

The advisory board worked with the hospital's billing department to help it see things from the patient's perspective. As a result, billing statements became more user-friendly. With the help of the advisory board, the department developed a brochure to explain things like Medicare, managed care and primary care networks.

"The billing department recognized a lot of problems," Luther recalls, "but as they worked with the board, they recognized they had some valuable information. They decided that maybe it is partly their job to help educate patients."

Another problem: dunning notices sent out by the collections department. As is often the case in hospital collection departments, the language used on the collection letters was accusatory. And, the timing of the notices left a lot to be desired. In some cases, patients would receive a notice even though their insurance company had already paid. On the advice of the board, a statement was added to dunning notices explaining to the patient, "your insurance company may already have paid the amount due."

Establishing an Advisory Board

At least one patient was chosen from each of the hospital's 11 lines, including orthopedics, pediatrics and cardiology. Nurses and medical staff from each line helped select former patients to serve on the advisory board.

"We told them we were interested in getting input from former patients about the care they received here and how it could be improved for future patients," says Ginny Gremillion, director of patient relations. "We also let them know we wanted their help on future endeavors such as patient brochures and patient surveys. One person thought we were joking. He didn't believe a hospital would be interested in his input."

Fifteen current and former patients were selected to serve on the board. The group met at the hospital about once a month, typically for a brief presentation about the hospital along with discussion of areas for improvement. In exchange for their time, they would be served dinner.

"They were all happy to be able to participate in this group and help improve things at the hospital, but it did take some time for the group to gel," she says, We've decided we need more ethnic diversity. To that end, we're looking at a new list of people we may be able to incorporate."

Board Helps Improve Brochures, Satisfaction Surveys

At an early meetings, board members were asked to review a new patient brochure. Suggestions included adding parking information, cafeteria hours and additional telephone numbers. The board's recommendations were well received by hospital leadership, and the information was added to the brochures. The board also helped improve the hospital's patient satisfaction surveys. Members mentioned they sometimes didn't feel safe walking through the halls of the hospital or the parking lot-understandable, considering the hospital is located in an urban area. Questions regarding safety were added to the patient satisfaction questionnaire.

Survey results revealed patients' perceived a lack of security. After seeing the results, the hospital's security department changed its uniforms so personnel could be easily identified as security.

Some of the board's ideas prompt more internal debate at the hospital. "We received a complaint from the daughter of a patient ... because we list the patient's age on the outside of the door. She thought it could be prejudicial. We presented the problem to the board, and most of them agreed the patient's age shouldn't be identified," Gremillion recalls.

After more research, Gremillion says they discovered that many hospitals post the patient's age outside the room. It helps the medical staff and nurses prepare mentally to meet with the patient. Also, the effect of some medications varies depending on age. Nevertheless, based on the board's advice, the hospital is switching to a system that will list ages more discretely.

"It's critical in this time of managed care and confusion among patients to make sure that patients are heard. I think now more than ever patients need to have a voice that is really listened to," says Gremillion. "The use of advisory boards is certainly a way to get that done."

Part II
Quality Theory And Practice

TOTAL QUALITY NOW!
Putting QI on the Fast Track

Frustrated with the slow pace of TQM projects, system leaders are finding ways for quickly implementing changes — some in as little as three-and-a-half days — and, advocates say, the results are just as good as full-scale TQM projects.

It was October 1994, and Robert Panzer, M.D., was at a Quality Management Network conference, listening to a speaker explain how Indianapolis' Methodist Hospital managed to slash $25 million from its budget in just a few months. The hospital had devised a fast-track cost-reduction scheme in response to the Indiana legislature's unexpected — and drastic — Medicaid reimbursement cuts.

Dr. Panzer, currently chief quality officer and associate medical director for the University of Rochester Medical Center and Strong Memorial Hospital in Rochester, N.Y., was impressed. But he recalls thinking, "That could never happen to us. We would never have so much to do in so short a time."

Just four months later, New York's governor and legislature indicated that they would take similar action, and Strong Memorial Hospital was looking at a $15 million deficit. "We knew on Feb. 1 that, effective in two months, we would have a $15 million problem with Medicaid reimbursement, and we were already into our budget year," Dr. Panzer recounts.

Hospital officials decided to solve most of the problem in the same way the Indianapolis hospital had — by convening teams of employees and empowering them to make cost-cutting changes in a hurry. By early May 1995, six teams with six members each were deployed for two weeks to a nearby university facility for daily, full-time work sessions. Their mission: to come up with a way to cut $3 million in hospital costs — in two weeks. Twenty-five part-time teams were charged with meeting weekly, with the goal of finding as much as possible of the remaining $12 million that needed to be cut over the next few months.

A six-member management team — led by the hospital's chief financial officer and operations director and including Dr. Panzer — worked for six hours a day for three months to help the other team efforts and to make salary and policy adjustments to cover the rest of the loss. The management team's job was to remove roadblocks, provide advice and help teams cross traditional departmental boundaries.

Before the whirlwind was finished, the six full-time teams had each on average figured out how to cut half a million dollars in expenditures, and two-thirds of the part-time teams had at least moderate success, cutting a total of almost $5 million. Among the team's actions were decentralizing phlebotomy functions and using expensive sedating and paralyzing drugs more selectively in intensive-care units. For a recommendation to take

From *The Quality Letter for Healthcare Leaders*, Vol. 9:11, 1997

effect, teams needed to win approval only from the management team that was empowered by the hospital's CEO to deliver necessary cost reductions.

Strong Memorial Hospital, which had previously had approximately one-half of the hospital's 5,000 employees trained in quality improvement methods and assigned to teams that typically met every two weeks for six to nine months, found the fast track a better way to make changes. "Accelerated improvement is better than slow improvement," he says. "It gets things done before the solution changes and while the team still has the energy to implement its ideas."

That sentiment is being echoed across the healthcare industry, as advocates of total quality management become frustrated with the snail's pace of traditional research-driven change.

Gaining Momentum

The slow pace of TQM "was driving people crazy," says Mary Williams, vice president of the Wilton, Conn.-based Juran Institute, a quality consulting organization. "Never mind that the problem was there for 30 years; they wanted it solved yesterday."

In fact, says Ms. Williams, putting TQM on the fast track means "responding faster to your customers, to senior leadership, to the payers. But the best part about speeding the process of change is that the teams are really very excited, and the momentum is very strong. They like the idea that there's light at the end of the tunnel and they're finished with the project quickly." Teams working under slower-paced models of change, she says, might wait a year or more to see their efforts bear fruit. "They'd get bored."

10 COMPONENTS OF SUCCESSFUL RAPID CHANGE EFFORTS

- A desire or mandate to finish the project quickly;
- A clear aim;
- A way to measure performance;
- Access to existing research;
- Good data collection on site, analysis and project management;
- Support from leadership;
- A willingness to make incremental changes;
- The ability to do quick, small-scale tests; and
- Impatience.

The results of accelerated change processes, she says, are "absolutely as good," as traditional TQM, which "costs too much and it takes too long. And customers aren't willing to tolerate either of those."

Sharon Englert, manager of TQM and patient relations at Central DuPage Health System in Winfield, Ill., agrees that market pressures require health systems to change constantly — and change quickly. Customers, she says, "expect state-of-the-art all the time" and, because medical information is so readily available via the Internet, they are becoming more savvy healthcare consumers.

"People have high expectations for the service components of healthcare," says Ms. Englert, who helped engineer a massive operations improvement effort that cut $16 million from the organization's $95 million in controllable expenses in swift increments. "They want what they want right now, they want it customized to meet their needs, and they don't want to wait. They're willing to pay if they see the improvement as having value."

And that's the bottom line in most fast-paced change methods: They eliminate the non-value-added components from a process or function within an organization. Where healthcare has become too wasteful, healthcare organizations such as Dr. Panzer's are coming up with ways to cut waste — and costs — from their daily routines.

Change Agents

A handful of consultants have designed fast-track methods for changing processes — one in as little as three-and-a-half days. Four have gained national attention:

Blitz improvement teams. A pioneer of accelerated improvement efforts, the Juran Institute advocates the use of "blitz improvement teams" to tackle cost-cutting projects. A team of health system employees with knowledge of the process in question meets with a facilitator — someone who works for or has been trained by the Juran Institute — four times over two weeks for up to four hours at a time to identify what Ms. Williams calls the "root cause" of a single process's problem. Then the team takes a week off and reconvenes for twice-weekly meetings for another two weeks. By the end of the cycle, the team has documented the root cause of the problem, designed a remedy, recommended a plan to implement a cost-cutting change and filled out spreadsheets that will help team members monitor progress and measure success. Later, the team engages in a "road show," says Ms. Williams, to sell the proposal to colleagues. Finally, the team implements its plan.

The effort often results in a protocol for medical staff to follow, which helps standardize behavior throughout the system and lowers costs. For the Rochester, Minn.-based Mayo Clinic, for example, a blitz team developed standards for peripheral vascular surgery after examining a year's worth of patient records. The records revealed vast variation in physician behavior, which led to variation in the cost of treating the patients. "They looked at every patient, every pill, every IV, every lab test," says Ms. Williams, who facilitated the effort. "We found that for those cases with higher costs, there were too many medications, lab tests and X-rays."

STEPS FOR BLITZ IMPROVEMENT TEAMS

1. Prove that a problem exists.
2. Identify the root cause of a process problem.
3. Design the remedy.
4. Formulate a plan to implement a change.
5. Develop spreadsheets to monitor progress and measure success.
6. Implement the remedy.

STEPS FOR THE BREAKTHROUGH SERIES

1. Facilitators search the literature for proven techniques to address an identified problem.
2. National experts in the topic area create a list of change concepts worth testing to solve the problem.
3. Organizational representatives to the collaborative effort meet to learn about possible changes.
4. Participants try out the changes within their organizations.
5. Participants meet again to share successes and problems, then try additional improvement techniques.
6. Participants meet in a final session to share results.

Breakthrough Series. The Boston-based Institute for Healthcare Improvement convenes panels of a dozen or so experts in a specific area of medicine to spend a day creating a list of "change concepts" worth testing in the field. Then representatives of healthcare organizations join in a collaborative group that meets for two days every few months to learn about possible changes that will achieve breakthrough results, lower costs and improve outcomes. Between meetings, collaborative members try out the initiatives in their organizations.

In a recent collaborative, for instance, 20 of 40 participating organizations reduced delays throughout their facilities by half. Organization representatives targeted various waits that plagued their facilities, met as a group for two days to pinpoint some possible improvements, and tested the changes for two months within their organizations. During the first two-day meeting, participants heard "a lot of good ideas about how to avoid delays" that had been identified through the literature, says Thomas Nolan, Ph.D., a statistician with the consulting firm Associates in Process Improvement in Silver Spring, Md., who worked with the collaborative. The group reconvened for two more days to review results and identify other changes to try over the next two months. At a final, daylong meeting four months later, participants shared their successes and problems. Between meetings, they communicated with IHI facilitators and with each other via e-mail and conference calls.

STEPS FOR PICOS

1. Identify wasteful practices in the process needing improvement.
2. Through observation, identify areas for eliminating waste by standardizing operations.
3. Meet with stakeholders to recommend an action plan.
4. Implement or schedule implementation of changes.

The added dimension that the Breakthrough Series brings to accelerated change efforts, says Dr. Nolan, is the rapid transfer of improvements to many organizations. And each collaborative concludes with a national congress open to all for sharing results and highlighting the improvements organizations achieved during the learning and testing periods.

STEPS FOR INTERACTIVE ACCELERATED REPLICATION

1. Search the database for ideas that might solve problems within the facility.
2. Create a plan to overcome resistance to change.
3. Implement identified problem-solving ideas.

PICOS. General Motors Corp., whose annual healthcare tab for its 1.5 million employees, retirees and family members tops $3.6 billion, developed the PICOS workshop, a three-and-a-half-day brainstorming session for hospital employees. By the end of the workshop, they generally come up with more than 100 suggestions for doing away with seven kinds of waste, encompassing time, effort and materials. Dozens of those recommendations are put to work before the workshop ends. PICOS involves front-line employees, who are relieved of other duties so they can devote their full attention to the workshop.

After using PICOS, the Cleveland Clinic Foundation cut from five hours to three hours the time it took for a patient to be discharged once a physician gave the order. In three-and-a-half days, employees at the University of Michigan Comprehensive Cancer Center's Ann Arbor campus came up with 213 ideas for increasing coordination among providers at its four sites for outpatient chemotherapy.

Interactive accelerated replication. There are three steps to this Internet-based change method. First, subscribers use the site's extensive database to find ideas that might translate into change at their own facilities. Second, they create a plan to help them overcome the inevitable resistance to change they will encounter from colleagues. Third, they implement those ideas in their organizations.

The site (www.interactivechange.com) is maintained by Premier, an 1,800-hospital alliance. Its database contains up-to-date articles from medical publications as well as success stories from healthcare organizations that have implemented change using the interactive method. Once an organization commits to making an improvement, managers take responsibility for implementing the change. Managers receive an electronic mail reminder from the site's administrator every day until committed changes have been implemented. For delayed implementation, the organization's senior leader sponsor, who is responsible and accountable for the project, also receives the reminder. Once changes have been effected, managers receive congratulatory messages.

In the meantime, if a manager meets with resistance at the facility, he or she may log onto a "discussion lounge," where managers from other organizations can offer advice and feedback.

Overall, organizations are encouraged to enroll dozens of managers in the program, and each one commits to making at least one change a month. Working on various problems throughout the organization can reap the solutions to numerous problems, says creator Chip Caldwell, Premier's senior vice president. He points to Toronto's Oakville Trafalgar Hospital, which saved more than $2 million in 60 days — 2% of its annual budget — using this approach.

Mr. Caldwell cites several advantages that this method offers:

- Every manager is involved; 75% to 100% of managers and clinical leaders are implementing changes simultaneously.
- Results begin immediately; budget reductions of 1% to 2% are expected within 90 days.
- Internet programming holds managers accountable for implementation.

SEVEN KINDS OF SYSTEM WASTE

PICOS workshop participants look for:

- ***Waste of correction.*** If an employee has to redo work or if a patient has to make an extra trip to the hospital because of a staff error, time and money are lost. Likewise, if employees suspect that the process has flaws, they will spend unproductive time double-checking work.
- ***Waste of overproduction.*** Producing more than is needed or completing tasks so quickly that those working on the next step in the process can't keep up can cause bottlenecks that affect both waiting patients and harried staff.
- ***Waste of motion.*** Keeping supplies needed for treatment out of reach means extra walking, reaching and bending for staff. That walking, reaching and bending is not directly related to treating the patient and, therefore, has no value to the patient.
- ***Waste of waiting.*** Patients wait for doctors; doctors wait for test results; staff waits for orders; even equipment waits idly to be used. Any time a resource — person or equipment — has to wait for something to happen, there's an interruption in the continuous flow of the value-added service.
- ***Waste of inventory.*** Some hospitals keep more equipment on hand than is necessary to keep a process running smoothly; others order supplies inefficiently so they pay for and use space for unneeded materials.
- ***Waste of processing.*** It's wasteful for patients or staff to fill out several forms that ask for the same information. Activities that add no value to the product often can be eliminated without consequence.
- ***Waste of material and information movement.*** While patients or materials are being moved (e.g., moving patients from the hospital room to radiology and back), no value-added activity is occurring.

Customizing Accelerated Change Efforts

It's not just healthcare consultants who are coming up with ways to speed the process of change. Like Dr. Panzer, quality leaders at other hospitals are finding ways to light a fire under their quality committees. They draw on their training in QI techniques to develop fast-track processes of their own.

At Intermountain Health Care in Salt Lake City, for instance, administrators abandoned a two-year effort to create protocols for 20 clinical processes that would do everything from standardize the treatment of knee injuries to cut the number of cesarean sections. Large committees were "doing good things, but they weren't making fast progress," recalls Brent James, M.D., vice president for medical research. "The responsibility for the work was falling back on physicians to do in their spare time," he says, and it was not getting done. Even though IHC paid physicians for their time serving on the committees, progress was often slow and attendance was poor.

So Dr. James and his colleagues created a different kind of committee — one in which just four people would gather for "high-content meetings" for two to four hours, once a week, then report to an oversight team of physicians every one to two months. One committee — devoted to the labor and delivery process — includes a quality expert, an administrator who could get approvals and resources from higher-ups, the physician head of women's medicine and an obstetrical nurse. And although it's too early to know the results of their changes, Dr. James says the tactic seems promising.

Outside the meetings, team members perform literature searches and analyze existing clinical data. During the meetings they develop conceptual flowcharts that describe care processes and share their conclusions with the physician oversight team and other practicing physicians to obtain their insights and get buy-in. The flowcharts have proved useful to organize practice protocols (e.g., for vaginal births after cesareans, or active management of labor) and to build an outcomes tracking system. The labor and delivery committee used its flowchart to identify a set of reports that tracks and manages the process within IHC's facilities, with sufficient clinical specificity to provide meaningful input to physicians. The outcomes tracking system distinguishes planned C-sections from planned vaginal births and the specific causes of C-sections within each category, such as C-sections performed for failure to progress (dystocia) among planned vaginal births. The entire outcomes tracking system routinely follows medical outcomes (like C-sections) and satisfaction and cost outcomes along a clinical process of care (like labor and delivery). The tracking system generates monthly reports by physician, hospital and region, comparing each to peers within IHC.

The initial set of outcomes reports showed wide variation in clinical performance among physicians and hospitals. For example, some physicians diagnose dystocia, leading to C-section, far more frequently than their peers. The committee shared those data with physicians and hospitals, to provoke a discussion among caregivers about appropriate indications to diagnose dystocia.

Based on the team's analysis, Dr. James predicts IHC's 15.8% C-section rate will drop within a year to around 14%, for annual savings of $800,000. "Based on our previous experience, if we show the physicians how their C-section levels compare with their colleagues, using clinically meaningful data, that is going to change C-section rates in our system," he says.

From start to finish, the committee's work took six months. Other teams in cardiac medicine and women's and newborn services are well along similar paths with total predicted savings of more than $2 million annually. And Intermountain officials plan to use the small-team system to make changes in its 60 most common processes. The total effort, predicts Dr. James, will take about four years. The team system, he says, "has greatly accelerated our ability to get things out. It's greatly accelerated our development and implementation of outcomes tracking and practice protocols."

Likewise, when administrators at Central DuPage Health System in Winfield, Ill., were faced with the need to reduce costs for managed care contracts, they set a goal to cut $20 million from their annual budget. So they devised an accelerated "operations improvement effort," in which more than 1,000 employees contributed to six major task forces and many subcommittees that examined dozens of processes to see where dollars could be spared. During the year-long process, committees had strict targets and timelines. When all was said and done, the committees, which met weekly "with a heavy dose of action items in between," Ms. Englert says, had won approval to cut $16 million and eliminated a quarter of the hospital management positions.

The effort, says Ms. Englert, was part of a push by administrators to "overcome the centrifugal force of our prior culture: slow decisonmaking, lack of accountability and satisfaction with the status quo. It was a recognition that outside of our own community, healthcare was changing rapidly."

"If we show the physicians how their C-section levels compare with their colleagues, using clinically meaningful data, that is going to change C-section rates in our system."

Brent James, MD
Intermountain Health Care

10 Critical Components of a Rapid Change Effort

Those who have implemented rapid change say there are 10 essential characteristics of a successful effort.

- **A desire or mandate to finish the project quickly**. Quality improvement teams can get distracted after working on a project for months, so picking up the pace can lead to better results. "Fast teams aren't saddled with working forever, and they can't defer decisions to some future committee meeting," says Dr. Panzer. "They have a target for completion, and then they're done." He says the tack is an especially effective one in healthcare because "that's very similar to how physicians and nurse leaders like to work. They focus more on achieving the outcomes than on the process of getting there."
- **A clear aim.** Before change can occur, system leaders should know exactly what it is they want to change. And the requested change should be as specific as possible, says Dr. Nolan. If the aim is to reduce delays in the emergency department, for example, leaders should narrow their goal even further, he says. "Do they want a 30%

reduction in the length of stay in the ER? In that case, if people are there for an average of three hours, I want it down to two hours."

- **A way to measure performance.** Continuing with the ER example, Dr. Nolan suggests one measure might be reviewing the experience of five patients a day to find out how long they stayed in the ER. As data accumulate and changes are made to reduce lengths of stay, the data — and the tool developed to measure reductions — can serve as the foundation for future quick-change efforts. Dr. James says the measurement tool is critical to the success of any rapid-change process: "You manage what you measure," he says.
- **Access to existing research.** Key to IHI's breakthrough collaboratives is the use of data that have been collected elsewhere. "We have a belief that scientifically grounded changes are available, and we don't have to reinvent them," Dr. Nolan says. Facilitators jump-start change, he says, by scouring the literature for information on the topic and tapping high-performing organizations that already have dealt with similar changes. Ms. Englert agrees that Central DuPage's efforts were hastened by the use of information garnered from literature searches. "We weren't reinventing the wheel," she says.
- **Good data collection on site, analysis and project management.** While accelerated change methods may take as little as three-and-a-half days of an employee team's time, a facilitator might spend several weeks before the group convenes collecting and analyzing data and developing a mission for the team.
- **Support from leadership.** For the team to persuade colleagues and managers to buy into their recommendations, the team needs support from the executive level of the organization. That is most easily accomplished by involving a respected authority in the team effort. At Lahey Hitchcock Clinic, Dartmouth-Hitchcock Medical Center in Lebanon, N.H., each team has a "champion leader," usually a physician or nurse leader who can speak for the administration. "You need senior leadership to give you a clear aim, infrastructure support, ways to collect data and time to do the work," says Marjorie Godfrey, M.S., R.N., Lahey Hitchcock Clinic's director of accelerating clinical improvement.
- **Willingness to make incremental changes.** An organization that wants to accelerate the pace of change should take small steps toward that goal, says G. Ross Baker, Ph.D., associate professor of health administration at the University of Toronto. "It's not attempting to design perfect systems and then install them," he says of any rapid-change method. "It's often making a lot of small changes and then judging the impact of those small changes."
- **Ability to do quick, small-scale tests.** Those tests generally are done in focused, short cycles of a few days to a few weeks, allowing the team to pilot one idea at a time rather than waiting to accumulate enough data for a systemwide fix. "We can learn from those tests and build our knowledge sequentially," says Dr. Nolan.
- **Impatience.** "The bottom line," says Dr. Nolan, "is that there's a rich

supply of good ideas — scientifically grounded ideas — for change that we can get from the literature or from good healthcare organizations; that's already available. We ought to be impatient about putting them into practice." Ms. Godfrey agrees: "One of the greatest things about accelerated change is that the concepts and theories of improvement can be folded into meaningful clinical work without formal classes. We're dealing with very busy clinicians. They don't have time to understand the concepts and theories of improvement, the flowcharts or whatever. The beauty of this is that they can begin to build improvement in their everyday work."

- **Follow-up.** The danger of putting cost-reduction ideas to work too quickly is that they might not last, cautions Mr. Caldwell. It's important for teams to devise a method of following up, "to go back and check and make sure you don't slip back into the old habits."

"The bottom line is that there's a rich supply of good ideas — scientifically grounded ideas — for change that we can get from the literature or from good healthcare organizations; that's already available. We ought to be impatient about putting them into practice."

Thomas Nolan, MD
Associates in Process Improvement

Holding the Gains

Members of fast-track committees should identify what they mean by "change" before setting out to make it happen, says David Gustafson, professor of industrial engineering and preventive medicine at the University of Wisconsin in Madison. Change, he suggests, is something permanent. "It's possible that we would change something and then in six months be right back to where we were in the first place," he says. "So we have to determine if these are lasting changes, or if we are really detecting a temporary change."

Maureen Bisognano, IHI's executive vice president, says just 16% of the improvement projects undertaken by U.S. healthcare organizations could be classified as highly successful — that is, the organization was able to sustain the results for at least a year.

To make sure results from fast-track improvement efforts last, Mr. Caldwell recommends establishing a systematic way to periodically revisit the process that has been changed — just as advocates of traditional quality improvement strategies do. The "plan-do-check-act" cycle, Mr. Caldwell says, is as crucial to the success of a fast-track model as it is to slower versions of quality improvement.

Another Tool, Not a Cure

Still, even the most strident advocates of accelerated change agree that quickening the processes can't cure all that ails healthcare.

"It's not a panacea," says Carol Jones, executive director of IHI's Quality Management Network. "That's not a shortcoming of it, but that isn't what it is."

"It's another tool that needs to be added to the managerial and clinical work chest," agrees Dr. Baker. "It's something that we need to be training more and more people how to do."

Sometimes, cautions Dr. Baker, working too quickly can have side effects. "For some, this is seen as a quick-fix mentality," he says. "It's almost as though you think you're buying a system that you can put in place."

In fact, says Ms. Englert, Central DuPage's accelerated overhaul was "angst provoking." The system changed so many things so quickly that "it left a wake of bad feelings that we're still dealing with. People have a lot of unresolved feelings about how it felt to be forced into that pressure cooker."

If she had it to do over, says Ms. Englert, she would make sure employees were better prepared for accelerated change. "We'd get people enrolled in it," she says. "We'd get their hearts and not just their feet."

Ms. Bisognano says taking on too much change too quickly also can lead to problems. "An organization can perceive it as being too easy and get too many balls rolling, and can fail," she says. "These projects are much more difficult than they seem on the surface. They require a level of investment in time, knowledge, skill building, negotiation and listening that is really substantial."

Her advice to heathcare leaders is to be selective about the projects they put on the fast track. Changes that affect several systems probably should not be accelerated. "Leaders should understand what it really takes to make a sustained change," she says.

For more information ...

Associates in Process Improvement
Contact: Thomas Nolan, Ph.D.
Phone: (301)589-7981
E-mail: apiwash@ix.netcom.com

Central DuPage Health System
Contact: Sharon Englert
Phone: (630)681-6627
E-mail: sharon_englert@cdh.org

Institute for Healthcare Improvement
Contact: Maureen Bisognano
Phone: (617)754-4800

Intermountain Health Care
Contact: Brent James, M.D.
Phone: (801)442-3730
E-mail: bjames@ihc.com

Juran Institute
Contact: Mary Williams
Phone: (203)761-1790
E-mail: mwilliams@juran.com

Lahey Hitchcock Clinic
Contact: Marjorie Godfrey, M.S., R.N.
Phone: (603)650-7487

Premier
Contact: Chip Caldwell
Phone: (704)679-5062
E-mail: chip_caldwell@premierinc.com

Strong Memorial Hospital
Contact: Robert Panzer, M.D.
Phone: (716)275-4064
E-mail: rpanzer@smhqm.urmc.rochester.edu

Tulane University
Contact: Gene Beyt, M.D.
E-mail: gbeyt@sprynet.com

University of Toronto
Contact: G. Ross Baker, Ph.D.
Phone: (416)978-7804
E-mail: ross.baker@utoronto.ca

University of Wisconsin
Contact: David Gustafson, Ph.D.
Phone: (608)262-4748
E-mail: dhgustaf@facstaff.wisc.edu

A Checklist for Accelerated Quality Improvement Efforts

Before initiating an effort to improve a process or system at an accelerated pace, be sure you're prepared.

A healthcare organization planning to put quality improvement on the fast track can borrow a process for accelerating change or devise its own. Whatever the choice, leaders should ask several questions about the effort in advance to gauge its chances of success. David Gustafson, professor of industrial engineering and preventive medicine at the University of Wisconsin in Madison, offers a checklist:

- A clear mandate
  - ❑ Have system leaders clearly described the change they desire?
  - ❑ Have they empowered a leader for the effort and established a firm time line?
- Resources
  - ❑ Are hospital authorities putting their money where their mouths are?
  - ❑ Are they allocating their own time to the effort, and making sure the teams have the resources they need to make the changes?
- Empowerment
  - ❑ Does the team have the authority — or enough access to higher-ups — to see its recommendations become policy?
  - ❑ Is the person in charge of the effort able to "sell" the team's recommendations?
  - ❑ Is the leader prestigious, powerful and committed to the changes?
- Support from the ranks
  - ❑ Were middle managers involved in the process of identifying changes?
  - ❑ How do they feel about the changes?
  - ❑ Are they committed to supporting them?
- Endorsement from informal leaders — those workers looked up to by their peers
  - ❑ How do these informal leaders feel about the changes?
- An understanding of customers

- How well do those responsible for making changes understand the organization's customers and what their needs are?

- Realistic goals
  - Is the change manageable?
  - Is the change such a radical departure from the way the system has done business in the past that workers won't support it?
- Evidence of success
  - Has the change been successfully implemented elsewhere?
- Training
  - Is staff sufficiently trained to change behavior?
  - How will their work environment change?
  - Will their job description, incentives or equipment change?
- Feedback
  - How will leaders know if staff is adapting well to the change?
  - Is there a method for staff to give feedback about what's working and what's not?

For more information ...

University of Wisconsin
Contact: David Gustafson, Ph.D.
Phone: (608)262-4748
E-mail: dhgustaf@facstaff.wisc.edu

Systems Thinking Applications in Healthcare: A Tool for Optimizing Change

Using this technique, managers consider how changing a single piece to solve a problem could have unintended consequences on other parts.

As is the case in most organizations, Baylor Health Care System's strategic planning efforts have historically been top-heavy. Senior leaders — mostly administrators — gathered around the boardroom table to hammer out a plan lining up the system's goals and objectives for the coming years.

This year, the Dallas-based system did things differently. The leaders invited physicians and staff from the system's various business units to help them pinpoint the organization's priorities. When they were finished, they asked the system's 12,000 employees — every one of them — for feedback.

Why? The system's leaders changed the way they think about strategic planning. Instead of translating a few individuals' perceptions into a plan that ultimately would affect every part of the system, they heard from people throughout. They looked at the whole, not its parts.

"At the very heart of the new methodology is this concept that you've got to look at the whole system," says Gerald Bryant, executive vice president for strategy development. "The parts don't operate in isolation from each other."

The result of the new thinking is a broad list of priorities that includes, as usual, financial, performance and market considerations. But a surprising objective — to enhance alliances with physicians — emerged as Baylor's top priority. "Before," recalls Bryant, "our planning group was made up almost exclusively of nonclinical people. We've come to understand that in the future, this business is going to depend absolutely on having alliances with physicians." Including physicians in the planning group influenced that understanding.

This kind of thinking, called systems thinking, often leads once-isolated decisionmakers to include the views and needs of others in their plans. The premise of systems thinking is that every organization is more than a collection of individual parts or departments or employees. The way each of those parts interacts is what makes the organization what it is, and every action taken by one part has the potential to affect some or all of the other parts — often unexpectedly. The system might be a healthcare organization whose parts are hospitals, home healthcare services, clinics, insurance plans, physicians and patients. Or the system might be a community whose parts include schools, police, churches, hospitals and residents. Dozens of leaders in the healthcare industry have latched onto systems thinking as a way to improve the quality of their service and the health of the populations they serve while maintaining respectable profits and market share.

From *The Quality Letter for Healthcare Leaders*, Vol. 8:9, 1996

“Clinicians have an innate understanding of systems thinking. It’s a biological model. Clinicians have always understood systemic relationships.”

Elaine VonRosenstiel

Looking at healthcare as a system may help unify what those inside and outside the field see as a widely fragmented industry. “People’s experience with healthcare is one of wandering through a maze of unconnected parts that don’t talk very well to each other,” observes Steve Durbin, director of quality management for Sisters of Providence Health System in Seattle, which used systems thinking to discover how seemingly unrelated hospital practices caused long emergency room waits for patients. Consultant Bette Gardner, whose Morgan Hill, Calif., consulting firm, Breakthrough Learning Inc., promotes and teaches systems thinking, agrees. “The current healthcare system in our country tends to be fragmented and not functioning very well by many measures,” she says. “And it’s not producing the results that people want it to produce. That’s a symptom of a systemic problem.”

New Life for an Old Concept

Systems thinking isn’t new; its biological roots explain living beings as systems that depend on relationships among their parts. The computer pioneer Jay Forrester in the 1970s developed a body of knowledge about what he called “system dynamics.” His theory was that many of the world’s problems actually had resulted or worsened because of policies designed to solve them. He called the problems “systems” and advocated burrowing deep to their roots rather than applying Band-Aids to their symptoms.

The research Forrester did at the Massachusetts Institute of Technology was global in nature and went over the heads of most. Then in 1990, Forrester protégé Peter Senge popularized the concepts in his book, *The Fifth Discipline*, and systems thinking took its place next to continuous quality improvement and total quality management as one of the decade’s hottest management techniques.

“It’s a natural path for us to understand systemic relationships,” says Elaine VonRosenstiel, vice president for policy and planning at Group Health Cooperative of Puget Sound. “It’s a natural for people who work in an integrated system like Group Health.” Besides, she adds, “clinicians have an innate understanding of systems thinking. It’s a biological model. Clinicians have always understood systemic relationships.”

Yet busy healthcare professionals rarely have time, in the push of day-to-day operations, to devote to learning a new way to think. “There’s so much press of day-to-day business,” says Mr. Durbin, “that it’s hard to have people step back and think, to take a learning approach to this stuff.”

The Big Picture

“Typically,” adds Keith McCandless, co-director of The Healthcare Forum’s San Francisco-based Leadership Center, “it’s the adage, ‘You can’t see the forest for the trees.’” Systems thinking tools, he says, “reveal the forest to people. They can still look at the trees, but for the first time, the forest emerges from the mist.”

Unlike continuous quality improvement, in which a manager dissects a piece of a system to figure out how to fix or improve that piece, systems thinking encourages managers to consider that the problem of a single piece could be influenced by other, seemingly unrelated pieces. Furthermore, this thinking says that changing one piece to cure its specific ills could have unintended consequences on other parts. And those consequences might not show up for months or even years. For example, a hospital administrator, in an effort to save money, might cut the number of people on the staff. In the short term, of course, the hospital will save money on salaries and benefits. But as the weeks and months drag on, the employees who are left to pick up the slack for their absent co-workers could show signs of burnout and resentment. Low morale could lead to expensive absenteeism or retraining when the stressed-out employees leave for better jobs. The administrator might not have considered the consequences on one piece of the system — the employees — when he or she decided to apply a quick fix to another piece — the budget. If the administrator employed systems thinking, the impact of the action on the whole system would have been considered.

OVERLAP OF QUALITY IMPROVEMENT AND SYSTEMS THINKING TOOLS

Best Use of QI Tools

Discrete processes (or systems) in which cause and effect relationships are observable and occur within a time frame that enables cycling through the plan-do-check-act wheel.

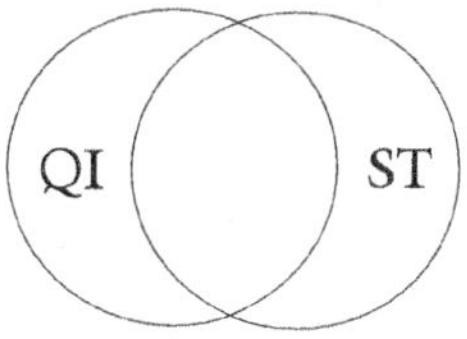

Best Use of ST Tools

Dynamic, non-linear systems (or processes) in which the complexity of interrelated variables and time delays obscure the ability to distinguish root causes and effects.

In our complex organizations, many problems or processes would benefit from application of tools from both disciplines. An integrated toolkit is needed.

© 1993 Bette H. Gardner. Used with permission.

That may sound obvious, but it isn't always easy to spot. "Structures within our organizations keep us from considering the consequences of our actions on other departments," says Rhoda Ryba, senior associate for Breakthrough Learning Inc. "If I'm a department manager and I have performance standards and I have a budget to manage and I have patients to take care of and patients to manage, I don't often take the time to step back and say, 'How is what I'm doing here affecting somebody somewhere else in the hospital?'"

Success Stories

Quality experts at Providence Medical Center in Portland, Ore., did that with resounding success — after a long, unfruitful stab at using traditional CQI methods to shorten the wait for emergency-room patients. They hypothesized that the long waiting times were caused when more patients than usual arrived for care, had especially serious problems or needed care on a weekend, when the Providence clinics are closed. Analysis proved them wrong. So they tried a systems thinking approach and looked at the emergency room as a part of a larger system — the hospital. From there, the analysts considered that the emergency room backup might be the result of interrelationships among many different parts of the hospital, all of which contribute to emergency care. And they were right. The problems were being caused by how the patients were handled once inside the system — not by their number, acuity level or day of the week. Once that was clear, emergency room managers opted to try out bedside lab equipment and add someone to the staff who could speed up lab work. They added flexibility to their system so that doctors and others from elsewhere in the hospital could help out in the ER in times of need. And they were able to reduce waiting time by 19%.

Systems thinking also helped dissolve a bottlenecking problem at San Jose (Calif.) Medical Center. Staff there found themselves turning away 35% of paramedic requests because they couldn't handle the workload. Frustrated after working unsuccessfully for two years to resolve the problem by improving hospital processes, staff turned to systems thinking, viewing the hospital as part of a larger system: the community. They quickly discovered that several hospitals in the community were routinely diverting paramedic patients and San Jose Medical Center had been trying to manage far more than its share. The problem was with the system, not the emergency room.

So San Jose Medical Center officials met with other community leaders, including the local government agency responsible for regulating the emergency medical system. The group agreed to establish new rules by which hospitals can divert paramedic patients, so a problem in one part of the system would never again have such a ripple effect. The medical center has since reduced its diversion rate to less than 5%.

HOW NINE HEALTHCARE ORGANIZATIONS ARE USING SYSTEMS THINKING

Abbott Northwestern — Staff in cardiologists' offices register patients for X-ray, labs and hospital admission.

Baylor Health Care System — Strategic planning, once the domain of administrators, now includes clinicians and other nonadministrative staff.

Group Health Cooperative of Puget Sound — Separate improvement efforts by operations and medical staff were brought together under the Clinical Planning and Improvement Division.

HealthPartners of Southern Arizona — Leaders and other employees are building a systems thinking culture that emphasizes continuous learning.

Kaiser Permanente — System dynamics help physicians understand the advantages of meeting demand on busy days rather than rescheduling patients for a later date.

Legacy Health System — Billing, once managed by each facility in the system, has been consolidated into a single process, increasing patient and physician satisfaction.

Providence Medical Center — ER backups, once thought to be the result of patient load, severity and day of the week, were found to be the result of how patients were handled in the system. Wait times have been reduced by 19%.

San Jose Medical Center — Agreement has been reached among community leaders regarding ER coverage, including criteria for diverting patients.

University of Nebraska Medical Center — Moving toward common classes for medical, nursing and other health professions.

Subtle Changes

Those are neat, quantitative examples of the success of systems thinking. But its results are rarely so tangible. Because systems thinking is most often incorporated into an organization's overall quality effort, it is often hard to tell which results are produced by systems thinking and which come from a combination of actions.

In fact, systems thinking is considered by most advocates as just one tool in a quality improvement effort. Planners and personnel experts at HealthPartners of Southern Arizona, for instance, are introducing systems thinking along with communications skills to leaders and employees in an effort to create what Senge, in *The Fifth Discipline*, calls a "learning organization." And while Lorraine Whittemore, director of human resource development, says she can't put her finger on specific improvements that have been made because the organization's leaders understand systems thinking, she says HealthPartners' staff are slowly "shifting toward a culture that's willing to learn constantly."

Taking Control

In practice, systems thinking can help bring order to situations that once seemed out of control. Before administrators used a systems thinking approach at the multihospital Legacy Health System, patients who visited more than one of the system's Portland, Ore., hospitals received different bills from each; individual facilities kept different patient records and insurance verification information. Policies, varied from one facility to the next, even though the facilities are all part of the same organization. This frustrated patients, physicians and health plans.

Enter systems thinking. "We said, 'Stop doing individual CQI efforts here. We're going to pull them together,'" recalls Ms. Ryba, a former Legacy vice president who headed the effort. "Planners were required to look upstream and downstream to see if we were all going to be doing the same thing," Ms. Ryba says. The result is a single billing process and other consolidated practices that have increased patient, physician and employee satisfaction.

A systems thinking effort can bring people from different disciplines to the same table to talk about common goals for an organization, as it did at Baylor Health Care System. Group Health Cooperative of Puget Sound has replaced separate improvement efforts with one Clinical Planning and Improvement Division under the leadership of both operations and medical staff. "It's breaking down a structural barrier and includes an increased understanding of the connections between improved clinical outcomes and service quality," Ms. VonRosenstiel says.

EXPLORING A LEARNING LAB

Learning labs vary in content and user interface, depending on the specific topic explored and the learning objectives of the group for which a lab is created, says consultant Bette Gardner of Breakthrough Learning Inc. in Morgan Hills, Calif.

The following steps are common in exploring a learning lab:

1. Examine information about the system to be studied.
2. Input key data to represent your assumptions and any unique conditions.
3. Establish performance goals or measures.
4. Design and implement a set of policies intended to achieve goals.
5. Run the simulation and see performance results over time.
6. Reflect upon results to understand why and how the underlying system is producing the observed behavior.
7. Repeat the above steps to deepen understanding and to gain insight about the effects of alternative assumptions, scenarios and policies on system behavior.
8. Consider how to put learning into practice.

Patients Benefit

Staff members aren't the only ones seeing changes resulting from systems thinking; patients are, too, although they might not know why. Heart patients of Abbott Northwestern Hospital in Minneapolis no longer have to register separately with a cardiologist, X-ray technician, lab and hospital admissions desk. They can do it once at the cardiologist's office, which will send the information to the others in the system.

Likewise, patients of Kaiser Permanente's physician groups may be finding access to their primary care providers improved, thanks to systems thinking. Kaiser Permanente uses computerized systems dynamics to help physicians understand the predictability and dynamic nature of patient demand over time. Daily average demand for appointments is predictable but, of course, there is variation. Individual physicians and teams of physicians adjust their availability to match the average expected demand, both urgent and routine, on the day it presents. However, there are unexpectedly heavy days when demand exceeds established availability. On those days, the temptation is to defer excess demand to the future. This solves the problem temporarily, but it may create later problems that quickly snowball. Backlogs can develop that seem insurmountable.

By demonstrating this phenomenon through computer simulation, physicians are able to compress time and see the downstream consequences of their decisions in seconds rather than in the days or months that separate decisions and consequences in the real world. What physicians can learn is that it is better to "work over" on busy days and see all patients wanting to be seen that day than to defer requests into the future. "It's better usually to meet demand when the demand presents itself instead of putting it off," sums up Steve Williams, medical group administrator for the Sacramento, Calif.-based HMO. "That's not intuitively obvious."

Computers Are Key

Although the computer is not a necessary tool for systems thinking, it's an effective one, by all accounts. Often, an organization that wants to teach systems thinking concepts to its leaders will gather them in teams in front of computers. The computers are equipped with software that simulates — like a video game — a common scenario in the healthcare field. Team members, using a computer mouse and following simple on-screen instructions, choose simulation parameters that parallel their organization. For example, a team might use computer simulation to look at whether its organization can improve the health status of the community's population without financial losses. The team would tell the computer how big its healthcare system is; the size, age and behaviors of the community's population; and other information that will personalize the scenario for the exercise. Then the team can try out its assumptions. Maybe one team member wants to invest heavily in prevention to accomplish the goal. The software will compute the consequences of that investment for the entire system over 20 years. It could turn out that the investment will put the system out of business unless the team also increases the system's market share. So a team member might decide to lower prices in order to raise market share. The computer may then show that competitors could also lower their prices, thwarting the team's plan. The exercise is designed to build shared understanding of strategy in complex systems and can last for hours.

"A team will go out of business together 20 or 30 times during a learning lab experience," says Mr. McCandless. "They learn a lot about each other and about how the system works as they struggle to find a sustainable 20-year strategy."

Going out of business on a computer-simulated exercise is a lot less risky

IMPACT OF DOWNSIZING

Rationale for downsizing: Staffing and staffing-related costs are roughly 70% of the total expenses incurred by a delivery system, thus downsizing will reduce expenses.

Impact over time: Downsizing decreases an organization's capacity to provide services, making it tougher for people to gain access. Over time, patients will leave, which will reduce revenue and, therefore, have a negative impact on profit.

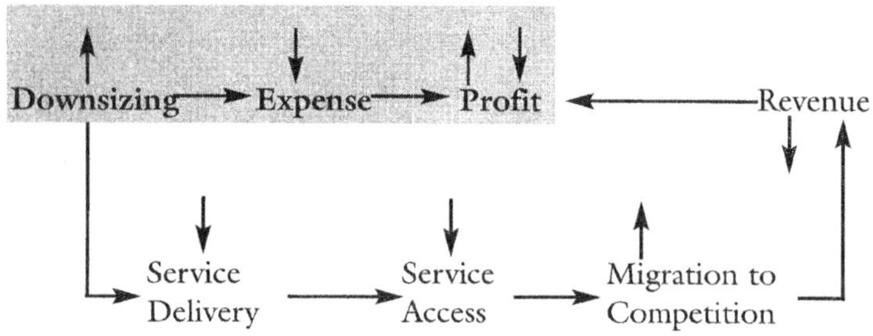

Adapted from: *Risky Business* simulation. Used with permission.

than putting these assumptions into practice in the real world. "If I implement these strategies and I fail, all I've done is fail a game," says Steven DeMello, director of healthcare practice at High Performance Systems Inc., a Hanover, N.H.-based systems thinking software and consulting firm. "We've yet to have anybody perform a career-limiting act by failing on the software." Mr. Williams agrees: "It's a practice field that's completely safe," he says. "Nobody's keeping score; nobody's going to be punished. It's a learning place."

In about four hours in the learning lab, Mr. DeMello says, a team of healthcare executives can test hundreds of combinations of a strategy. "They play a little, talk a little ... They can share what they learned and what didn't work."

As the computer simulations help the administrators see the consequences of their actions, they also teach them the concepts of systems thinking. Software can be designed to simulate actual changes a system is considering — how cutting the budget or downsizing might affect the organization over the next 10 or 20 years, for example.

"You can run five years in five minutes," explains Mr. DeMello. "You can get a sense of, 'I look great in the first year, but what happens in year two or three?' Because the computer simulates performance over time, you can experience those ups and downs."

Systems thinkers use other tools instead of or in addition to the computer as well. Among them is the popular board game Friday Night at the ER, which simulates 24 hours in a hospital emergency room and allows players to see the systemwide consequences of their decisions. Others use a technique called mapping, which involves causal-loop diagramming — a pen-and-paper way to show relationships among pieces of a system and the actions taken by each one. Most often, organizations set up intensive training sessions for leaders who want to apply systems thinking to strategy development or improvement efforts. The training can include lectures about the concepts and a demonstration of mapping techniques, board games or computer simulations and can take anywhere from four hours to two days. Trainers marvel over the vigor with which senior hospital executives play the learning games: "We've found very few people who aren't fighting for control of the mouse" within a few minutes of starting the exercise, says Mr. McCandless.

"We have spent years as an organization talking the talk, and it's not quite as easy to walk the walk. It's more difficult to implement systems thinking than to talk about it."

Terrence Weeks
Director of System Planning
HealthPartners of Southern Arizona

Ups and Downs

Still, understanding systems thinking and putting it to work in a healthcare organization are two different things. "If we can't figure out how to apply it, then there's not a lot of value in it," says Mr. Bryant. Putting it into practice isn't always easy. "Not too many people can demonstrate successful implementation with high levels of confidence," says Terrence Weeks, director of system planning at HealthPartners of Southern Arizona. "We have spent years as an organization talking the talk, and it's not quite as easy to walk the walk. It's certainly much more time-consuming to have all the appropriate data elements put into place. It's more difficult to implement systems thinking than to talk about it."

TRAINING IS COMPLEX

Learning the difficult concepts of systems thinking using a learning lab full of computers and game-like simulations can be fun, say those who have taken part in such exercises. Those who are teaching systems thinking to teams within an organization must take care that training sessions don't turn into games.

"You don't just send the technology out and say to people, 'Go play this game,'" says Elaine VonRosenstiel, vice president for policy and planning at Group Health Cooperative of Puget Sound. "It's not Nintendo."

In fact, those who develop and sell the software that enables healthcare leaders to plug in their own situations and assumptions for a computer-simulated ride into the future agree that these training sessions should be guided by a trained facilitator, who is steeped not only in systems thinking concepts but in keeping a group of learners on track.

Facilitators are usually system leaders, quality managers or human resources directors who advocate systems thinking. After their training, which takes about a day and a half, they design labs ranging from a few hours to two days for their own organizations.

According to Keith McCandless, co-director of the Healthcare Forum's Leadership Center, which trains facilitators, the group leader should:

- Know the fundamentals of systems thinking.
- Understand the attributes of the healthcare system whose leaders are being trained.
- Understand the difference between analysis — in which you break things apart — and synthesis — the relationships that serve as a system's glue.
- Make people comfortable using the computer mouse and software.
- Help the teams articulate their perceptions about the system.
- Move players from team to team so they can get new ideas.
- Coach participants who aren't "getting it" toward self-guided exploration.
- Encourage team members to see how their expertise is critical yet only one part of the whole.
- Ask questions rather than give answers.
- Talk about organizational values in relationship to the strategies that are being tested in the learning lab.
- Teach others how to read causal-loop diagrams and understand relationships.
- Help leaders transfer what they learned in the lab to the real world.

The concepts can be difficult to grasp, as well. A common criticism of the discipline is that it is time-consuming to learn and takes even more time to implement. And there are other hurdles to implementing systems thinking:

- Some dismiss it as an academic exercise. "It's considered to be fairly esoteric, something that academicians do," says Randall Benson of World Class International in Seattle. "It's something people would use to understand systems in general, but it's not something that they would apply to a real problem in their organizations. Being a consultant, I can spend the time to dig deep into the theories and figure out how to apply it in my work. But if I were a nurse on a nursing unit, and I had to ask myself, 'What's the value to me to learn systems thinking, and how can I apply it?' it would be a tough decision."

- Not everyone is comfortable working with computers — even if they are set up like video games. "Computer phobia is alive and well in healthcare," says Mr. DeMello.

- Systems thinking has its own language. Learning lab participants speak of mental models, dialogue and mapping. And it requires participants to learn how to use those systems thinking tools.

- Practice makes perfect, but it also takes time — a rare commodity in a busy healthcare executive's workweek. "It's analogous to learning a language," says Mr. DeMello. "If you don't apply it, if you don't practice it, you'll fall out of fluency with it. You'll be less likely to use it." Mr. McCandless agrees: "It has to be somebody who is willing to spend time in a study period in which confusion and learning are all you get. It works for people who are willing to invest enough time in something that is not going to give them immediate results."

Systems thinking requires administrators to lay their cards on the table.

For computer models to correctly simulate a system's situation, the team using the model has to program in its assumptions about where the system is, where it's going and what members think should happen. Sometimes the computer — or other team members — shoot down those ideas. "Some people say, 'I'm not willing to do that,'" says Mr. DeMello.

Some organizations, however, are primed for putting systems thinking into place. The groups that do it best:

- Have a history of practicing process improvement, which requires working in teams. Gaining understanding, learning a new language and using new tools are activities these organizations' employees have done before. At both Providence Health System and Group Health Cooperative, for instance, teams of employees routinely work to apply other management techniques in their organizations. Using the teamwork required by systems thinking is a natural progression.
- Demonstrate a high level of curiosity and discussion. "This tends not to be a really good tool in organizations where the CEO makes pronouncements and everybody else says, 'Yes,'" Mr. DeMello says. Ms. Menke notes that nurses at the University of Nebraska Medical Center particularly welcomed the new concepts. "They said, 'Hey, this is what I do all the time,'" she says. "They are extremely creative with the options that systems thinking opened to them."
- Are committed to education and learning. At HealthPartners of Southern Arizona, human resources staff constantly encourage employees to attend in-house seminars that cover nonmedical topics such as communications skills.
- Do a good job of integrating doctors and managers. It's a scientific process: You lay out your premises and test them. Ms. VonRosenstiel says leaders at Group Health Cooperative of Puget Sound are whittling away at the division between physicians and nonmedical staff, and each is beginning to appreciate the role the other plays in the system's success.

A Look Ahead

Even the staunchest systems thinking advocates say the healthcare field is a long way from putting the concepts to wide use. "Structures die hard," says Ms. Ryba. "Those structures that have been around for a number of years are very difficult to take down and change."

And while she and others say the concepts are here to stay, it could be a while before they take hold. "The tension between how the current market is and the need to act — and act quickly — makes it difficult to develop these systems thinking capabilities," says Mr. McCandless. "But I think the time is right for it. The way our society has fragmented itself into parts has reached its limit."

Ms. Whittemore agrees. "We can't keep up with the current change in the environment behaving the same way we always have," she says. "We have to change our whole outlook, or else we're just going to keep doing the same thing. There's a lot of short-term thinking going on."

A Systems Thinking Toolkit

An inviting array of products — from board games to computer simulations — helps systems leaders apply systems thinking techniques to solving problems.

It's not easy for people to change their views of the world. Each of us has what systems thinkers call "mental models," which Peter Senge describes in *The Fifth Discipline* (Currency Doubleday, New York) as "deeply held internal images of how the world works, images that limit us to familiar ways of thinking and acting." The challenge for would-be systems thinkers is to break free of those models and broaden their thinking.

A number of tools are available for people to use to learn — and apply — systems thinking:

- **Causal-loop Diagrams**

A group of executives from a healthcare organization can connect circles, or loops, on a flip chart to help members understand relationships among all parts of their company. These cause-and-effect diagrams help show how an action taken in one part of the organization can have a positive or negative effect — even an unintended one — on other parts of the organization.

Generally, members of the team select a specific problem for the diagram to address. They come to the table armed with statistics that show how the issue has been handled in the past and present. On the diagram, the group plots the behavior of key variables, identifying relationships in specific detail so that what has been happening in the system becomes clear. Then, team members can form assumptions about what will happen in the future as they work to resolve the problem.

Causal-loop diagrams are useful only to a point, some systems thinkers claim, because a diagram that is detailed enough to show many specific relationships can become cumbersome. Also, for team members to test their assumptions, more data must be collected. It's difficult for people to retain so much information about so many different relationships without the help of a computer that will do their calculations. Systems thinking, by definition, deals with complex systems; many systemic problems are too complex to be solved without the aid of a computer.

- **Computer Simulation**

The hottest systems thinking tool resembles the hottest thing in America's shopping malls — the video arcade. Computer-simulated models of a healthcare system or a community that includes a healthcare system are becoming popular with systems thinkers in the healthcare field. Unlike a diagram, a computer can calculate how today's actions will affect tomorrow's reality. Most simulations can show a user how one decision made this year might play out every year between now and 2016.

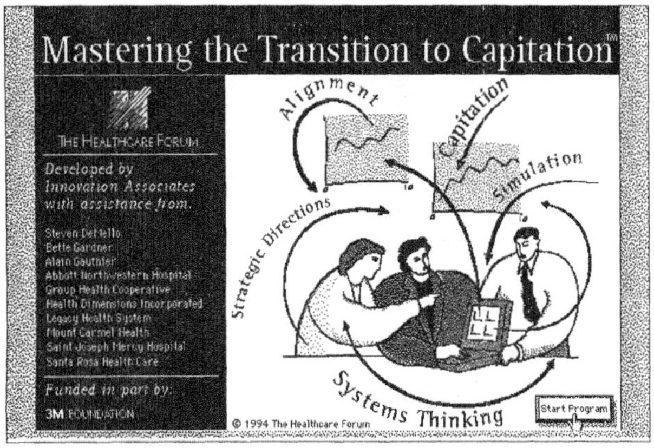

At the same time, the computer can forecast how an action taken by one department or hospital or clinic will affect all the other departments and hospitals and clinics in the system. Often those consequences are unintentional. "Every solution creates new problems," explains Elaine VonRosenstiel, vice president of policy and planning at Group Health Cooperative of Puget Sound. "The problems you're facing today as a manager are often the result of solutions someone else devised a year ago or five years ago."

Organizations can tailor software programs to help their senior leaders delve into the consequences of specific proposed actions. Several groups sell software that guides leaders through general problems in the healthcare industry while teaching systems thinking concepts. Three popular computer simulations *(see margin)* are available from The Healthcare Forum in San Francisco:

✓ ***Mastering the Transition to Capitation.*** This computer exercise walks teams through the shift from fee-for-service to capitation and helps participants understand the dynamics of the changing healthcare environment. As players make choices for their organizations, they witness the delayed impact their actions have on other parts of the healthcare system.

✓ ***Risky Business: Mastering the New Business of Health.*** With this computer simulation, teams try to optimize the health of their organization's patient population while enhancing the company's financial performance. Along the way, team members learn systems thinking concepts.

✓ ***The Community Builder.*** Many healthcare organizations look at their own systems as part of an even larger one: the community. The Community Builder is meant to be used by community leaders in politics, public safety and education as well as healthcare. The goal of this 20-year simulation model is to help participants allocate resources in a manner that will improve life in the community.

■ Learning Laboratories

Computer simulations generally are set up in situations called learning labs, in which a trained facilitator gathers up to 40 participants around computer screens. Some healthcare organizations have rooms permanently set aside for this purpose; others have purchased laptop computers so they can create a learning lab anywhere. Still others move their leadership team off-site for one- or two-day learning lab sessions in meeting rooms equipped with computers.

Work with computers and software is just one piece of the learning lab. The facilitator generally talks about the concepts of systems thinking before starting the simulation. Team members then play out the simulations, stop and talk about the results, and then play some more. Trainers claim it is an effective way not only to help healthcare leaders find solutions to real-world problems, but to teach them to think about the impact of their own actions on the system as a whole.

Facilitation is key to the success of the learning lab, says Ms. VonRosenstiel, because the simulations are colorful, interactive and, by most accounts, fun to use. "These can quickly become games," she warns. "You need to structure people's use of the software so that they obtain insights about the systemic relationships and they actually learn about how one part of the organization — one person's actions — affect another. It's not Nintendo."

■ Noncomputer Simulations

Systems thinking is a concept that may be best taught through experiential learning tools; that is, if its students can learn the theory by applying it to a relevant, real-world problem, they pick it up more easily. Computer simulations are an effective tool for teaching systems thinking concepts, and so, say those who have used it, is a table-top board game called "Friday Night at the ER."

Developed by consultant Bette Gardner at Breakthrough Learning Inc. in Morgan Hill, Calif., the game simulates the challenge of running a hospital during a typical day. Players are assigned specific functions and quickly realize that they depend on each other as they try to solve common problems. The game is usually played under the watchful eye of a facilitator.

■ Literature/CD-ROM

The Fifth Discipline describes five disciplines of a learning organization: systems thinking, personal mastery, mental models, building shared vision and team learning. Senge and others at MIT also have published *The Fifth Discipline Fieldbook*, which uses examples, games and exercises to teach the concepts of the five disciplines. Both books are available at most bookstores, or from their publisher, Currency Doubleday. Senge and Gardner plan to release an interactive CD-ROM that explains the five disciplines.

High Performance Systems, the publisher of the I-Think software, which serves as the platform for the simulations, has released a new interactive CD-ROM, "Why Systems Thinking." The program is designed to help participants understand why and when they might want to use the principles of systems thinking.

TOOLKIT SOURCES

The Healthcare Forum, 425 Market St., 16th Floor, San Francisco, Calif. 94105:

- *Mastering the Transition to Capitation*, computer simulation
- *Risky Business: Mastering the New Business of Health*, computer simulation
- *The Community Builder*, computer simulation

Breakthrough Learning Inc., 17800 Woodland Ave., Morgan Hill, Calif. 95037:

- *Friday Night at the ER*, board game

Currency Doubleday, 1540 Broadway, 18th Floor, New York, N.Y. 10036:

- *The Fifth Discipline*, by Peter M. Senge
- *The Fifth Discipline Fieldbook*, by Peter M. Senge et al.

High Performance Systems, 45 Lyme Road, Suite 300, Hanover, N.H. 03755:

- *Why Systems Thinking*, CD-ROM

Transforming Patient Feedback Into Strategic Action Plans

Patients' perceptions provide valuable insight into areas for improvement and opportunities for strategic planning.

Driven by market and regulatory forces, measuring quality in terms of both clinical outcomes and patients' perceptions has risen to the forefront of health services research. A recent survey of managed care organizations found that patient satisfaction was second, after price, as a common criterion for evaluating providers. Although patient satisfaction information is being collected by many health service organizations, methods for utilizing these data in strategic planning are scarce. A case study approach, focusing on patients as the primary customers of care, provides new insight into the usefulness of patient feedback.

Increased satisfaction with health care services is beneficial to an organization as well as to the health of the patient. High levels of patient satisfaction can be not only a desired outcome measure, but also a legitimate measure of quality. Increased patient satisfaction means better patient compliance and cooperation and may also improve access to care by making patients more likely to return for care if they are satisfied. In turn, a high level of patient satisfaction also enriches providers' sense of a job well done.

Frameworks for Understanding Patient Feedback

If asked properly, patients can provide information on: (1) their expectations for treatment outcomes, (2) their assessments of the goodness of care in meeting their needs and (3) their perceptions of the health benefit that they have derived from care. Moreover, patients can answer open-ended questions on their experiences and report on (1) good surprises or sources of delight, (2) bad surprises or sources of disappointment and (3) their suggestions for areas for improvement.

Noriaki Kano suggests three types of customer expectancies that influence satisfaction: must be, expected and delighting characteristics of quality.

Patients consider certain aspects of care must be characteristics. If these features of care are not met, the patient has high dissatisfaction. For example, one must be characteristic of care may be physician skill. Once the must be quality characteristics are met, the patients then judge quality of care in terms of certain expected traits. For example, one expected characteristic of the visit may be caring nurses. These expected traits serve as indicators of better value. Levels of satisfaction follow a direct relationship as expected characteristics are fulfilled: The more expected characteristics encountered the higher the level of satisfaction, and the fewer characteristics the lower the level of satisfaction.

From *Quality Management in Health Care*, Vol. 5:3, 1997

Besides must be and expected, a third category emerges containing the exciting or the delighting characteristics. An example of a delighting characteristic may be a follow-up telephone call from the provider. Delighting characteristics are not noticed when they are absent, but cause exceedingly high satisfaction when they appear.

With the understanding that patients are a resource from which to gather information for strategic changes, patient feedback can be transformed into organized and usable data and subsequently employed to make changes in the way health care is delivered. The aim of this article is to demonstrate one method of how patient-based information on quality of care can identify drivers of satisfaction and can ultimately help to form specific strategic action plans.

Development of the Case Study Setting

The Lahey Hitchcock Clinic is a regional, multi-specialty group practice that serves more than 150,000 individuals in New Hampshire, Vermont and Massachusetts. This physician-led, trustee-guided practice operates with more than 850 physicians in more than 75 locations. The LHC, which handles approximately 2 million outpatient visits per year, is part of an integrated delivery system that has a desired core competency of delivering quality care. As a part of its measures of system performance, LHC regularly gathers a series of customer-based quality measures. Outpatient satisfaction measures are collected by surveying 32 outpatients a month at each of its New Hampshire clinic sites (Concord, Keene, Lebanon, Manchester and Nashua). Summary high-level information is reported each month. Special reports of in-depth analyses of patient satisfaction help develop specific strategic action plans that promote the achievement of higher levels of satisfaction.

The study examined two groups of outpatients from LHC. In the northern region (Lebanon division) satisfaction measures from specialty patients were analyzed. In the southern region (Concord, Manchester and Nashua divisions) satisfaction measures from primary care patients were analyzed.

Satisfaction Survey Method

All patients who kept an appointment with a primary care provider, surgical specialist, medical specialist, or other provider (e.g., physician assistant) from LHC were eligible. Patients under the age of 15 were included in the sample, but the interview was conducted with the person who took the minor to the clinic for care. Patients visiting LHC for ancillary services or mental health visits were excluded from the sample. A systematic sample of every 100th patient was drawn, and a professional survey research firm conducted the interviews.

The response rate, calculated by dividing the number of patients who agreed to the interview by the number of attempted contacts, was 85%. The cooperation rate, calculated by dividing the number of patients who agreed to the interview by the number contacted, was 94%.

Authors:

April S. Levine, MS, is a doctoral candidate at Dartmouth Medical School in the Evaluative Clinical Sciences and a Research Associate of Quality Education, Measurement and Research, Lahey Hitchcock Clinic, Lebanon, N.H.

Stephen K. Plume, MD, is President, Lahey Hitchcock Clinic, Lebanon, New Hampshire, and Professor, Department of Surgery, Dartmouth Medical School, Hanover, N.H.

Eugene C. Nelson, DSc, MPH, is Director, Quality Education, Measurement, and Research Lahey Hitchcock Clinic, Lebanon, New Hampshire, and Professor, Department of Community and Family Medicine, Dartmouth Medical School, Hanover, N.H.

Analysis Methods

Quantitative analyses included correlation analyses of the independent variables to the overall visit satisfaction, stepwise multiple regression of overall visit satisfaction and control charts of overall visit satisfaction for trended data. Qualitative analyses included verbatim content analysis of responses to questions concerning what patients bragged and complained about, what good and bad surprises patients experienced during their visit, and what improvements patients thought could be made to better the care they received.

When patients were asked what they bragged about and what good surprises they experienced during their visit, the number one source of delight for the primary care patients in the southern region was caring by providers.

From Results to Recommendations

Based on the analysis of the results, strategic action recommendations for improving patient satisfaction in the two markets were developed.

Primary care patients in the southern region

When patients were asked what they bragged about and what good surprises they experienced during their visit, the number one source of delight for the primary care patients in the southern region was caring by providers. After caring, the next most frequent causes of delight were, in rank order, choice of physician, competence and appointment ease. When patients were asked what they complained about and what bad surprises they experienced during their visit, choice was most frequently mentioned. Caring, coordination and the monetary aspects of the visit were also cited as characteristics of disappointment.

The southern region drivers of overall visit satisfaction were provider caring, provider choice, provider communication, perceived health benefit, and office wait time. These five variables accounted for almost two-thirds of the variation in overall visit satisfaction (R-square = 0.62).

Strategic Actions

The combined qualitative/quantitative results suggest that the southern region should focus on two key areas: caring for patients by clinicians and choice of clinician by patients. The recommended strategy for caring is: Strive to make each patient feel that their physician is concerned, first and foremost, with the welfare of the individual patient.

The patients' comments showed that senior leadership must remove the barriers that prevent clinicians from spending sufficient, useful, uninterrupted time with their individual patients when these patients come in for an office visit. Moreover, the clinicians must learn and use interpersonal skills that demonstrate their commitment to caring for patients in a way that each individual patient appreciates.

One patient comment hints at the kinds of actions that both senior leadership and front line clinicians should take to improve patients' perceptions of caring:

"Well, I guess maybe I would say that ... maybe she's [Dr. X] taking up too many patients [and I] don't feel like there's any personal touch."

This comment clearly suggests that improvement actions need to be made at both the front-office and front-line levels of the organization.

Choice is the second quality characteristic that should be concentrated on to improve satisfaction of southern region patients. The recommended strategy for choice is: Aim to make it possible for patients to talk with their clinician of choice. This clinician is usually the physician they consider to be their personal physician.

Provider choice, particularly for primary care patients, is an extremely important, high-visibility item in today's managed care markets. A patient's answer to the question, "What did you complain about?" provides a window into the problem of choice:

"The inability to schedule ahead. ... It's very difficult to get an appointment with a particular doctor. Sometimes it takes two months! A month should be all it takes."

Progress on this strategic action will require improvement in both office visit scheduling systems and in patients' telephone access to clinicians. The southern region will need to identify what aspects of its system — telephone access, provider scheduling, provider office hours or any other process — in which delivery settings are substantially limiting patients' ability to see or talk to their clinicians when they want to.

Specialty Patients in the Northern Region

When patients were asked what they bragged about and what good surprises they experienced during their visit, the number one source of delight for the specialty patients in the northern region was caring. The characteristic of caring, from all providers of care, generated the most delight in this sample. After caring, the next most frequently mentioned

SOUTHERN REGION: WHAT DID YOU BRAG ABOUT/COMPLAIN ABOUT?

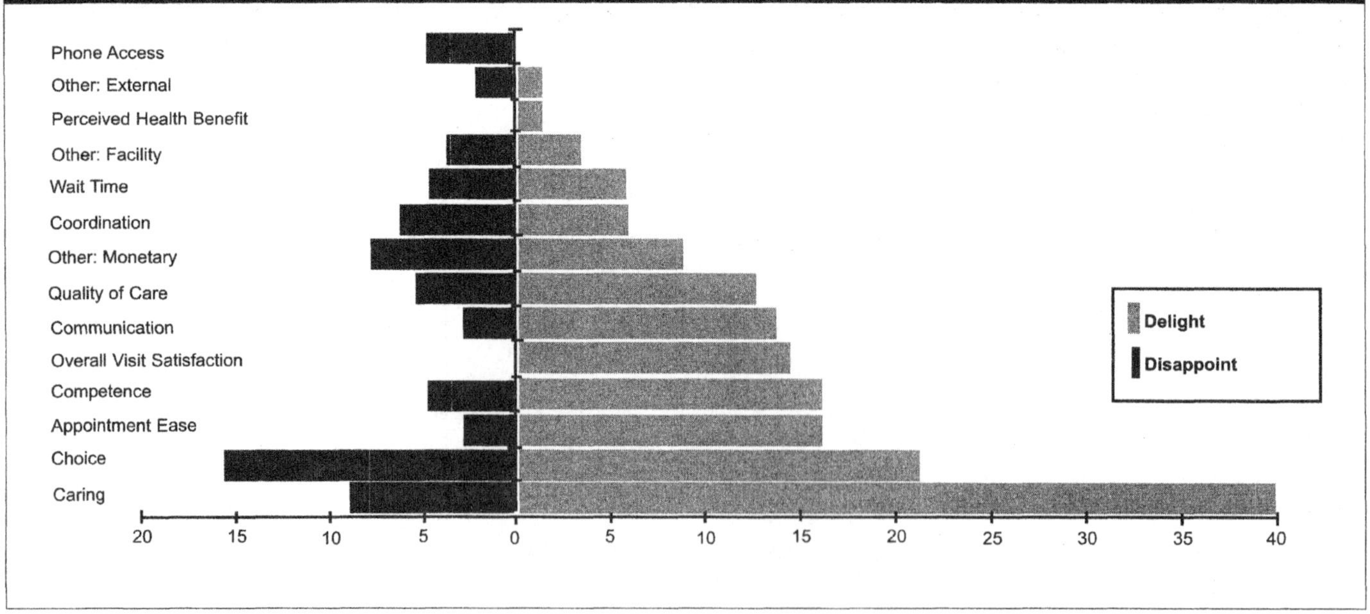

determinants of delight were, in rank order, overall visit satisfaction, characteristics of the facility, quality of care and competence. When patients were asked what they complained about and what bad surprises they experienced during their visit, communication was most frequently mentioned followed by caring, wait time and choice.

Strategic Actions

The combined qualitative/quantitative results for specialty patients in the northern region suggest that the northern region can improve by focusing on four areas: caring for patients, communication of information, competence of clinicians and office wait time for patients at time of visit.

Once again, caring was the leading source of delight and the second most mentioned reason for disappointment. Communication, however, was the reason most mentioned for disappointment. The recommended strategy for caring and communication is: Make each patient feel that his or her physician is concerned, first and foremost, with the welfare of that individual patient and always attempts to identify and meet that patient's information needs.

The verbatim comments suggest action is needed both by the front office and the front line. For example, one patient complained:

"I get the sense you [LHC] don't respect me as much as you respect the work you have to do to get ready to see me ...! And [those work processes] don't work well enough for you to be available to me and my needs."

Leadership will need to remove barriers between physicians and patients spending quality time together, and clinicians must be aware that their patients sometimes believe that caring is a facet of providing care that is sometimes overlooked or lost in the shuffle of production.

Patients' perception of clinical competence is the second source of high strategic leverage. Competence was commonly offered as a source of delight (ranked fourth by specialty patients) but, more important, it was the leading variable in explaining variation in overall satisfaction. The strategic recommendation is: Encourage clinicians to recognize that patients judge the competence of their physicians. Even though many patients lack technical knowledge that would enable them to evaluate technical quality accurately (i.e., that the physician is doing the right thing, at the right time, in the right way) they nevertheless do make judgments about competence that strongly affect perceptions of satisfaction. Thus, clinicians should endeavor to let their patients know what they are doing and why they are doing it so as to provide information that will enhance patients' perception of medical know-how.

Last, specialty patients frequently complained about office wait time, and it also emerged as a driver of satisfaction. Hence, the third recommendation is: Improve the scheduling and appointment processes to ensure that patients visiting their physicians are seen promptly.

Office wait times should be less than 15 minutes; other sources of

"I get the sense you [LHC] don't respect me as much as you respect the work you have to do to get ready to see me...! And [those work processes] don't work well enough for you to be available to me and my needs."

Patient

information (i.e., correlations between office wait and satisfaction) show that dissatisfaction increases sharply if patients think they are kept waiting for more than 15 minutes. Consequently, interdisciplinary clinical/management process improvement teams should be chartered by senior leadership to work with departments where wait times have been problematic with the aim of ensuring that no patient has to wait longer than 15 minutes.

Action Steps for Both Regions

Common to both regions was the highly valued factor of caring, the interpersonal aspect of medical care. From all aspects of judgment — satisfaction, delight, and dissatisfaction — caring by clinicians, as well as others involved in the visit, was extremely important. Senior leadership must remove barriers that prevent providers from spending more productive time with their patients.

Across both regions, individualized care that met specific, patient-identified needs created extraordinary levels of satisfaction. Seamless care plays an important role in delighting patients, as do efficient cycle times for appointments and being seen by the physician of choice.

Conclusions

Patient feedback can be used to improve performance of health care organizations. Once gathered, organized and analyzed, the information can then be translated into specific process changes and improvements. For this case study in particular, the recommendations for the following strategic action steps were made:

Southern region: Primary care patients

- Remove barriers to length of time providers spend with each patient.
- Reemphasize the importance of a caring manner to providers.
- Search for process improvements with regard to provider choice; examine the areas of scheduling, office hours and telephone access.

Northern region: Specialty patients

- Remove barriers to length of time providers spend with each patient.
- Reemphasize the importance of a caring manner to providers.
- Develop an understanding among providers that patients evaluate care based on perceived levels of competence of the provider.
- Develop a team to analyze process flow problems created at the appointment with the goal of minimizing wait times for patients.

REFERENCES

Batalden, P.B., and Stoltz P. "A Framework for the Continual Improvement of Health Care: Building and Applying Professional and Improvement Knowledge to Test Changes in Daily Work." *Joint Commission Journal on Quality Improvement 19* (1993): 424-47.

Bergmann, P. "Study: Employers Consider Cost Over Quality in Health Purchases." *Hospitals and Health Networks* (March 1994): 54.

Deming, W.E. *Out of the Crisis.* Cambridge, MA: Massachusetts Institute of Technology Center for Advance Engineering, 1986.

Gerteis, M., et al., eds. *Through the Patient's Eyes: Understanding and Promoting Patient-Centered Care.* San Francisco: Josey-Bass, 1993.

Hays, R.D., et al. "Hospital Quality Trends: A Short-Form Patient-Based Measure," *Medical Care 29* (1991):661-68.

Joint Commission on Accreditation of Healthcare Organizations. *1994 Accreditation Manual for Hospitals.* Vol. 1. Oakbrook Terrace, IL: Joint Commission, 1994.

Nelson, E.C., et al. "Report Cards or Instrument Panels: Who Needs What?" *Joint Commission Journal on Quality Improvement 21* (1995):155-66.

Shiba, S., and Walden, G.A. *A New American TQM.* Portland, OR: Productivity Press, 1993.

Vuori, H. "Patient Satisfaction — An Attribute or Indicator of the Quality of Care?" *Quality Review Bulletin* 13 (1987): 106-08.

Part III
Quality Tools And Measurement

Health Status Assessment — A Vital Sign for Planning Patient Therapy

Patients' perceptions of their health status need to be weighed along with blood pressure and lab results to choose the best course of treatment, these physicians say. They're using health status surveys to get the information they need.

Milton Seifert Jr., M.D., a family practitioner in Excelsior, Minn., recalls the case of a 22-year-old man who came to see him for a seasonal allergy problem. Soon Dr. Seifert discovered that his patient had a host of other, potentially more serious problems, including work-related stress, alcohol abuse and smoking. He also learned that the man disliked his job intensely and often felt angry and depressed.

This information put the man's allergy symptoms in a new context, as a clearer and more comprehensive picture of his health emerged, Dr. Seifert says. "What I was looking at was the way he felt about life in general," he explains. "I told him, 'When you treat these other things, the allergy symptoms may not seem so bad.'" Dr. Seifert says he is trying to help the man solve his lifestyle problems.

How did Dr. Seifert become so attuned to his patient's inner life? The answer lies in his incorporation of health status assessment into his everyday clinical practice. Dr. Seifert routinely asks his patients to fill out a form called the SF-36 Health Survey *(see box, page 125)* and a health behavior survey he designed that includes questions on exercise, diet, sexual activity, work, seat belt use, safety and other lifestyle issues.

The two surveys, known collectively as the Health & Disease Questionnaire, are loaded into a handheld computer. Patients take a few minutes to enter their answers on the computer, and Dr. Seifert quickly scores them, so that when he sits down to talk with a patient, he has concise, "real-time" information. He also has a clearer picture of what is going on with his patients' health — which he can flesh out as needed during his consultations.

Such health status assessment — the use of standardized, patient-based surveys to obtain information about different aspects of health — is slowly moving into the mainstream of clinical practice. For some time, researchers have recognized the value of patient behaviors and perceptions in measuring and assessing clinical outcomes and quality of life. Now, a few physicians are going a step further — making health status assessment part of their practice routine and using survey-based information to improve care for individual patients. No one really knows how widespread the practice is, but the peer-reviewed literature is an indicator. In the early 1990s, only six articles mentioned use of the SF-36; during 1996 and 1997, more than 100 articles on its clinical use were published.

From *The Quality Letter for Healthcare Leaders*, Vol. 9:10, 1997

Some physicians have begun using health status assessment to gain new insights into their patients' problems, communicate better with their patients, improve care and target their resources more efficiently. These physicians say that health status assessment has helped them bring their patients' needs and perspectives more fully into healthcare decisionmaking.

Viewing Care Through the Patient's Eyes

"We started out from a relatively skeptical point of view," recalls Klemens B. Meyer, M.D., director of dialysis services for Boston's New England Medical Center. Nephrologists spend a good deal of time with their patients, who generally come in several days a week for dialysis treatment. "We were very proud of giving personalized care to our patients, and we felt we knew our patients very well," Dr. Meyer says, adding that he and his colleagues expected the SF-36 results to merely reaffirm what they already knew intuitively. But that view changed after Dr. Meyer and his colleagues studied their experiences using the form among their dialysis patients.

For example, one patient felt he was doing significantly worse than did his physicians, who learned that they had greatly underestimated his disability during recovery after surgery to repair a fistula. Another patient perceived that he was doing better than his physicians did. It turned out that, unknown to his physicians, the patient had felt significantly impaired by hip pain. When the patient started taking ibuprofen on his own to relieve the pain, his overall view of his health improved substantially. "We had been attending to all sorts of things with great solicitude, but not the hip pain," Dr. Meyer notes.

Those and other experiences, Dr. Meyer says, illustrate that "there are a number of aspects of health that are hard to see through somebody else's eyes."

That is where generic health assessment surveys like the SF-36 come in. These instruments were designed to capture patients' perceptions of their health on a range of dimensions — systematically, effectively and efficiently.

BENEFITS OF HEALTH STATUS ASSESSMENT

A number of benefits accrue to practitioners using properly designed health status assessment techniques:

- ✔ Patient care is improved.
- ✔ Patients are able to participate more fully in disease management and health maintenance.
- ✔ Practitioners can help purchasers and business owners improve employee health and reduce costs.
- ✔ Practitioners acquire scientifically sound data useful in negotiations with other entities within the healthcare system.
- ✔ The technology is nonintrusive, preventing practitioner stress. The patient does the work.
- ✔ Healthcare and healthcare research merge into one process.
- ✔ The technology supports and improves the interaction of clinician and patient. This adds value to the service.

Getting the Data Takes Only Minutes

Physicians applying health status assessment to patient care acknowledge its challenges, but they are not insurmountable. Generally, a standardized survey, such as the SF-36, is administered to a patient during an office visit. These surveys may be combined with disease-specific or other questions such as those Dr. Seifert developed. Patients can fill them out in a few minutes. The information may be processed through an optical scanner and translated almost immediately by computer into graphs that illustrate a patient's scores in eight health-related domains:

- Physical function
- Role limitations as a result of physical problems
- Role limitations as a result of emotional problems
- Bodily pain
- General health perceptions
- Vitality
- Social function
- General mental health

Practitioners with limited computer capabilities can send completed survey forms to a service vendor by fax or telephone using voice recognition technology; the vendor's software computes the scores and transmits the results within minutes.

Low Scores Shed New Light on Problems

The choice of technology makes little difference, physicians say. What's important is to have those scores available to share with patients during consultation. And that, they say, is when the real discovery process begins. By clarifying patients' perceptions of the reasons for their low scores, physicians may unearth important information that places their patients' problems in a whole new context for diagnosis or treatment, says Donald Lum, M.D., president of a consulting firm called Living Lab Inc.

"I used to say health status assessment paints a word picture of the patient," says Dr. Lum, who's also a practicing family clinician at the Allina Medical Group's River Valley Clinic in Northfield, Minn. "My new analogy is that it's actually like the picture frame that surrounds a presenting complaint or chronic illness with the mind-body connections."

Advocates say they're learning to understand their patients more completely, more efficiently and more effectively. They warn that administering forms such as the SF-36 to patients is not a substitute for talking with them. It is a tool for engaging in more productive dialogues.

"In the old days, we'd ask, 'How are you doing?'" says allergist Don Bukstein, M.D., of the Dean Clinic in Madison, Wis. "Now we have a much broader ability to really say how that patient is doing beyond just

ABOUT THE SURVEY INSTRUMENTS

The SF-36 Health Survey is a multipurpose survey that yields an eight-scale health profile as well as summary measures. The SF-36 — which stands for short form, 36 questions — has been used to monitor general and specific populations, compare the relative burden of different diseases, assess health benefits produced by different treatments and screen individual patients. Permission to use the SF-36 routinely is granted royalty-free to individuals and organizations for their own use by the Medical Outcomes Trust.

The Health Status Questionnaire by the Health Outcomes Institute in Minneapolis adds three items that are disease-specific mental health measures to the 36-item form.

Another survey almost identical to the SF-36 is produced as the RAND 36-Item Health Survey; this less-often-used version recommends a different scoring method on two of the eight scales.

Information on the SF-36 is available on the World Wide Web at http//www.sf-36.com, or call the Medical Outcomes Trust at (617)426-4046. For information on the HSQ, call (612)858-9188. Information about the RAND 36 is available from RAND at (310)393-0411.

overt symptoms. And if people don't think that asking patients is important, they're wrong, because patients' answers are very accurate and sometimes lead to important questions."

Dr. Seifert says that combining the SF-36 with the lifestyle survey he designed has helped him probe into health and disease as "two interdependent topics." The SF-36, he notes, is a "good measure of the impact of disease," but he also wanted to assess lifestyle habits related to patients' health. Together, he says, the two instruments have enabled him to "create a language of health negotiation" with his patients.

One of his cases involved a 32-year-old woman with Crohn's disease, who, despite significant health-related problems, put on a show of optimism. Using the SF-36, Dr. Seifert says he quickly discovered that she had a low health perception and low vitality. "She said she thought she was going to die," he recalls. Upon hearing that, Dr. Seifert arranged for a team of providers — an internist, a nutritionist, a digestive disease specialist and a health educator who teaches life management skills — to work with her and get her back on track. The test scores will be used to mark her progress.

Like Dr. Meyer, Dr. Seifert says he initially had low expectations regarding the usefulness of health status assessment. "I wasn't prepared to know that there could be that much improvement," he says. "We are finding the test results to be very reflective of our patients."

INTERPRETING HEALTH STATUS ASSESSMENT RESULTS

The real value of health status assessment data comes into play when the physician shares the results with his patient and uses the assessment as a basis for discussion and decisionmaking, notes Donald Lum, M.D., president of Living Lab Inc., Northfield, Minn. Dr. Lum outlines four steps in that process:

1. Explain the meaning of each measure to the patient.
2. Identify measures in which the patient scored low.
3. Ask clarifying questions to determine the patient's perceptions of the reasons behind those low scores.
4. Use this information in clinical decisionmaking.

"Assessment," notes Dr. Lum, "is an interactive process."

Start a Dialogue

Systematic use of the SF-36 has helped Dwana Bush, M.D., a family practitioner with Atlanta Family Medicine, involve her patients more in their own healthcare by identifying health-related goals and deciding on steps to achieve them. The SF-36 scores serve as a basis for discussion between patient and clinician. "A graph depicting a patient's current health status is the most important 'vital sign' for planning patient care," she notes. "If you get a graph of the scores and the two of you are looking at the graph and at data trends, you can solve problems together and evaluate effectiveness of treatment." For example, a patient with a low vitality score may reveal that she is feeling stressed by work. A new objective emerges: to minimize that stress and its effects.

Dr. Bush says that use of the SF-36 also has heightened her awareness of depression among her patients. The survey's depression screen (less than 60% of the total possible score for mental health) flags potential problems. As a result, she has redesigned her care processes to evaluate and treat depression and other mental health problems in the daily course of primary care. Dr. Bush notes that diagnosis of depression is particularly important in treating patients with chronic diseases, such as diabetes or asthma.

The real payoff, physicians say, comes with time, after several rounds of scores have been compiled and patterns begin to emerge. "If your patient improves or deteriorates, you can do a process of discovery to find out what's making the difference either positively or negatively," explains Dr. Lum. In real life, he says, patients with complex problems often require a number of interventions, and figuring out which one made an impact can be difficult. For a patient with both depression and diabetes, a physician can use health status scores as a launching point to identify the relative effects of antidepressants, cognitive therapy, intensive insulin management and diet. "You will have your own perspectives about these things, and patients will have theirs," Dr. Lum says.

In addition, Dr. Bush notes that her use of routine health status assessment has helped her use resources more efficiently. By zeroing in on patients' problems and responding to them earlier and more appropriately, she's reduced her use of diagnostic tests and referrals. She's been using the SF-36 for four years, and she can see patterns and can quickly identify changes in a patient's status — and quickly respond.

Assessment Predicts Patient Use of Resources

Health status assessment can be extremely useful in managing risk, says John E. Ware Jr., Ph.D., senior scientist at the New England Medical Center's Health Assessment Laboratory and the principal architect of the SF-36. "A big part of managed care is risk management — deciding what a patient's care is going to cost, what her risks are and how she should be managed," he notes. "That's going to help with capitation a lot." Clinicians agree. Dr. Bush observes that patients who score low on the SF-36 tend to consume more healthcare resources. Dr. Bukstein says that scores are highly predictive of resource use among asthma patients. And Dr. Seifert notes that taking on intentional accountability buys clinicians reasonable and appropriate autonomy — which piques many practitioners' interest.

Dr. Bush has demonstrated in one managed care population that her patients' low initial mental health scores have, on the whole, improved by 20% — of interest to managed care administrators looking for quality outcomes documentation. "Functional health status measurement and identifying trends can get the patient, provider and purchaser all reading off the same page," she says.

FOUR KEYS TO SUCCESS

- ✔ **Unwavering support from local administrators.** This support empowers the team to effectively implement new clinical care processes by clearing roadblocks, gaining access to resources and sponsoring a mandate for innovation and change.
- ✔ **Well-organized clinical teams.** Respected opinion leaders from multiple disciplines, they act strategically to embed clinical innovation into the everyday work processes at the site.
- ✔ **Strong clinical champions.** Highly respected by their peers for excellent clinical skills, they demonstrate a high degree of interest and competence in teaching new clinical skills to other clinicians.
- ✔ **Clinical mentors.** Successful dissemination of the skills to clinicians depends on effective mentoring and coaching.

Invest for Long-Term Gain

One nagging question remains: If health status assessment is so beneficial, why aren't more clinicians incorporating it into their practices?

Consultant Harry Wetzler, M.D., M.S.P.H., a senior vice president at Health Process Management Inc., Doylestown, Pa., and a clinical outcomes specialist with the American Medical Group Association, has several theories.

First, he says, the clinical quality arena is crowded with activity. Many practices are caught up in efforts to keep up with accreditation requirements, contracting demands by managed care organizations and multiple pressures for data. In addition, health status assessment may seem vague to the uninitiated. "They're not sure what they can get out of this," Dr. Wetzler says. Chances are it won't be reimbursement.

Clinicians also may be afraid of addressing new issues that will cut into their productivity. "There's no question in my mind that health status assessment gives you insights on patients' psychosocial lives that are often swept under the rug or missed entirely," Dr. Wetzler asserts. "There's a disinclination to deal with these issues out of concern that 'If I touch this, I'm tied up for 30 minutes.'" That, he believes, stems from a misconception of what productivity means in healthcare delivery. "Right now, physicians think in terms of 'How many people can I see?' We feel that productivity should be equated with 'How much health am I producing?'"

Some physicians say they consider health status assessment neither time-consuming nor difficult. Others say that although health status assessment does require a little additional time up front, it generally saves time down the road by helping them to focus on important problems early and prioritize treatment. "It is a time investment, but it is time-efficient," claims Dr. Lum.

Overcome Barriers to Implementation

But even staunch supporters of health status assessment in clinical practice say there are some nuances to it.

Dr. Lum led a collaborative group practice project in the Allina Health System that centered on health status assessment. Of seven sites that started with the project, only three completed it. Dr. Lum says those practices shared three characteristics: strong clinical champions, well-organized clinical teams and unwavering support from local administrators. "At the micro level, those three things are probably the most important transformation drivers," he notes. As a corollary, he recommends heavy emphasis on clinical mentoring and coaching for successful dissemination of the skills to clinicians. (Dr. Bush, he notes, was his clinical mentor.)

Dr. Meyer agrees with Dr. Lum about the need to train and educate physicians in health status assessment. "We're not taught how to interpret a change in physical functioning or in role limitations due to physical problems," he observes. "It takes some figuring out."

Explaining to clinicians what they should do with the results can be tricky. These practitioners offer four key steps to successful application:

- **Start small.** "Don't try to do too much too quickly," Dr. Wetzler says. Keep in mind the impact of assessment on staff, and don't lose sight of the fact that some financial investments are necessary. "Costs here don't have to be extraordinary, but you can't do it on a shoestring either," he warns.

- **Be prepared to process the data.** Technical needs can run the gamut. Dr. Meyer says at first it was a matter of remembering to have enough pencils for his patients to fill out their forms. Others describe their experiences with different types of scanners, computer programs and fax services. Dr. Bush says she believes that many people expend too much angst on high-tech hardware. "I tell people to invest in a little laptop that they can take around to process graphs on site," she says. Dr. Wetzler believes that technology — especially in the outpatient arena — needs more integration. "You want to automate this as much as possible by tying it in with appointment and billing systems," he notes.

  Dr. Ware is upbeat about technology. The development of phone/faxback, computer, Integrated Voice Response and Internet technologies, which currently are being merged with television, he notes, has made seamless use of health status tools in practice "much more feasible." And some two dozen vendors now have software to process the forms.

- **Put referral systems in place to support needed actions.** Dr. Bush's experience with depression in patients is a case in point. "We found that approximately 30% of our patients have low mental health scores, which suggests that they need to be further evaluated for depression," she says. "You need to have an algorithm to follow for treatment and monitoring — and deal with the condition without creating a traffic jam." Referral systems need to be in place. "You need to have an individual and systemwide approach to dealing with mental health scores," Dr. Bush asserts.

  Dr. Bush notes that "people tend to overmeasure and underrespond. You don't want to document that 30% of your patients have low mental health scores and then be unprepared to respond."

- **Verify and understand the results.** This interaction with patients "is the first thing you do," Dr. Meyer says. That means talking to patients and probing beneath the surface. Even then, "whether you do something about it depends on the information," he adds.

Dr. Ware is optimistic about the future of health status assessment in clinical practice. "We're on the verge of a whole new generation of tools," he predicts. The reliability and sensitivity of the instruments will improve and they will become even cheaper to use than they are now; a number of firms are marketing their assessment services for a few dollars or less.

Training programs in talking with patients to assess their health status also are being developed, including the educational series produced by HealthStat Productions and a twice-yearly conference sponsored by the Integrative Health Institute in Atlanta.

"The real challenge is going to be: Who knows what to do with outcomes data and has the will to do it?" Dr. Ware says.

For more information ...

Milton Seifert Jr., M.D.
Phone: (612)474-4167

Harry Wetzler, M.D.
Phone: (206)780-5092
E-mail: HWetz@aol.com

Atlanta Family Medicine
Contact: Dwana Bush, M.D.
Phone: (404)255-5774
E-mail: DwanaBush@MindSpring.Com

Dean Clinic
Contact: Don Bukstein, M.D.
Phone: (608)252-8000

The Health Assessment Laboratory, New England Medical Center
Contact: John E. Ware Jr., Ph.D.
Phone: (617)636-8645
E-mail: john.ware@es.nemc.org

HealthStat Productions Inc.
Contact: Ken Nochimson
Phone: (732)636-6930
E-mail: HStatProd@aol.com

Integrative Health Institute Inc.
Contact: Dorothy L. Rece
Phone: (404)255-5774
E-mail: jebcleo@peachnet.campus.mci.net

Living Lab Inc.
Contact: Donald Lum, M.D.
Phone: (507)645-5094
E-mail: dlum@mr.net

New England Medical Center
Contact: Klemens B. Meyer, M.D.
Phone: (617)636-0372
E-mail: klemens.meyer@es.nemc.org

University of Colorado Center for Health Services and Policy Research
Contact: Kathryn Crisler, M.S., R.N.
Phone: (303)756-8350

Wake Forest Clinics Become Better Performers With Creative Approach to Performance Standards

"There may be 50 ways of accomplishing a goal; I'm not concerned about how you get there, as long as you play by the same rules."

This edict was issued to staff members at the Wake Forest University School of Medicine to spark creative problem solving.

An academic medical center's ability to satisfy referring provider and patient expectations of access and customer service is critical to survival in a competitive health care market.

As the new associate director of clinical operations, I found Wake Forest University School of Medicine Physicians faced with dismal scores in the critical areas of access and service.

Referring provider surveys indicated that community physicians were very satisfied with the quality of care. However, WFUP did not provide timely referral appointments. In fact, staff often advised patients to call competing providers, not network-affiliated providers, if a clinic appointment wasn't available.

Established patients complained about the inability to see a physician in an acceptable time frame. In addition, the call center, which assists new patients in becoming established with a WFUP physician, found next available appointment slots to be a month away or even closed to new patients in several specialties.

A consultant's report confirmed other serious customer service problems and access barriers. The report revealed that the typical patient experienced lengthy phone rings and periods on hold, multiple transfers and curt staff members. It also indicated several other areas needing improvement.

Action Plan

To tackle this problem, we developed and implemented an action plan to improve WFUP's response to the service demand.

The initial step involved establishing an accountability structure and sharing knowledge about the poor performance not only with physicians but with the department staff as well.

We used the "mystery shopper" concept to obtain snapshots of the typical patient appointment scheduling experience. Each department and service was assessed on appointment availability and customer service through the use of predetermined scripts requesting appointments for chronic, acute and emergent scenarios. In addition, we collected data from the patient relations department on all registered complaints of the prior six months regarding communication, no return or follow-up phone call, appointment wait time and rude behavior.

From *Inside Ambulatory Care*, Vol. 5:2, 1998

We used managed care quality standards and provider feedback to establish goals for telephone accessibility, appointment availability, and customer service.

Each department chairperson selected one staffer and one physician representative as the key clinical contact to be responsible for effecting the necessary behavioral changes in this and other improvement efforts.

All clinics were represented in the data via a slide presentation and ranked in each category of access, customer service and patient related complaints. The first KCC meeting of staff and physician members focused on sharing these indicators. The KCC members were provided with the information for discussion with their clinic staff and physicians.

We used managed care quality standards and provider feedback to establish goals for telephone accessibility, appointment availability, and customer service.

These standards were then endorsed by the WFUP executive committee and made more tangible through clear performance expectations. Definitions based on levels of visit urgency were developed to assist the staff in handling appointment requests efficiently.

Appointment Planning

To minimize resistance, we allowed each department to develop its own appointment availability compliance plan.

Within one month, each department submitted its individualized appointment availability compliance plan based on its unique practice pattern, which would accomplish the established service standards and performance expectations.

Every department chairperson, section head and clinic manager was required to endorse the plan by signature.

There were four required plan components:

- who would be responsible for self-assessment of the department;
- how often the self-assessment would occur;
- how the self-assessment would be performed; and
- how often each area would report its performance to WFUP clinical operations.

Each department received a performance assessment checklist modified to suit its unique plan. A score of 85% or above represented adequate performance.

Each of the 26 compliance plans was different, but all outlined how to accomplish the established standards within the department. Some creative methods to meet the service standards included:

- Monitor hold times, number of rings and "lost" calls via the phone system;
- Centralize the patient appointment scheduling phone calls in one area, rather than having various staff members and physicians answer incoming calls;

- Designate certain access lines for referring provider-only appointment calls;
- Block internal phone calls from using appointment scheduling lines;
- Use decision grids to guide staff through handling calls based on levels of visit urgency;
- Use the call center to triage all incoming patient calls based on department protocols;
- Increase available appointment slots by adding additional clinic sessions and physicians;
- Designate specific physician and physician extenders as "on call" for same day acute and emergent appointments; and
- Establish early morning clinics in which appointments requested through the call center after hours could be seen before regular clinic hours.

The next month was devoted to the KCCs educating their staff through self-assessment reports, inservices and instruction on how to make the best use of the call centers.

Plan Status

By the December 1997 mystery shopper snapshot, we made significant gains in appointment availability for patients and referring providers.

WFUP was recognized as a "better performer" in a referring provider survey sponsored through University HealthSystem Consortium, although there are still significant improvement opportunities in customer service. We'll compare the self-assessment reports to the mystery shopper audit in order to identify enhancement opportunities in data collection, as well as areas for further performance improvements. These will include the following:

- Improve customer service feedback to staff members;
- Improve referral network education;
- Implement patient satisfaction surveys;
- Establish a clinic cancellation policy;
- Standardize visit types within subspecialties;
- Update master schedules;
- Provide call center appointment scheduling for primary care providers;
- Assess the need for additional providers;
- Develop a schedule for appointment availability reporting; and
- Develop a staff training/education plan on appointment scheduling, registration, referrals and managed care.

Author Sherri De Shazo, RN, MHA, MBA, is associate director of clinical operations at Wake Forest University School of Medicine in Winston-Salem, N.C. She can be reached at (336)716-4775.

Patient Surveys Motivate Unit Staff to Improve Service

Can a patient survey really be a catalyst for change? It was at the Intermediate Care Unit at Saint Margaret Mercy Healthcare Centers, South Campus.

In 1996 and early 1997, the 32-bed unit in northwest Indiana received low scores on the Press Ganey Patient Satisfaction Survey. Patient satisfaction in IMCU ranked lower than every other unit in the hospital. These scores prompted the IMCU staff to implement an innovative plan that would better meet the needs of their patients, families and visitors.

Staff targeted eight focus areas: nurses' promptness, nurses' friendliness, nurses' attitude, nurses' attitude toward visitors, staff concern for privacy, staff concern for well-being, time to wait for discharge and noise level.

Nurse Promptness

To improve patient satisfaction in the area of nurses' promptness, the unit established a goal to respond to call lights and address the patient's request within three minutes. Ownership of the patient's request, and ensuring that the patient's request or need was being addressed became the responsibility of the person who responded to the call light. Unit clerks and patient service assistants also were incorporated into the plan.

This team approach to patient care assisted in ensuring quality service to patients, families and visitors by breaking down the barriers of a "that's not my patient" mentality. Additionally, IMCU networked with the Volunteer Services Department to acquire additional support for a hectic 3 p.m. to 11 p.m. shift. A volunteer was assigned to the nurses' station to assist with answering the telephone and call light system.

Nurse Attitude and Staff Concern

A plan for improving nurses' attitudes and staff concern for well-being included a review and discussion of past patient surveys. Role playing was an effective tool to educate the staff on patient perceptions. The key areas addressed were tone of voice, response time to call lights, and follow-through with patients' requests. A QA tool was developed and implemented to monitor patient satisfaction. This assisted the staff in identifying potential problems for quick resolution.

To address the nurses' attitude toward visitors, "Going the Extra Mile" was emphasized when educating the staff regarding visitors' perception. Attention was focused on offering comfort, information and direction to visitors. Additional chairs were made available in patient

From *QRC Advisor*, Vol. 13:9, 1997

rooms, and visitors were personally escorted to an area of the hospital instead of being provided with directions.

Time to Wait for Discharge

An Admitting/Discharge Nurse program was implemented on the 7 a.m. to 3 p.m. shift to improve the time to wait for discharge. The nurse (usually the charge nurse) was assigned to a "team" of patients but was primarily responsible for completing the admission/discharge process. Implementation of this program did not increase the budgeted staffing for IMCU.

Noise level

"Noise level" on the unit was the most difficult area to address. IMCU consists of a central nurses' station surrounded by several patient rooms and long hallways. Heavy fire doors at the end of the hall are frequently used to exit the hospital or access other departments of the hospital. A sign was placed on each of the doors to increase staff's awareness of the noise created in a patient care area. Conversations were limited to the nurses' station, particularly on the evening and night shifts.

Speed of Admissions

Discharge responsibilities were returned to the patient's primary nurse. This change provided the patient with more thorough discharge instructions. The admission nurse was not assigned to a "team" of patients; rather, her "team" was built throughout the shift with admissions and transfers to the unit.

CATEGORY	Percent of Satisfaction per Category		
	2ND QTR.	1ST QTR.	% POINT INCREASE
Noise Level	74%	79.9%	5.9%
Information Regarding Diet	68.9%	79.8%	10.9%
Nurses' Friendliness	93.5%	94.3%	0.8%
Nurses' Promptness	85.9%	91.2%	5.3%
Nurses' Attitude to Call	89.1%	92.3%	3.2%
Nurses Took Problem Seriously	88.0%	93.7%	5.7%
Nurses' Attention to Special Needs	85.7%	90.9%	5.2%
Nurses' Information Regarding Test	84.4%	89.1%	4.7%
Technical Skill of Nurse	89.4%	92.5%	3.1%
Nurses' Attitude Toward Visitors	89.9%	93.7%	3.8%
Adequacy of Information Given Family	86.1%	90.8%	4.7%
Time to Wait for Discharge	77.0%	83.5%	6.5%
Adequacy of Advice for Home Care	87.7%	90.7%	3.0%
Staff Concern for Privacy	88.5%	91.0%	2.5%
Staff Sensitivity to Inconveniences	86.5%	90.7%	3.5%
Likelihood to Recommend Hospital	87.5%	92.1%	4.6%
Staff Concern for Well Being	86.3%	92.8%	6.5%

Inconveniences

IMCU used brainstorming to create a list of daily routine activities that a patient would not be able to accomplish due to hospitalization — going to the bank, caring for their pets, driving a car, wearing their own clothes, or being in their own bed, etc.). This list was displayed to staff to demonstrate the changes in lifestyle each patient faced.

Dietary Information

A Nutrition Services Department task force created a file for dietary discharge instructions and developed information to give to patients when they are released from the hospital. Additionally, the dietician's name and telephone number were provided to the patient and family should questions arise at home.

Home Care

A second task force developed guidelines to assist the staff in identifying patients who would benefit from a home health referral, as well as a QA tool to monitor the adequacy and thoroughness of the instructions provided to patients. Nurses were assigned to review copies of the instruction sheets provided to patients upon discharge. The case manager collaborated with the social service and respiratory departments and the home care coordinator to facilitate the discharge process.

Overall Improvement

Although IMCU focused on 12 specific areas for improvement, there was a dramatic increase in the overall unit scores. Each quarter, the staff chooses several focus areas and develops a plan for continued improvement. Their efforts and commitment to patient satisfaction through effective team work have assisted the staff of IMCU to become leaders in patient, family and visitor satisfaction.

Author Karen A. Bogdan, RN, BSN, is the manager of ICU-IMCU at Saint Margaret Mercy Healthcare Centers, South Campus, in Dyer, Ind.

Visual Control: Using Simple Graphics Can Eliminate Errors and Boost Quality

Many organizations have completed extensive change initiatives to improve processes and reduce costs. But even when an organization is in pretty good shape in terms of productivity and efficiency, there are continuous improvement opportunities that should not be overlooked. Ongoing improvement is necessary for anyone trying to stay competitive, satisfy shareholders and better serve customers.

One tool with great potential for continuous improvement is called visual control and has the potential to eliminate a world of waste and error. It costs virtually nothing to implement and has the potential to knock out one-third of the everyday inadvertent errors.

Seeing Is Believing – and Doing!

Visual control, sometimes called visual communication, is a technique imported from Japan. In the early 1970s, U.S. executives went on tours of Japanese industry to see why they were beating the United States so badly in terms of quality. They noted that the workplaces were filled with pictures and diagrams of what to do ... and what not to do. With the way things were displayed, anyone passing by (whether a U.S. executive or a new employee) could actually sit down and do the assembly without knowing the Japanese language.

They brought back a lesson. The optimum place for instructions and communications is not in lengthy memos or thick procedure manuals, but in the workplace itself, where the work is done.

Taking the First Steps

There are a few fundamental rules that can make any visual control program more effective:

Make It Employee-Driven

Let the process start with the workforce — let them own it. After all, it applies to them the most. Explain the concept of visual control to the staff, and let them elect how to make the changes. Show them how a color-coded key on a key ring and a matching piece of colored tape under a lock eliminates waste and frustration. Chances are, they'll carry on from there. Because employees are often most affected by these errors, they are likely to have the most to gain by having things done right. Ask them to come up with visuals that will guide or instruct the newest employees and help everyone do things the right way the first time.

From *QRC Advisor*, Vol. 14:8, 1998

Make it Obvious

Use diagrams or colors for the visuals; they're easier for the mind to process than text. Just as icons are intuitive for computer users, so visual controls are to employees. To be sure the visual is complete, ask, "Is it obvious who should do it, how it should be done, when it should happen and where it goes next?" If the answer is yes, keep going!

Make Problems and Abnormalities Stand Out

Subtlety is not the idea here. Visuals should be attention-getters and clear in meaning. For example, place striped tape around a restricted area with a universal "no parking" symbol if you want people to comply. One chemical plant suggested obvious bright colored splash designs in those areas where previous spills had occurred.

STAFF AIDS AND PROCEDURES

To remind staff of important procedures, dates, times and other helpful information, consider these visual controls:

- Staff assignments and procedures can be placed on staff lockers as important reminders.
- Need to count days, months or weeks of treatment? Wallet-size calendars can be posted near phones or other places where this information is needed.
- A pocket guide for student nurses or float staff can help accelerate learning and increase productivity.
- The back side of an ID badge can be the perfect spot for important telephone numbers, critical clinical values or emergency procedures.
- Poster inservices can be placed in staff restrooms so all staff have an opportunity to see them.

Samples of Visual Control in Health Care

The goal of visual control in health care is to get the instructions as clear and close to the point of action as possible. Below is a series of examples of visual control that can and have been used successfully by health care organizations.

How Does This Equipment Work ... Again?

How often do people remember exactly how to work a piece of equipment when it is rarely used? To help refresh memories, visual controls can ease their frustration by offering tips on equipment operations. A few examples follow.

- Common instructions answering basic computer questions can be laminated to the frame of the computer screen.
- Put fax-problem codes and their meaning laminated on the fax machine for quick reference. Common fax numbers can be laminated on the fax to reduce searching or calling for the number. Try putting the toner replacement order number or the repair phone number on the equipment to speed problem-solving.
- One hospital laminated the operating instructions for the hospital day bed onto the bed itself, behind the cushion. During hospital admission, patients and families are shown the diagram behind the cushion. The procedure has saved staff time, and has offered more control to patients or family members.
- Replacing paper in an EKG machine can be made simpler by laminating instructions on the underside of the door to the paper. A diagram depicting EKG lead placement on the body was affixed outside of the machine.

Coordinating Services

- An essential part of care coordination is understanding who's who and who's doing what. These visual controls can help each care giver become acquainted with the multidisciplinary environment. To help doctors and other members of the care team locate a patient's nurse, place pictures of nurses next to their names on the patient assignment board.
- Stickers can be used on patient records to identify the consulting physician on the case. Staff can write the consultant physician name and phone number on the sticker and place it on the front of the chart for quick reference.
- Marker boards can be placed in patient rooms to display the names of the care givers, the day, the patient's goals and the patient's special needs.
- One organization used visual cards attached to clothespins to clue all staff as to what outstanding needs are for the patient going for surgery. The clothespins were clasped to the privacy curtains or to IV poles. Without a word, one quick glance showed the anesthesiologist which patients needed to be evaluated.
- To support patient confidentiality efforts, computer screen savers were set to appear after two minutes of down time.
- When staff leave the patient unit for breaks and other off-unit trips, a sign can be used to communicate "Sign-out" and coverage.

MAKING A STATEMENT

Visual controls can be used to convey subtle messages that support the organizational philosophy, mission, vision and goals. For example, buttons periodically worn (and recycled) can remind the work force to be sensitive to patient needs, such as "Noise Annoys," "Patients First," "Mobilize," "Lab Casual Day — Our Dress is Casual But Our Attitude Is Not," "Clean Hands, Caring Heart."

Patient Care Reminders

- Many individuals enter and leave a patient's room each day, and it is critical that certain special precautions, therapies and instructions for patient care be followed consistently by all. Visual controls can be extremely useful in communicating basic instructions to a wide audience.
- Stickers can be used to remind transporters of easily forgotten steps such as notifying the telemetry monitor technician or nurse that the patient is leaving the unit, and notifying the unit staff of the patient's return.
- An Isolation card placed on the patient door can effectively communicate who it applies to, what is to be done and proper procedures to follow.
- "No Liquids" stickers can be easily converted to illustrations that can be understood by patient populations representing multiple languages. For example, use a picture of a meal place setting and draw an "X" through it. Patients can write on their menus all foods and liquids they have consumed, and place their menus in an envelope.

- One hospital uses "No Caffeine" signs (Mug with a slash across it and list of overlooked items such as decaffeinated drinks) to help gain compliance with dietary requirements before stress tests.
- If an arm or leg should be kept free from IV sticks, consider placing a large neon sign near the patient and affixing an armband that displays the message, "Do Not Use Right Arm."
- To track and encourage ambulation progress, one organization used "Walk-a-Mile" laminated sheets. They also placed distance markings on hallway walls, every 25 feet, to track distances achieved by beginning ambulators.
- To help bring services and projects to a close, use "Target Date: ______" stickers that provide a goal for all to see.

Customer Service Hints and Signs

- Personalize patient care by having the care team sign "Now That You're Home" get well cards.
- An "Instruction for Home" packet can be used to collect discharge instructions, and related material. Inserted is a business card with a number to call for belated questions and a medication wallet card with lists that itemize the take home medications.
- Remind staff of "Telephone Etiquette" by placing a card with tele-tips by the phone.
- Each patient room can use a "Do Not Enter" door hanger. One side can be used to indicate a procedure (for example, bath or examination), the other can remind staff that the patient is resting.
- When rooms are cleaned while the patient is away, a "Your Room Cleaned By ____" tent card can be placed on the counter to inform the patient that work was done.
- Provide pencils and pads in patient rooms upon admission.
- Ask patients/family members for patient's nick name, hobbies and occupation to help a nurse quickly make the patient feel comfortable with their environment. Place the information on a form that accompanies the chart to aid staff in relating to patient's interests.
- Picture communication cards help tracheotomy and foreign patients communicate common requests.
- To keep the environment quiet for patient recovery, use periodic reminder signs displaying a mime picture and the words "Shhh! Patient resting," or "Healing in Progress." These should be conspicuously placed in staff gathering areas around computer terminals or nurses' station.

COST REMINDERS

- In one organization, a "Blood Tubing Only" sticker was applied to units of blood that did not require the use of a filter. The sticker helped save $6 every time it was followed.
- A "Do Not Sit" tent card on unused beds in semi-private rooms can save time in remaking the extra bed.
- To reduce the accidental release of biohazardous materials going down the trash chute, one hospital placed "Good Trash Only" on the trash doors. Similarly, a "Linen Only" sign can be placed on linen chute doors.

- A colorful laminated sign inviting patients to educational class can be posted in rooms to increase attendance and subsequent outcomes.

Getting in Control and Staying There

Attention to these five dimensions of visual control, if judiciously applied, will eliminate most errors in the workplace:

1. Sort through and sort out. Make sure that what is needed is available — and what is not is out of the way. The trial-and-error door keys example is a type of waste detected in "sorting through and sorting out." Our systems and workplaces can't afford to have more than what is needed, because clutter requires searching or pushing things aside to get to the needed item. At the same time, we still need to have the resources, tools and communications necessary to complete our jobs nearby.

2. Set things in order. The key motto here is: a place for everything and everything in its place. Visually designate where everything goes so when the order is upset, or something is out of place, it is obvious and looks awkward.

3. Shine. "Shining" is a type of visual inspection. Look around the workplace for all preventable errors. Remove things that are out of order or put in the wrong place, and search for anything that lowers the level of quality or efficiency.

4. Standardize. Where standardization can drive out the variability of doing the wrong thing, just do it! But here's a warning: Do not allow standardization to become an end in itself or to sub-optimize the whole. A one-size-fits-all procedure can be your best friend if employed appropriately — or your worst enemy to work around if not.

5. Self-discipline. Quality should become second nature to the workforce. When people are given the liberty and accountability to create and maintain a visual environment, they take charge of the process.

Standards, procedures and checklists are essential, but they should be at the point where the work is done instead of in a remote procedure manual. If these messages can often be even more effective if described in diagram or color-coded fashion — without words.

Author Duke Rohe is a Performance Improvement Specialist at M.D. Anderson Cancer Center in Houston.

Establishing and Achieving Team-Based Organization Performance Measures

"No margin, no mission" is a frequent refrain among health care executives. While we have done a good job of tracking financial performance, few of us can measure other "softer" elements of our missions as readily. Even if we succeed in establishing performance measures for attributes such as quality, clinical outcomes or partnership, most of us continue to struggle to motivate employees to focus on organization — rather than individual — performance.

The Healthshare Group in Petoskey, Mich., parent organization of seven health care companies, has developed a measurement system to analyze the basic tenets of its mission: quality, partnership and stewardship. This system now drives our organization's strategic plan, motivates employees and has allowed our organization to accomplishing its mission.

Mission Development

Some organizations develop a slick mission statement behind closed doors, frame it, post it and then expect everyone to embrace it in their everyday behaviors. At the Healthshare Group, we took a more circuitous, but collaborative route: We conducted a beliefs audit to identify our collective values. These values became the basis of our mission: to improve the health and quality of life of the communities we serve.

A good measurement framework enables you to routinely collect feedback to determine whether or not you are on course toward achieving the mission. We studied five basic elements: community health status, organization performance measures, patient care outcomes, key work processes, and workforce competence. Examples of these measures include, but are not limited to:

- **Community Health Initiatives.** We worked collaboratively with several community agencies to conduct a 21-county community health assessment. The assessment provided a baseline on health status, access to care, education levels, lifestyle behaviors, demographics and projected population growth.
- **Key Organizational Work.** We identified 17 key work processes in the areas of patient care (example: pain management), care support (example: registration) and business (example: human resource management). Measures included access, timeliness and utilization of service.
- **Patient Care Delivery.** We collect and report measures on nine top volume patient care aggregates such as cardiology or oncology, measuring clinical results, functional health, cost and utilization.
- **Mission/Values and Business Strategies.** We collect and report

From *QRC Advisor*, Vol. 13:9, 1997

> **“We found ourselves lacking the ability to sift through the data and find meaningful information to make decisions and prioritize improvement initiatives. The result: analysis paralysis.”**

measures on patient satisfaction, accreditation and net margin, which constitute 30% of every nonmanagement HSG employee's performance appraisal.

- **Workforce Competence.** We've defined five levels of competence and have redesigned our performance review to assess the employee's competence for each of the work processes he or she performs. The data are aggregated organizationally and used to develop curricula to improve competence.

Establishing a Uniform Approach

We recognized that without a common "map" to follow, we would soon be on divergent paths. We found a model that incorporated the basic tenets of our mission in *The Health Care Manager's Guide to Continuous Quality Improvement.* The model not only improves process but provides a uniform approach to conduct business.

Interpreting Results: Turning Data Into Information

After collecting data according to our measurement framework and performance improvement model, we recognized that we're more comfortable collecting data than interpreting it.

Three Levels of Accountability

Level 1 — Organiation Performance Measures
For managers: Organization performance measures are considered "circuit breakers" and if not met, will cut off any further consideration of additional pay increase, regardless of individual performance.
For nonmanagement staff: Organization performance measures constitute 30% of the individual employee's performance review.

1996 **Target** Performance	**Patient Satisfaction**	**Accreditation**	**Net margin**
	94.7% of patients indicate their likelihood to recommend was "good" or "very good" on the Press, Ganey survey, benchmarking our system to others nationwide.	All HSG companies either attain or maintain required accreditation status.	2%
	94.8% of patients indicated their likelihood to recommend was "good" or "very good" on the Press,Ganey survey benchmarking our system to others nationwide.	All HSG companies either attained or maintained required accreditation status.	6%

Level 2—Team Accountabilities — Tactics that drive the strategic business plan were established at each company in the HSG system. Again, these are business imperatives that individual managers are either directly responsible for or indirectly support. At The Healthshare Group, more emphasis is placed on achieving the team accountabilities than on individual performance.

Develop and implement system clinical paths, performance measures and case management pilot across the Continuum of Care.	Develop and implement system human resources management processed to align system and employee risk and reward.	Develop and implement plans for targeted wellness programming and primary care outreach services through partnership.	Continue to position the system for participation in managed care contracting.

Level 3 — Individual Accountabilities — Each manager identified two or three imperatives within his/her scope of responsibility to achieve within the year. Achievement of these goals constituted the remaining percentage of his/her overall performance bonus.

Position	**% Team**	**% Individual**
CEO	90%	10%
Vice President	80%	20%
Director/Manager	70%	30%
Medical Director	70%	30%

We found ourselves lacking the ability to sift through the data and find meaningful information to make decisions and prioritize improvement initiatives. The result: analysis paralysis.

Breaking through this data jam required us to go back to our work processes and our customer expectations, streamline the data collection process, teach breakthrough thinking and simplify the reporting process. Now the reports look the same, are easy to interpret and contain meaningful information that directs our attention and decision making toward achieving our mission.

Aligning Incentives With Organizational Goals

Frequently, organizations talk about collective performance but continue to recognize and reward only individual performance. The result often is the perpetuation of empire building, turf battles and individual "stars" on the corporate horizon. At the Healthshare Group, the executive team, with consensus from the full management team, adopted three levels of accountability.

Customer Expectations and Job Performance

The Healthshare Group bases job descriptions on the key work processes of the position. Once the processes are identified, the process steps are listed and customer expectations are defined for each step. These customer expectations then become performance expectations in the performance plan. Data from the customer become the basis for the annual performance review. Thus, the employee begins to look out to the customer for approval rather than to his/her boss.

Communicating Results

Because our compensation is directly tied to results, we must improve the way we communicate and celebrate our results. We use the Press,Ganey Patient Satisfaction Survey to tabulate our results, and our internal research department interprets the statistical significance of the data. We also have created a multidisciplinary team called the Performance Improvement Council to review results, prioritize improvement initiatives and incorporate this information into our strategic planning process.

The author, Diane M. Banks, MSEd, is the director of learning resources and organization development for The Healthshare Group, 416 Connable Ave., Petoskey, Mich. 49770; (616)348-7807; Fax: (616)348-4552; e-mail: dbanks@freeway.net

Nicholas Michels, DNSc, RN, CHE, also contributed to this article. He is vice president of hospital operations, The Healthshare Group, Northern Michigan Hospital.

References: Leebov, W. and Ersoz, C.J., *The Health Care Manager's Guide to Continuous Quality Improvement,* American Hospital Association, 1991.

Taking a Critical Look at Technology: Smarter Purchasers Make Smarter Users

That new technology being lauded in today's medical journals may not be just what the doctor ordered for your healthcare organization. The decision to use it, these experts say, should rely on a thorough assessment of cost, quality and, especially, patient outcomes.

Healthcare technology no longer is about keeping up with the Joneses. Continued pressures to keep costs at bay and the realities of living under capitation have forced many hospitals and other providers to view costly technological breakthroughs with a more critical eye. At the same time, however, they must remain focused on quality and on the potential impacts — positive and negative — of new technologies on patient outcomes.

"Providers have to balance two things," says Earl P. Steinberg, M.D., M.P.P., vice president, Covance Health, Economics & Outcomes Services Inc., a healthcare consulting firm in Washington, D.C., and director of its Quality Insurance and Improvement Services, Inc. "They have to be able to deliver care at a competitive price, but they still have to have the technology that serves as a draw for patients." The dilemma, he says, boils down to: "What do I need to remain competitive, and what can I afford to remain competitive?"

To resolve that dilemma, providers must be able to evaluate the impact of new technologies on clinical outcomes, utilization and costs in their own practice settings. They must also take a hard look at their own needs and capabilities to determine whether a device or procedure is a good strategic fit for their institution.

Some providers have launched technology assessment (TA) programs to deal with the complex issues surrounding the state of the art. They are probing into questions of outcomes, effectiveness and costs; demanding solid evidence to justify their purchases; and saying "no" when the answers don't add up. They are trying not only to become smarter purchasers of high-tech items, but also to become smarter users, so that their acquisitions — whether they're devices, procedures or drugs — are applied effectively and appropriately.

Assessment Activities Expand

"The whole practice of technology assessment is becoming more prevalent throughout the healthcare industry," says David A. Natale, director of TA at the Charlotte, N.C., office of Premier Inc., a group purchasing alliance of more than 1,700 hospitals. Mr. Natale says his department fields about 150 requests a month, of which two or three are from hospitals seeking advice on how to set up their own TA programs.

From *The Quality Letter for Healthcare Leaders*, Vol. 9:8, 1997

Although the market forces of managed care and decreasing reimbursement are the impetus for providers to intensify their TA activities, quality and effectiveness must remain their primary concerns, emphasizes Melanie Swan, M.P.H., a senior TA associate for ECRI, a not-for-profit TA and research organization in Plymouth Meeting, Pa. "The first question providers have to answer is: 'How does this technology affect patients?'" she says. That means examining such issues as mortality, disease-free survival, infection,S quality of life, daily functioning and return to work. These issues vary in significance depending on the disease or technology.

QUESTIONS TO ASK WHEN ASSESSING TECHNOLOGY

- ❖ How does this technology affect patient outcomes?
  - Mortality
  - Disease-free survival
  - Infection
  - Quality of life
  - Daily functioning
  - Return to work
- ❖ Do I need this technology to compete in my market place?
- ❖ Is appropriate use assured once the equipment is purchased?
  - Physicians support it
  - No political issues remain unresolved
- ❖ Do I have enough information to make a decision?
  - Regulatory approval status
  - Technology development status — Have the bugs been worked out?
  - Safety
  - Care delivery — Can we meet the requirements?
  - Operational requirements
  - Financial impact of purchase

Methods for Evaluating Technology: From Decisionmaker to Information Resource

Providers are far from uniform in their methods for evaluating new technologies. "There are probably as many different processes for technology assessment as there are institutions," says Karl Matuszewski, M.S., Pharm.D., director of TA for the University Health-System Consortium, an alliance of academic health centers based in Oak Brook, Ill. Three elements, however, are essential.

■ **Organize a TA program.** Most providers that approach TA seriously establish a program with a TA department and a physician-driven, multidisciplinary committee. This helps assure a focus on clinical quality consistent with the organization's needs and interests. The TA committee usually is separate from the pharmaceutical and therapeutics committee, and generally does not evaluate new drugs. The size of the committee generally ranges from 10 to 16 members, and they may include several of the organization's top financial and purchasing administrators. Mr. Matuszewski says few institutions have formal committee meeting schedules, preferring instead to meet on an ad hoc basis. Those that do establish schedules generally hold them to once a month or less.

Committee membership should be as varied as possible. In addition to financial types, the ideal panel would also include members from pharmacy, imaging, nursing, medical administration, and devices and diagnostics.

■ **Establish level of approval authority.** The power of the committee panels varies: Some panels have final say over whether a high-tech purchase goes through; others may issue advisory opinions.

For example, at North Mississippi Health Services — a healthcare system that includes a 650-bed hospital in Tupelo, four rural affiliate hospitals, a large home health service and 23 primary care clinics — every clinical capital budget item theoretically falls under the purview of the TA committee.

However, the committee conducts different levels of review depending on the item's cost and whether it is a new, replacement or additional item. Big-ticket items — those that cost $100,000 or more — are put under the microscope. The committee gets from 15 to 20 requests for such items each year, according to Jess Mark, director of planning and TA.

FLOW CHART OF THE DECISION-MAKING MODEL

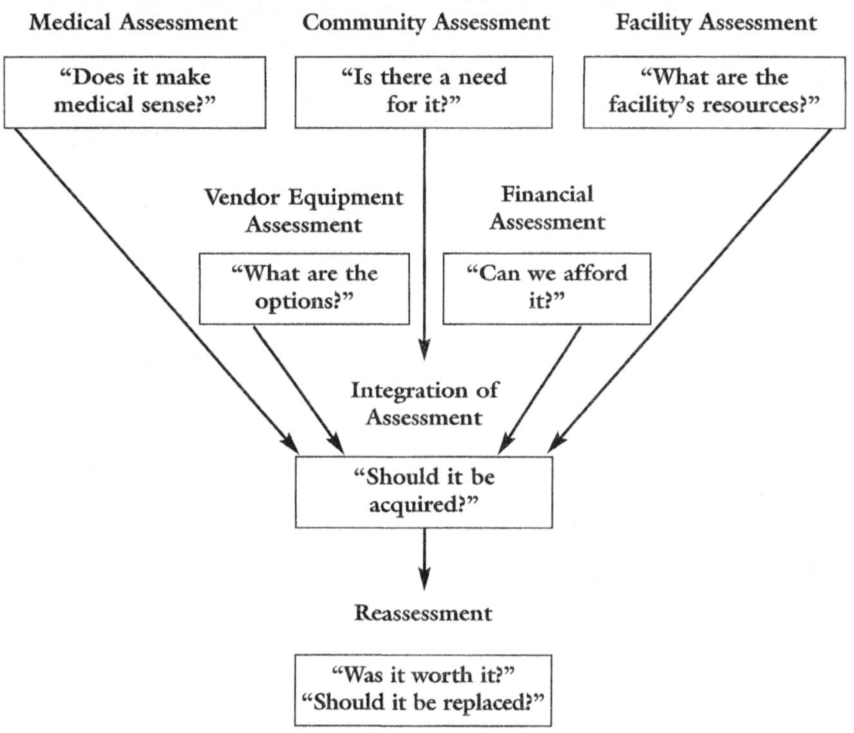

Source: Healthcare Association of New York State. Used with permission.

The University of Texas Health Science Center in Houston chose a different method. "We did not want to function as a unit of the administration," explains Jay H. Glasser, Ph.D., a professor at the university's School of Public Health. "We wanted to be more of a resource for people who are considering or proposing these technologies." The 12-member multidisciplinary committee, which has a staff of three full-time-equivalent employees, offers advisory opinions on whether to acquire, replace or expand the use of certain technologies at the health center and its affiliated teaching hospital, Hermann Hospital.

At Sarasota (Fla.) Memorial Hospital, a 952-bed public hospital, the TA department also views itself as an "internal consultant" for physicians and is available to help them find the information they need to support their requests before the TA committee, says Vicki Weingart, manager of TA and planning. In fact, the department encourages clinicians to scout out new products and procedures. "We really solicit new technologies, because we want to stay on the cutting edge, and we encourage staff members to be our ears and eyes in the field," she says. "Maybe they're not technologies that we should buy today, but we want to follow them."

The TA committee at Sarasota Memorial wields approval authority on technology-related purchases. Ms. Weingart says purchase requests are more likely to get the go-ahead now than they were before the committee was established, when the hospital's cost-containment committee, an administrative body, often turned them down. Now the hospital is reassigning its capital budget review process to the TA department. It has its work cut out. "We're allowed about $10 million, and requests came in at $34 million," Ms. Weingart explains. "So now we're trying to go through and slim down from $34 million to $10 million without having a negative impact on our strategic plan or on patient care."

■ **Ensure a champion for each request.** Most TA programs use a fairly straightforward review process. When a purchase request is involved, the burden of evidence falls on the clinician championing the request, who is asked to supply research references or copies of studies and other information to support his or her case. "We tend not to be too excited about vendor brochures," notes North Mississippi's Mr. Mark. Dr. Glasser says that his department networks extensively with other hospitals and organizations that do TA to get needed information. "A very important part of this is not reinventing the wheel — or at least not reinventing a square wheel," he says.

TA committees vary in terms of the criteria they use to make their decisions; those criteria often include regulatory approval status, development status (Have the bugs been worked out?), safety, complexity of care delivery, operational requirements, financial impact and impact on patient outcomes. TA program directors say they're looking for evidence that the technology not only is scientifically sound and beneficial but also matches their organizations' needs and objectives. "Is it going to have a significant impact in reducing the disease burden of the 500,000 people that we hold ourselves responsible for?" asks Mr. Mark.

The Decision Becomes Clear

Usually, TA officials say, the decision is clear once the evidence has been reviewed.

Does the science make sense? "When you give the data thoughtful consideration, the things that don't make sense just don't make sense, and the ones that do make sense generally are blindingly obvious," Mr. Mark says. "It's rarely that difficult."

For example, research clearly showed that biliary lithotripsy was ineffective and "bad science," despite the success of lithotripsy with kidney stones, Mr. Mark recalls. On the other hand, "kidney lithotripsy was a home run," he says, particularly because it provided a solution to a problem that caused a great deal of pain and suffering. A similar case, he notes, could be made for laparoscopic cholecystectomy.

Does the technology fit system needs? The science may be sound, but the product may not fit the system's needs. The committee has turned down three requests to adopt positron emission tomography "because it's just inappropriate for our circumstances," Mr. Mark says. PET works well for certain indications, he acknowledges, but North Mississippi's patient base could not come close to generating the volume needed to justify the technology's $5 million price tag, let alone the multimillion-dollar operating costs.

Is watchful waiting appropriate? Scientific evidence is not always definitive. Because technology is a moving target, watchful waiting is sometimes the right choice, Ms. Weingart observes. It may take time to develop enough information to make a decision about a technology's impact on patient outcomes. Also, providers may have issues of their own to resolve before they can make good use of a technology.

For example, Ms. Weingart says, Sarasota Memorial's nurses were inter-

TECHNOLOGY ASSESSMENT BENEFITS

- Cures the problems that made technology assessment necessary
- Saves money
- Ensures that the appropriate technology is available for patients requiring it
- Promotes "organizational" perspective as opposed to "departmental" perspective, thereby ensuring that decisions are made based on what is best for the organization rather than what's best for the department
- Minimizes conflicts between medical staff and management
- Helps prioritize technology decisions in the capital budgeting process

ested in a wireless telephone technology that they thought could help them communicate better with each other and with physicians. Initially, the proposal seemed to mesh well with plans to redesign the nursing units to eliminate overhead paging and other noise. But when the TA committee tried to determine the impact of the wireless system on the hospital's existing phone and other communication systems, it decided it needed to address communications systemwide within the hospital. The committee is still examining the issue.

"For some questions, you can give a definitive answer, particularly if there's a goal in mind," remarks Dr. Glasser. "But in other situations, the answer might really be a set of alternatives, recognizing that all these technologies are evolving at such a rapid pace that you're in part trying to forecast where these things will be two years from now. In those latter cases, it's more likely there is no real definitive answer."

Does the technology have physician support? In one case, Ms. Weingart recalls how the TA committee turned down a request for a harmonic scalpel because there was little support for it among the hospital's surgeons. Six months later, the situation had changed. Surgeons had learned more about the technology and were now interested in it. The TA department did some research, found the device had merit and educated the medical staff on how the device could help them and how to use it.

ECRI's Ms. Swan notes that physician support and training are essential to adopting and implementing new technologies. If physicians don't support a new device or procedure, they won't refer patients or use it themselves. And that not only is a waste of money but also affects quality. For example, if surgeons want to perform stereotactic breast biopsy but cannot because radiologists are the only ones meeting credentialing criteria, then the surgeons are unlikely to refer the patient for the stereotactic breast biopsy procedure. They likely will keep the patient and perform the traditional excisional biopsy. "These things are all tied together," she observes. "If the surgeons don't buy into a technology, they're not going to refer patients. This raises concerns about clinical proficiency and patient outcomes. You can't look at any of this in a vacuum."

Politics can also affect use of new technologies, Ms. Swan says. For example, stereotactic breast biopsy is a controversial issue in many hospitals — not because of questions about its effectiveness, but because of the turf wars it has sparked between radiologists and surgeons. "The places where we've seen this work are where the surgeons and radiologists had a great relationship. In other places, the issue really drives a wedge between them," says Ms. Swan. As a result, physicians at those hospitals are less likely to become skilled in using the technology, which costs $300,000 to $500,000 to acquire.

Track Performance to Avoid Inappropriate Use

Tracking a new technology can be as important as assessing it before acquisition, although Ms. Swan says that few providers do this. "We tell hospitals it's very important to look back a year after you've acquired a technology — both from a financial and a patient outcomes perspective —

and then to periodically reassess throughout the life of the technology." UHC's Dr. Matuszewski agrees. "Unless you look at a technology periodically and systematically, there's a huge potential for inappropriate use," he says.

North Mississippi's TA committee assigns a multidisciplinary team to implement each new technology acquisition. This team supplies the information the committee needs to track the technology's performance over time. For example, once the decision was made to open a sleep disorder center, the TA committee pulled together a group of physicians, other clinicians and purchasing administrators to develop an action plan and set certain benchmarks for the new lab. Mr. Mark says his top concern is uti-

COLLECTING AND USING TECHNOLOGY ASSESSMENT DATA

Data that permit head-to-head comparisons of new technologies on outcomes and cost-effectiveness often are scarce. As a result, healthcare organizations are evaluating and using data from multiple sources to assess state-of-the art devices, drugs, procedures and biological products.

Identify best available evidence. "Generally, we try to understand the nature of the clinical problem and identify the best sources of evidence to address that problem," explains Naomi Aronson, Ph.D., director of the Blue Cross and Blue Shield Association's Technology Evaluation Center. For certain conditions, data from randomized clinical trials may be critical to performing an adequate evaluation. But other conditions might not require that level of evidence, she notes. Then it's a matter of making the most of the best available evidence, choosing from a number of statistical analysis methodologies, Dr. Aronson says.

The Blues association launched TEC in 1985; since then, it has issued more than 250 assessments of medical interventions. In 1993, recognizing that the scope of the task had broadened, TEC began working collaboratively with Kaiser Permanente and established a medical advisory panel of nationally recognized experts.

Cost-effectiveness is not among TEC's evaluation criteria, which focus mainly on clinical outcomes and effectiveness. However, Dr. Aronson says that TEC has performed cost-effectiveness analysis case studies during the past two years. For example, an analysis of PET for coronary artery disease found that it conferred virtually no clinical advantage relative to the less expensive alternative, SPECT. In another study, TEC is examining the cost-effectiveness of new cervical cancer-screening technologies. "One of the important things about the Pap smear is that it's very accessible and inexpensive and it leads to successful interventions," Dr. Aronson notes. "If you are looking at such a well-established and useful technology, you want to understand how any changes you might make would alter cost, accessibility and so on."

Analyze clinical outcomes, then cost-effectiveness. Dr. Aronson says TEC hopes to increase the use of cost-effectiveness analysis, but it believes that clinical analysis should come first. In addition, she notes, although methods for conducting cost-effectiveness analysis have improved, they still need further standardization.

Mitchell Sugarman, technology assessment manager for Kaiser Permanente's Permanente Federation, says "far too little" rigorous evidence is available for many technology evaluations. That's particularly true when trying to compare new technologies with conventional therapies.

Mr. Sugarman says that at Kaiser Permanente, data are collected from as many sources as possible and rated for rigor before the managed care giant's Interregional New Technologies Committee reviews the data. Sometimes, he says, when the data are found wanting, the committee must make decisions that are less than absolute. "We try to exercise a great deal of caution." In addition, he says, it's important to inform patients of the potential benefits and drawbacks of new technologies and the validity of the information that was used to evaluate them.

Like Dr. Aronson, Mr. Sugarman says he'd like to be able to conduct more cost-effectiveness analyses, but the data usually aren't available. In any case, he adds, questions of cost are secondary to questions of safety and effectiveness. "Otherwise, what's the point?"

Alan L. Hillman, M.D., M.B.A., associate dean of the University of Pennsylvania's School of Medicine in Philadelphia, says that methods for conducting cost-effectiveness analysis have become more standardized during the past few years.

"There's more cognizance of what is a good study and what's not a good study, and I think the technology for lization — making sure that the product or service meets its target. He followed the sleep lab closely for several years before he was satisfied that it was on track. When utilization targets are missed, he says, the committee will step in to find out why. "Sometimes we wind up correcting the science," he notes.

Over Time, Assessment Becomes Easier, Saves Money

Program directors say systematic TA can be hard work, particularly when it's tied to capital budgeting. But Mr. Mark suggests that done properly, TA becomes easier over time because the assessment cures some of the

COLLECTING AND USING TECHNOLOGY ASSESSMENT DATA (Cont.)

cost-effectiveness analysis is being used within the industry and by insurers as an in-house method to assist decisionmaking in an informal way," he says. "More insurers and corporations have people on staff who can run a research model and who can read the literature properly, so that they can discuss these things in their internal reports and meetings."

But formal use of cost-effectiveness analysis is spotty at best, particularly with respect to formulary design, Dr. Hillman notes. That's partly because the Food and Drug Administration doesn't allow pharamaceutical companies to market their drugs on claims of cost-effectiveness unless those claims pertain strictly to on-label uses, Dr. Hillman says. "Managed care wants to see how things work in the real world, but the FDA won't allow that information to be marketed."

In addition, he notes, many pharmaceutical purchasers still harbor suspicions about cost-effectiveness studies and analyses performed or funded by drug companies, although Dr. Hillman believes that those doubts have abated somewhat. Pharmaceutical manufacturers, he says, would be well-served to work more closely with purchasers to produce the kind of information they need to make smarter formulary decisions.

Barbara J. Zarowitz, Pharm.D., director of ambulatory clinical pharmacy services for Detroit-based Henry Ford Health System, agrees that it's difficult to get hold of any kind of outcomes or comparative data, beyond what are required for FDA approval. "We plead with the drug companies to give us outcomes data," she says. Ideally, she explains, she'd like to be able to compare not only costs but also physician visits, time lost from work, side effects and emergency admissions among competing therapies. "My frustration is that often that information is not available until a year or two after the drug has been released," she says.

Dr. Zarowitz says HFHS's ambulatory care formulary committee tries to start evaluating drugs as early as possible, by tracking them before they receive FDA approval and collecting all available information. Some of that information comes from drug companies, but Dr. Zarowitz says usually a wealth of independent research is available on new drugs by the time they win regulatory approval. In addition, HFHS consults its own clinical experts for opinions on new drugs, she says.

Producing timely outcomes and cost-effectiveness data early in a technology's life is difficult, says Neil R. Powe, M.D., M.P.H., M.B.A., an associate professor of medicine, epidemiology, and health policy and management at the Johns Hopkins Medical Institutions in Baltimore. In addition, he says, to truly understand how the technology will perform under different clinical circumstances, it's necessary to conduct a whole series of studies.

Look at new uses of existing products. For example, Dr. Powe recently headed a national study on the impact of recombinant erythropoietin, which is used to stimulate red blood cell growth, on patients with kidney disease. Dr. Powe's team examined numerous issues, including how well the drug worked among different patient types; its impact on hospitalizations and how that offset other associated costs; and the effect of different reimbursement methods on provider use. "We looked at it very comprehensively and performed a cost-benefit analysis," comparing erythropoietin with conventional blood transfusion, he says. The bottom line boiled down to "not just whether you use the drug, but under what circumstances and how."

But these types of analyses appear to be few and far between.

problems that made it necessary in the first place. For example, capital budget proposals by department heads have become much more reasonable over the years, he notes. "We've cured them of the 'wish list' syndrome," Mr. Mark says. "We don't see much of that anymore."

The savings from good TA can be substantial. Ms. Weingart figures that the TA program has saved Sarasota Memorial close to $3 million. If anything, she says, that estimate is low because it is based on acquisition costs that were avoided — not the downstream costs associated with integrating and implementing new technologies that were rejected. In addition, she notes, "a whole lot of dollars are saved by making the right buy" but are difficult to quantify.

Ms. Swan offers this example of a technology evaluation that she believes combined consideration of quality, cost and strategic fit. Several years ago, cardiologists at a hospital that ECRI was assisting proposed the use of stents for primary therapy. The physician who chaired the technology committee agreed that although stents were very important for emergency situations, patient outcomes data were inadequate at that time to support the use of stents in primary therapy over the gold standard, angioplasty. Next, Ms. Swan reports, the committee considered cost. At this hospital, patients with stents were given heparin therapy and recovered in the ICU. This meant that the hospital's per-patient cost for using a stent was $25,000 to $27,000, compared with about $7,000 for angioplasty.

The committee turned down the request to use stents for primary therapy, but agreed to reconsider the proposal as more patient outcomes data became available. Because very little long-term outcomes data existed in the literature, the committee decided to follow its own patients in whom stents were used in emergency situations (e.g., threatened abrupt closure of the vessel during cardiac catheterization) — a solution applauded by Ms. Swan as "thoughtful" and balanced.

Lessons Learned

TA program directors and experts offer this advice to providers thinking of starting their own TA programs:

- **Make sure your process is physician-driven**, drawing from multiple disciplines throughout the organization. This ensures physician buy-in and promotes decisionmaking that is both clinically sound and rooted in a broader perspective of what is good for the entire organization — not just one department.
- **Keep politics at bay.** Make sure your review criteria are applied consistently and fairly. You will also need the full commitment of your organization's top administrators to ensure that disgruntled department heads don't bypass the review process by going through the back door. One solution is to recruit your facility's financial administrator to serve on the TA committee. But the best way, Mr. Mark says, is simply to do a good job. One reason North Mississippi's TA program has its CEO's full support is because "he never gets any calls from the doctors about equipment," Mr. Mark notes. In addition, program officials should be willing to acknowledge and fix mistakes

when they make them.

- **Hold your physicians accountable for their requests.** Ms. Weingart notes that, at Sarasota Memorial, each request to the TA committee must have a "champion" who assumes responsibility for making the case to acquire the new product or capability. This is particularly important in determining who at the hospital will actually use the technology. Tracking is another effective means for holding technology champions accountable.
- **Consider using a consultant** when designing your program. Sarasota Memorial relied heavily on ECRI's expertise for setting up its program, and Ms. Weingart says she still taps ECRI for help on specific technology issues. Outside consultants can help bring focus and objectivity to a TA project and reinforce important messages, she says.
- **Figure out what technology your organization already has** and how those technologies are being used now before you start considering new ones. "You have to know what you have before you can determine what you need," Ms. Swan notes.
- **Educate your medical staff about technology** and how the purchase and use of technology affect the organization as a whole. This will help promote that broader perspective that program directors say is so important to their success. Ms. Weingart says her department also educates clinicians on how the TA process works and how they can use it effectively. "We want to show them that it's a rational, objective process, and we also want to show how to make their lives easier," Ms. Weingart says.

For more information ...

Blue Cross and Blue Shield Association
Contact: Sally Bleeks
Phone: (312)440-5583
E-mail: us993slb@ibmmail.com

Covance Health, Economics & Outcomes Services Inc.
Contact: Earl P. Steinberg, M.D., M.P.P.
Phone: (202)508-6540

ECRI
Contact: Melanie Swan, M.P.H.
Phone: (610)825-6000, ext. 163

The Johns Hopkins Medical Institutions
Contact: Neil R. Powe, M.D., M.P.H., M.B.A.
Phone: (410)955-4128
E-mail: npowe@phnet.sph.jhu.edu

North Mississippi Health Services
Contact: Jess Mark
Phone: (601)841-3033
E-mail: jmark@mmhs.net

Premier Inc.
Contact: David A. Natale
Phone: (704)679-5237
E-mail: dave_natale@premierinc.com

Sarasota Memorial Hospital
Contact: Vicki Weingart
Phone: (941)917-1295

University HealthSystem Consortium
Contact: Karl Matuszewski, M.S., Pharm.D.
Phone: (630)954-1709
E-mail: matuszewski@msgate.uhc.edu

University of Pennsylvania School of Medicine
Contact: Alan L. Hillman, M.D., M.B.A.
Phone: (215)898-9400

University of Texas Health Science Center at Houston
Contact: Jay H. Glasser, Ph.D.
Phone: (713)500-9173
E-mail: jglasser@utsph.sph.uth.tmc.edu

Part IV
Quality In Care

Identifying and Meeting Community Healthcare Needs — From the Beginning

Effective community health improvement depends on appropriate needs assessment, development of an action plan and the right mix of people to make it happen.

Somerville and Cambridge were proud of their "melting pot" characteristics; the combined population of the two Massachusetts cities is about 172,000, of which roughly a third is immigrants.

But community leaders of the cities have grown concerned in recent years that the influx of new populations was exacerbating communications barriers that led to inadequate healthcare. About 26% of the area population live 200% below the poverty line, many of them immigrants from Portugal, Central America and Brazil. "Some immigrants were not getting any healthcare; some had no insurance and did not understand ways to access services because of language and cultural barriers," says Mark Rukavina, program director for the Somerbridge Community Health Partnership. Figures for 1995 showed that 39% of all medical visits in the Somerbridge area were with non-English-speaking patients.

"We needed a way to identify the critical issues so that we could develop the best plans for action," Mr. Rukavina continues. Together, Cambridge Hospital and Somerville Hospital (which now have been merged under the Cambridge Public Health Commission) established the Somerbridge Community Health Partnership in 1996. Its aim is to build healthier individuals, families and communities through new managed care offerings, improved community outreach in preventive and primary healthcare and a concerted effort to overcome language barriers. Other groups, including the Community Action Agency of Somerville, the Cambridge Department of Public Health and the Cambridge Economic Opportunity Committee, joined as full working partners. Building on a community health agenda prepared by the city of Somerville in 1992, the community partnership won a $225,000 grant from the Community Care Network Demonstration Program of the American Hospital Association's Hospital Research and Educational Trust.

The Somerbridge program spent the past year completing various surveys about immigrant health needs, one of the first actions of its Immigrant Health Task Force. At the same time, Somerbridge began working with Multilingual Services of Somerville Hospital and training healthcare providers and others to keep them abreast of national welfare reform and immigration policy changes, which have greatly affected resources available to immigrants.

Now the hospital and its affiliated community health centers have 11 Spanish-speaking primary care providers and 20 others who speak nine more languages. Full-time and on-call interpreters provide 24-hour coverage for the top three most-requested languages. During the first six

From *The Quality Letter for Healthcare Leaders*, Vol. 10:1, 1998

months of 1997, Multilingual Services staff provided roughly 1,300 interpreter-patient contacts each month and translated more than 150 documents.

Somerbridge also helped to found a certificate program for medical interpreters through Bunker Hill Community College, and it will offer its first course this month.

"We couldn't have learned as much about our community as we did without targeted assessments — for example, in a housing development and among the people who have used interpreters — to learn where there are still gaps in care," Mr. Rukavina says. While there still are no comprehensive data on immigrant health status, findings from the assessments will help Somerbridge plan for action centered on continuous quality improvement. Anecdotally, access to care and usage of services has improved as communication has improved, and in another year solid data should be available, Mr. Rukavina says.

Somerbridge is an example of a community health improvement program that has gathered the proper staffing and funding and drafted clear plans and schedules to meet its health priority goals. The program is evolving alongside federal policy changes, subpopulation growth and changes in healthcare delivery, including the expansion of managed care and facility consolidations.

10 STRATEGIES FOR SUCCESS

- ✓ Gather together individuals with differing strengths so that all aspects of the community assessment, planning and action will be covered. Get a commitment to action from all partners.
- ✓ Include individuals in the CEO's confidence who can act explicitly but who may have more time than a CEO for group activities.
- ✓ Broaden the definition of health. Put out a general call for interested partners and pursue nontraditional local assets that may prove valuable (*e.g.*, school assistance, religious organizations, environmental groups, refugee organizations).
- ✓ Strive to keep the project on schedule. Busy managers as well as retirees want to see results as soon as they can.
- ✓ Work to keep all members at the table and find ways to satisfy each organization's specific needs before launching a project.
- ✓ Use existing assessment tools, but tailor them to the local situation.
- ✓ Don't think that data must be up-to-the-minute and perfectly refined. Data must be credible, however, to all partners before action can be taken.
- ✓ Pursue funding from all possible sources — from grants and corporate programs to small local donations.
- ✓ Keep communication lines open through a steering committee that oversees projects and understands "the big picture."
- ✓ Define projects based on real local needs. Build in an evaluation piece at the beginning and monitor the projects to learn what is working well and what needs to be modified.

Getting Started

Most community improvement efforts begin with one or two organizations or agencies that want to gather information and community support for such an effort. Community assessments are performed to learn about healthcare needs, local assets and resources. Then a health improvement committee or task force develops an action plan and implements it, often one program at a time. Most often, communities focus on their costliest healthcare problems or on solutions that will make the greatest beneficial impact.

Hospitals and other healthcare facilities in many communities have banded with other groups to create economical and effective systems to improve the delivery of care and to promote wellness. Some are spurred to action by high rates of certain chronic diseases and the need to introduce public prevention efforts like increased safety belt use or strength training in older patients prone to falls. Still others have recognized underserved populations with growing needs. The mission or values of a healthcare organization also may dictate a community assessment and improvement program. Whatever the reason, community health improvement actions, involving a number of different organizations and consumer groups, are becoming commonplace.

Assessing Community Needs

Today's community assessments often are initiated by public health departments that want to identify prevalent diseases or environmental factors affecting health, as opposed to the governmental health planning launched in the 1970s, says Raymond Baxter, Ph.D., a senior vice president with the Lewin Group, a research firm in Fairfax, Va. Hospitals may use foundation money to conduct assessments. Large employers or business coalitions also may ask for an assessment of health problems or a demonstration of how well the delivery system is performing. Employers, who for years have paid rising premiums for healthcare, now want to learn the results of their increased investments, and some are asking for results in the form of improved patient health outcomes. *(See box at right for four types of needs assessments.)*

Because the scope of community assessment projects varies so much from place to place, it is impossible to say how long an assessment should take or what a typical schedule looks like. A community assessment project may be as straightforward as defining a single problem without an action plan or as complex as assessing and planning for action on a number of different fronts.

After concerned organizations have come together to investigate and assess community health, they need to agree on a collective vision for their project, says Claude H. Hall Jr., who directs the CCN demonstration program, which distributed grants to 24 communities besides Somerbridge. The organizations must agree on the purpose for conducting an assessment and define the scope of the project.

TYPES OF NEEDS ASSESSMENTS

Claude H. Hall Jr., director of the Community Care Network Demonstration Program, who oversees many different community health networks, notes that there are four common types of multiorganizational needs assessments, which are:

1. Performed in conjunction with health departments, through state mandates or local voluntary efforts;

2. Performed by key informants and leaders of major institutions (*e.g.* hospitals), chambers of commerce or academic institutions that are embarking on "vision" efforts for the community;

3. Performed by hired consultants for major local institutions, including broad-scale community surveys or hosted focus groups; or

4. Commissioned by a group, but with no particular ownership by any one institution. For example, a university professor might perform a communitywide survey and share results with the multiorganizational committee.

Once the vision is defined, research into the issues begins with data collection. Several dimensions can be explored during a community health assessment, according to research conducted by the Lewin Group for Grantmakers in Health in Washington, D.C., an educational organization serving trustees and foundation staff members. Some of these dimensions are health status and risk factors, utilization of resources and capacity, community assets, unmet needs and dislocations, system responsiveness, healthcare programs, major disease categories, and population age groups. Each community must determine the particular dimensions to include in an assessment. Each dimension is best measured by a different set of indicators, many of which are readily available.

The appropriate data collection method should be determined by looking at the scope of the assessment. Most groups select a researcher or research firm to perform the actual collection and analysis. Communities that want more detailed information generally combine both primary data collected through interviews and surveys and secondary data from existing public sources.

Understanding the resources that will be available for a health improvement effort is "just as important as gathering the data from the assessment," Mr. Hall stresses. A group's resource, time and economic constraints will determine the type and quality of the information to be collected, he says.

After analysis, the data must be summarized in a meaningful report that can be readily understood and embraced by the community health improvement members.

The final step of an assessment, Mr. Rukavina says, is revising goals, refining data collection techniques or monitoring methods and engaging additional people as the health improvement effort progresses over time.

"Every partnership that imagines it wants to do a needs assessment really needs to think about how it could configure the potential methods of assessment to the individual community and environment," says Mr. Hall. His organization awards grant money and is a collaboration of the Hospital Research and Educational Trust of the American Hospital Association, the AHA, the Catholic Health Association of the United States and VHA Inc. Each of the communities that has received a CCN grant has conducted some form of assessment.

In most communities, a number of groups come together to perform the needs assessment, as in Virginia's Nelson County, where several healthcare and community action agencies gathered to explore unmet county needs.

Mr. Hall offers a counter-intuitive piece of advice: Rather than pool resources to get a comprehensive needs assessment, let different partners perform different needs assessments to capture what various segments of the population might need. Then devise an omnibus report that can be presented to the funding agency. "There is a seductive attractiveness to the notion of an integrated needs assessment, but the price paid is administrative difficulty for the partners engaged or surprises down the road," Mr. Hall says. For example, if a group joins an integrated needs assessment effort after startup, that group sometimes can derail the effort with its own expectations of the assessment.

KEY COMPONENTS OF A COMMUNITY NEEDS ASSESSMENT

- ✓ Once the community improvement group has been established, work on defining a specific vision for healthcare in the community and, thus, the scope of the project.
- ✓ With the vision defined, decide which dimensions of healthcare the group wants to study (*eg.* health risk factors, utilization rates, unmet needs, system responsiveness).
- ✓ Collect data from primary and/or secondary sources.
- ✓ Analyze data and summarize the information in a meaningful report.
- ✓ Determine resources or assets in the community that could contribute to improved healthcare.
- ✓ Present data to members for review and discussion. Collect further data if necessary to create buy-in and to sharpen project goals.
- ✓ Over time, collect further data to monitor progress toward goals or to define new goals. Revise goals and engage additional people when necessary.

Using Assessment Tools Wisely

Many workable tools for healthcare needs assessment are available. Mr. Hall suggests using existing models for needs assessment, particularly the PATCH and APEXPH tools *(See box, page 166)*. He stresses that these tools should be used only as guides, however, not as to-the-letter cookbooks. "You need to understand the personalities of the partners and purposes of needs assessment, all of which must be managed appropriately," Mr. Hall says.

Dr. Baxter notes that data are extremely important and should be collected as objectively as possible, by a neutral collector if resources for one are available. "It is so easy for the participants to become defensive. Hospitals may feel that purchasers are picking on them, for example. If all partners feel the information was collected by a neutral party, they can all come together around the information, rather than using the information as ammunition," he says.

Dr. Baxter also warns groups not to become bogged down by the amount of data or the way it has been adjusted. Remember that the information is merely a tool to help those involved in the effort to get a clearer picture of the community. "The data will never be completely current, or as refined as you want them to be. The group has to move on — to say, 'We have enough information to identify the major problems, so let's figure out what to do about them,'" he says.

"The data will never be completely current ... The group has to move on — to say, 'We have enough information to identify the major problems.'"

Raymond Baxter, Ph.D.
Senior Vice President
The Lewin Group

The timeliness of the assessment and of subsequent actions also is important. Many groups want their data collection to be methodologically sophisticated, which means that it will be extremely time-consuming as well as labor intensive. If the assessment takes a long time (significantly longer than an original schedule), the people involved become disinterested and momentum — and, therefore, the project — is lost, Mr. Hall and Mr. Rukavina warn.

Assessments can function as unifying political tools, not just planning tools. In California's Solano County, a data aggregation report pulled together facts and figures related to community health issues such as birth and death rates, cancer incidence, and violence. "We arranged and presented the data both at a county and a city level. It did act as a linchpin and was a cause to bring people together," says Patrick S. Hughes, Ed.D., who is the project coordinator for Healthier Solano Communities, a CCN grant program that is part of a larger community coalition effort.

Remembering Your Audience

Dr. Baxter says that a common pitfall is performing an assessment without thinking through the process of how the information will be used or considering the audience for the information. "If you haven't prepared the soil and gotten people in the effort ready to receive the information, think about it and engage in planning, the information will not go anywhere, other than as a line in the newspaper when results are released," Dr. Baxter says. Let constituents or stakeholders know in advance what the assessment is designed to do, and they will feel ownership of the information, be willing to develop a plan and help boost the plan into action.

Knowing your constituents and being sensitive to their needs are essential. Many people who work in community health improvement efforts are provider representatives, who are busy and have a brief threshold of time they can commit, Mr. Hall says. Other members often are people from the community who are retired or who have a select set of interests. "They need a way of feeling good about their ability to improve things. They want to make their impact soon," Mr. Hall cautions. He suggests a realistic and thoughtful approach to the amount of time that will be spent in assessment and thereafter. "Once you set up a schedule, move heaven and earth to stick to the schedule," Mr. Hall advises.

A tricky part of most efforts is satisfying all members of a coalition, at the outset and as plans progress. The Solano Coalition for Better Health, which began in 1988, serves an ethnically diverse rural and urban population of about 400,000. And members of the coalition are competitors for patients in the community.

Kaiser Permanente has a large presence in the county and enrolls 50% of the population. "The Kaiser Permanente physicians were not used to working with other physicians" when they united to form the Solano Partnership Health Plan (a private, not-for-profit Medi-Cal managed care plan) to provide access for poor and underserved patients, says Steve Graham, director for Community Health Partnerships for Kaiser of California and the Kaiser Permanente liaison for the SCBH. "The HMO's physicians wanted to be sure that the Solano Partnership Health Plan would allow them an equitable portion of the Medi-Cal (Medicaid program) patients."

Another partner, Sutter Health System, which had a medical center and a new birthing center, needed assurance that Kaiser Permanente would not enroll more than its share of women of childbearing age.

"We had to do some fine tuning, remember the final goal and then sit down at the table and examine the best ways we could all provide care to those who were not receiving it," Mr. Graham says.

COMMUNITY ASSESSMENT AND ACTION TOOLS

PATCH (Planned Approach to Community Health)

This comprehensive health planning program has a six-step process designed to be ongoing and adaptable to the changing needs of the community. The PATCH manual provides information on the collection, analysis and presentation of data and contains training information.

Centers for Disease Control, Community Health Promotion Branch, (770)488-5438, manual free of charge.

APEXPH (Assessment Protocol for Excellence in Public Health)

This voluntary process for organizational and community self-assessment includes implementing planned improvements and continuing evaluation of the organization and its activities. APEXPH comprises a three-step process: organizational capacity assessment, community needs assessment and incorporating the information from the needs assessment into ongoing activities and a move toward policy development.

National Association of County & City Health Officials, (202)783-5550; workbook is $20 for association members, $60 for nonmembers.

Community Health Assessment: A Process for Positive Change

This comprehensive 182-page book describes how healthcare organizations can join the larger community and assess and develop strategies for local health issues. It addresses strategic fit and the philosophical basis for such an effort, how to implement a six-phase process, and key challenges and solutions that can arise throughout the six phases.

VHA, (800)468-6842, $40 for members (first copy free), $65 for nonmembers.

CHART (Missouri Community Health Assessment and Resource Team)

This set of five manuals contains tutorials on how to initiate, develop and sustain community initiatives. This set was designed by Anderson Consulting, tailored to the state of Nebraska and Republic of Slovakia, and a more comprehensive version is being released.

Missouri Hospital Association, (573)893-3700, ext. 1305, $30 for in-state purchase; price under negotiation for use outside Missouri.

For many more useful publications and programs, consult *Background and Resources for a Community Health Status Focus*, September 1996, The Hospital Research and Educational Trust, 1 North Franklin, 29th Floor, Chicago, IL 60606.

When Nelson County began its project, members identified different needs in measuring results, according to Peggy Whitehead, director of the Rural Health Outreach Proram based in Arrington, Va. The county's health improvement team wanted to show the two major neighboring hospitals in Charlottesville, which are participants in the effort, that the rural Nelson County effort to improve health is making a difference. The hospitals wanted the outcomes information as an incentive for their participation in the rural health effort. Future funding also may depend on the outcomes that are reported, she adds. Thus, during the planning phase, the group began developing a system for monitoring results to meet these different needs.

Uncovering Local Assets

Local resources that can assist in the health improvement push should be identified during the assessment phase. "Organizations are often not aware of each other's existence," Dr. Baxter says. One way to enhance the search is to define health as broadly as possible, not just focusing on hospitals or healthcare organizations. He notes that religious groups, for example, often are organized and willing to make healthcare improvement a priority.

"We had to do some fine tuning, remember the final goal and then sit down at the table and examine the best ways we could all provide care."

Steve Graham
Director, Community Health Partnerships
Kaiser of California

In the Lehigh Valley community health improvement effort in eastern Pennsylvania, members learned to stretch their definitions of health and wellness to include quality of life and well-being for disabled individuals.

The initial community improvement group, which included internist Mark J. Young, M.D., who also is professor and chair at the Department of Health Evaluation Sciences at Penn State University College of Medicine in Hershey, and colleagues at Lehigh Valley Hospital, brainstormed to come up with a list of nontraditional healthcare elements, including the environment. They contacted Hawk Mountain Sanctuary, which became a surprise partner to many in the healthcare improvement effort. The wildlife preserve, dedicated to raptor preservation and other environmental concerns, sponsored a forum and explained the project it wanted to pursue — a handicap-accessible area in one overlook. Another partner organization, the Center for Independent Living, worked with the preserve on the overlook's design.

Other Lehigh Valley assets included: 1) schools' participation in an asthma care campaign; 2) the local health bureau's funding for home visits, which was used to visit children; and 3) a college that had assigned an undergraduate with an interest in epidemiology and statistics to collate and organize findings for the communitywide health indicators report.

In Solano County, SCBH Medical Director Michael Policar, M.D., envisions a continuum of care that includes offices outside of healthcare walls. Dr. Policar says that medical providers also must partner with organizations that provide such services as psychosocial counseling, transportation and child care to create a successful "social model" of healthcare.

Knowing When to Act

Action is possible when the following pieces are ready:

■ When Staffing Is in Place

Mr. Hall advises being clear from the beginning about the skills and staffing requirements for a communitywide effort. You'll need people with leadership and management skills, but not necessarily CEOs who are pressed for time. You'll need support from leaders to act on your findings. And you'll need people capable of wearing several hats, who can focus on making steps happen. Once all players are assembled, a project is poised for take-off.

A steering committee is needed to be the centralized eyes, ears and voice for the many projects that are planned, say these experts. In Nelson County, for example, an interagency council provided oversight of local rural outreach activities. Now all members of that council are part of a steering committee that oversees daily activities. Members include representatives from the Jefferson Area Boards of Aging, Monticello Area Community Action Agency, the social services department, the health department, two city-based hospitals, the community medical center and community services, as well as consumers and interested citizens such as retired physicians.

The interagency council is seen as a communications tool. "Coordination of our various programs is easy, because of a tight referral network," Ms. Whitehead says. "We all feel free to call each other about patients and the care they need to receive. That has been a significant factor in our success." The council also helps determine gaps in care and how to avoid duplication of services.

■ When Funds Are Secured

Funding can be found in many places. For example, the medication assistance program in Nelson County basically pays for itself, through the help of pharmaceutical firms, many of which donate drugs for impoverished patients as goodwill and good public relations. Ms. Whitehead says that the county uses the Pharmacy Connection software developed by the Virginia Healthcare Foundation and offered free to facilities in Virginia. The software helps to identify some 80 pharmaceutical companies' programs for making particular medications available to the needy and explain the often-complex processes and requirements for obtaining those medications. Since October 1996, Nelson County has provided $100,000 worth of medications through pharmaceutical company foundations and programs.

Nelson County's program overall has relied on outside grants, but also local business donations that Ms. Whitehead says are helpful in a county with no large industry. In 1991, three-year grant funding from the federal Office on Rural Health Policy launched the rural outreach program for the county. Once that funding ended in 1994, the CCN program and four other grants have allowed the initiative to keep its staff of three — Ms. Whitehead as director, a nurse practitioner and a certified nurse's aide.

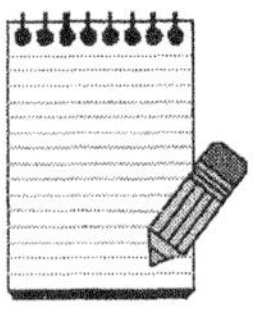

You're ready to act when:

- ➤The appropriate staff are in place;
- ➤The necessary funds have been committed;
- ➤Enough data have been collected; and
- ➤The improvement project has been well defined.

An education coordinator also is working with the group temporarily as an anthropologist and translator for the Spanish-speaking migrant workers in this farm belt. A grant from the U.S. Public Health Service is used for patient transportation.

Thanks to a local foundation gift, Lehigh Valley was able to give grants of $15,000 to some local agencies to be used for measuring results of agency efforts to improve community health. The agencies have developed wide-ranging projects, from prejudice reduction in schoolchildren to fitness activities. It's too early for the outcomes of those projects to be known, Dr. Young says, and it remains to be seen if smaller agencies that have challenges of their own will be able to stretch and do something measurable for healthcare improvement.

■ When Data Are Ready

Almost anyone could guess that a community's major problems are heart disease, cancer and diabetes, but each community must collect enough data to make sense of the reasons for disease prevalence. "If you want to find a solution, you'll need more defined data on more issues," Mr. Baxter says. Is everyone sicker than in the average community? Is it an environmental issue? Is it a problem of how medicine is being practiced? Is there inadequate access to care?

Besides having to collect the right data on the right issues, the group must ensure that the audience believes in the data. "Different audiences will ask for different levels of detail, particularly if they disagree with what seems to have been found," Mr. Baxter says. There must be enough information to respond credibly to critics, but not so much that you never stop collecting data, he warns. When the group generally agrees that the data are sound, understood and acceptable to members, the action plans can be drawn.

SOMERBRIDGE'S VISION AND PRIORITIES

VISION:

The Somerbridge Community Health Partnership was created to develop a prevention-focused, integrated service delivery system accountable to the residents of Somerville and Cambridge.

GOALS:

Substance Abuse: to reduce substance abuse in the community by increasing primary prevention and improving intervention, treatment access and efficiency.

Elder Health: to improve health status for residents more than 65 years of age by expanding primary and preventive services and developing lower cost noninstitutional treatment; to provide elderly residents with information on changes now taking place in the Medicare system and with a forum from which to advocate improvements to the current systems and to reduce injuries caused by falls among community-dwelling elders.

Immigrant Health: to improve the health status of the immigrant populations. This includes ensuring access to culturally appropriate preventive and primary healthcare while addressing underlying causes of poor health outcomes. It will also involve developing strategies for ensuring access for those immigrants most affected by recently enacted welfare reform efforts.

Source: The Somerbridge Community Health Partnership, supported by the Community Care Network Demonstration Program.

■ When a Project Is Well Defined

Mr. Rukavina of the Somerbridge project notes that progress has been slow and steady, and others echo this. He suggests that such progress is achieved with clearly defined priorities and goals. *(See box above for Somerbridge's priorities and goals)*. In addition to immigrant health programs, the Somerbridge community effort has launched a project to reduce the number of falls among the elderly. That project has a clearly defined mission, a statement of the project's importance, literature searches and a schedule for data collection and revised aims based on findings. A well-organized plan makes it easy to implement such a project, Mr. Rukavina says.

Community health efforts should "not be afraid to embark on projects that might seem oddball at first," counsels G. Kent Ballantyne, senior vice president of the Oregon Association of Hospitals and Health Systems and staff member for the Oregon Health Systems in Collaboration, a coalition working on community health improvement. He cites the example of head lice, a problem that was well defined by an initial grassroots exploration of health concerns.

The metropolitan Portland community implemented plans with schools, pharmacists, other healthcare providers and families to solve the problem as soon as it became evident. The local drive against head lice had an unanticipated benefit: Nurses who visited the homes of patients with lice were able to uncover other needs that healthcare workers could help with, such as education on diabetes, immunization and nutrition. Building an immunization database is another project under way.

Mr. Ballantyne emphasizes that success is based on full cooperation and thinking "outside the box." Large medical systems, "which may be more concerned with providing trauma and transplant care to the community, should see their role also in problems such as head lice," he says.

Acting on Well-Laid Plans

Dr. Baxter says he sees two common approaches to taking action. One is focusing on the most expensive healthcare problems. The other is focusing on an effort that will make the greatest impact, usually on the causes of premature death.

Lehigh Valley's actions stemmed from two surveys that gradually refined the picture of healthcare problems and resources. In 1992, a regionwide health assessment initiated by a hospital foundation found that access to care was a major issue among the uninsured. Local hospitals set up the Partnership Health Plan and founded their own HMO for Medicaid patients. The hospitals created a plan based on "co-opetition," a termed coined by Novell Network software founder Ray Noorda to mean cooperation without competition. Then the hospitals capitalized the HMO.

A second survey, the 1997 Partners in Health survey (a follow-up to the 1992 survey) is a health status measurement that is part of Measurable Enhancement of the Status of Health. MESH's goals are to engage local providers and caregivers in clinical projects with measurable health-related outcomes, such as Vascular Prevention and Outcomes Research Team for reducing the incidence of vascular disease in the region. The MESH clinical initiative is a collaborative venture of the Lehigh Valley Hospital, the hospital's healthcare trust, and community organizations that develop grassroots strategy and partner with clinicians.

Solano County has succeeded with several projects, including a countywide effort to reduce asthma problems, because the coalition laid substantial groundwork. "Rather than performing an initial traditional health assessment study, with a data expert exploring the issues, the Solano

County coalition decided to embark on a community health organizing process," says Dr. Hughes. He helped to organize seven teams of community members and health experts in each of the seven cities of the county. Then each of the seven teams performed its own assessment of a variety of health-related issues, including violence and school attendance. Each team now is responsible for encouraging healthy lifestyles and implementing a community health outreach system for neighborhoods and individual families, thanks in part to the CCN research grant. The seven teams have since come together to "cross-pollinate their ideas" with the help of Dr. Hughes and hospital healthcare providers. A countywide steering committee, with members from each city, helps the seven teams share information about projects and what they have learned.

Solano's community organizing effort linked various community partners for the best delivery of care. For a program to reduce expensive hospitalizations associated with childhood asthma, Solano Partnership Health Plan providers focused on developing a mutually agreeable set of practice standards. The health plan's provider-relations professional staff made sure the providers received the practice standards, that the standards were understood by all and that any extra education for providers was available. "They provided a supportive effort rather than a distant, regulated approach," Mr. Graham says.

Case managers were assigned to patients with asthma for close oversight of their health. Gradually, school nurses and school assistants (where no nurses were available) were called on to help with proper medication assistance and education through the schools, where many asthma attacks occur.

GETTING READY FOR ACTION

What do community teams need to start the improvement process?

❶ Focus: A clear aim

A core group of people can use data to define a focused aim. For example, a small group from a hospital and a public health department wished to work on preventing injuries caused by falls in the elderly. Hospital data helped them identify the most vulnerable population. From this information they defined the aim as "preventing injuries from falls among people more than age 75, who live alone or with one other person and who have a history of a fall or falls injury."

❷ Measurement: A way to measure progress toward the aim

At the beginning of a project, a team must determine the way it will know if it is making headway. It must collect baseline data and design a system for obtaining and plotting data on an ongoing basis. The "falls" team has baseline and ongoing data from the hospital on the number and characteristics of injuries as well as falls-injury rates reported annually by the public health data system.

❸ Team: The right group to resolve the problem

Once the aim and the initial measurement are defined, the core team identifies the different parts of the community system that have the potential for accomplishing the aim. For falls-injury prevention, this includes the primary healthcare system, visiting nurses, home health aides, family and neighbors, elder affairs departments, senior centers, exercise and balance programs, and elders themselves. The core team now expands the team composition to include these key system components. As other key groups are identified, they will be represented as well.

❹ Potential interventions: Things that are known to be effective

For most community health problems, one intervention will not achieve the aim. A multifaceted, coordinated approach is usually required. For falls-injury prevention in the elderly, this means identifying the key factors in prevention — exercise and balance training, home environment safety, nutrition, comprehensive healthcare with medical and diagnostic work-up, education and behavioral changes.

❺ Test interventions: Plan, Do, Study, Act

Using small PDSA cycles, the team or sub-teams will identify potential areas for improvement and test changes. The team should meet regularly to reflect on what it is learning, develop strategies to deal with barriers to improvement and define the next improvement cycles. For example, in the falls project, the team learned that every patient hospitalized with an injury from a fall was given a check-sheet for safety on discharge. The visiting nurses, wishing to learn its usefulness, reviewed six patient records and found none contained completed check-sheets. The nurses tested a small intervention by completing the form, one-on-one, with homebound elders, and found that both the elders and nurses learned useful information by completing the form together. Elders learned how to protect themselves from falls, and nurses learned how best to communicate this information.

In another example of cooperation, the Solano health plan dramatically reduced the number of low-birthweight babies, from 4.2% to 1.7% of births in its first year. The Growing Together Perinatal Program case management assessed the risk level of a pregnancy and then provided the patient with educational resources, referrals, free transportation and incentives for participating, such as gift certificates for attending appointments. Outreach workers were added to work with clients in their neighborhoods and collaborate with local social service and community-based organizations. Postpartum home visits were added. The first year's savings was $99,000, even after hiring four community outreach workers.

Willing Partners and Early Planning Are Keys to Success

What communities want from their efforts is a mixed bag. Some want a quick snapshot of problems or an idea of local assets, just for informational purposes. Most, however, want a detailed assessment with some form of follow-up, Dr. Baxter says. He emphasizes that any communitywide effort should be viewed as a balancing act that must proceed cautiously, with reasonable expectations about how long measurable results will take.

Finding willing partners and building on their skills are important, Mr. Hall notes. Then you can find ways to manage these partners, keep them engaged, gather the best-skilled staff, define the scope of your project, make research actionable and engage others such as the media who will be important down the road, he says.

Early planning is critical. "The needs assessment is a great process for inventorying who you need now and who you'll need later," Mr. Hall says. "If you view the assessment as a mechanism for change and for being operational down the road, you will be able to keep your project timely, communicable, actionable and relevant. All of those things will ultimately lead you to success."

For more information ...

G. Kent Ballantyne
Oregon Association of Hospitals and Health Systems
Phone: (503)636-2204

Raymond Baxter, Ph.D.
The Lewin Group
Phone: (703)218-5500
E-mail: rjbaxter@lewin.com

David Bor, M.S.
Cambridge Hospital
Phone: (617)498-1018
E-mail: dbor@warren.med.harvard.edu

Steve Graham
Community Health Partnerships, Kaiser of California
Phone: (707)651-3672
E-mail: steve.graham@ncal.kaiperm.org

Claude Hall Jr., M.A., M.H.A.
Community Care Network Demonstration Program
Phone: (312)422-2637
E-mail: chall@aha.org

Patrick Hughes, Ed.D.
Healthier Solano Communities
Phone: (707)651-3681

Mark Rukavina
Somerbridge Community Health Partnership
Phone: (617)666-4440, ext. 179
E-mail: mrukavina@cphc.org

Peggy Whitehead
Rural Health Outreach Program
Phone: (804)263-4000
E-mail: rhoppw@aol.com

Mark J. Young, M.D.
Lehigh Valley Hospital
Phone: (610)402-2446
E-mail: Mark.Young@lvh.com

The Population-Based Approach to Chronic Care

Many acute care episodes among the chronically ill can be avoided, providers say. Probing patients' history to understand the causes and setting up interventions are key to prevention.

It wasn't just one of the patients with diabetes working at the Salt Lake City plant who had high a hemoglobin A_{1C} level; it was a whole group of them. So it didn't make sense for the company's health plan, an Intermountain Health Care product, to investigate what was bothering a single worker without figuring out what that employee had in common with the others.

An earlier IHC health promotion assessment aimed at improving the well-being of all the plant's employees had revealed that the company employed a group of workers with diabetes. An IHC nurse care manager stationed at the company began educating these patients about how they could help prevent swings in blood-sugar levels by carefully scheduling their meals and exercising.

Further examination of why individuals were having difficulty revealed that the patients continuing to have problems worked the night shift and were unable to eat the right foods at the right times during the day or fit exercise into a schedule dotted with interrupted sleep and wake schedules. "No healthcare person thinks about how to manage diabetes on the night shift," says Jill Hoggard-Green, R.N., Ph.D., assistant vice president of Intermountain Health Care. They do now. The company's care manager immediately added to the worker education schedule a series of classes on how to manage diabetes on the night shift and swing shift.

IHC's strategy for treating patients with diabetes is a bit off the beaten path. More often, says Dr. Hoggard-Green, those who suffer from chronic conditions such as diabetes find themselves in a doctor's waiting room or even in the hospital when unexplained symptoms persist, as they often do with a disease noted for its complications. But because the health plan embraces a population-based approach to treating diabetes, administrators there say they hope consequences ranging from absenteeism to diabetes-related blindness will be less common in Salt Lake City in the future.

Data Aid Prevention

Most health plan administrators might not have noticed that the sick workers in Salt Lake City had anything in common at all. But because Intermountain Health Care made a point of assessing the company's employees in an effort to improve the wellness of the enrolled population, it had the data to crack the case.

From *The Quality Letter for Healthcare Leaders*, Vol. 10:2, 1998

A population-based approach means looking at the needs of a population rather than the episodes that land an individual in the hospital, explains John Fletcher, regional director of health services integration at Providence Health System in Portland, Ore. "Healthcare traditionally has been somewhat episodic in nature," he says. "Someone has an episode, and you take care of that episode." But the population-based approach, he continues, involves "looking at the overall condition of the population and then setting up systems of care addressing those conditions. Then when an episode occurs, you have a system in place to deal with it, and sometimes you can prevent episodes from occurring."

For patients suffering from chronic conditions — diabetes, asthma, depression or congestive heart failure, for instance — such an approach is touted as a way to help a broad spectrum of patients manage their disease and, as a result, enjoy a better quality of life and require fewer trips to the emergency room. "It's a way to step back and say, 'What are the groupings of patients, what are their common characteristics, what are their risk factors and how might we identify them earlier?'" says Chuck Hawley, vice president of continuum development and long-term care at Sisters of Providence Health System in Seattle. "We're looking at how we can better coordinate care across provider, place and time in order to ensure better healthcare outcomes."

THE CHRONICALLY ILL

- ✓ 99 million Americans have chronic illnesses
- ✓ In 1987, 17% of Medicare recipients used 47% of the system's healthcare resources for chronic conditions.
- ✓ At Intermountain Health Care, an estimated 20% of the health plan's enrollees who suffer from chronic ailments consume 50%–60% of the system's resources.
- ✓ In 1990, chronic care cost an estimated $659 billion:
  - $425 billion in direct costs; and
  - $234 billion in indirect costs.

Driving Healthcare Costs

Providers have long recognized the high cost of treating patients with chronic conditions. Today, more are warming to a strategy that ferrets out patients suffering from similar illnesses and finds ways to systematically and routinely ensure that each of them takes advantage of preventive treatments. These providers are becoming more willing to intervene with patients, their families and even their communities to ensure the patients are taking care of themselves so that they will require less institutional care later. They're willingly entering into once-unheard-of partnerships with the patients and with other caregivers — from social workers to nursing homes to home health workers — to ensure that patients are following doctors' orders between visits or after an acute episode.

Given the statistics, it's no surprise that providers are opting for alternatives to the tried-and-true methods of treating chronic conditions. The National Chronic Care Consortium reports that the 99 million Americans who suffer from these persistent, recurring ailments have propelled chronic care to become the highest-cost and fastest-growing segment of the healthcare industry. In 1987, according to researchers at the Henry J. Kaiser Family Foundation, Medicare recipients with chronic conditions used 47% of the system's healthcare resources, even though they accounted for just 17% of the population. Based on data from the National Health Interview Survey, the Kaiser study estimates that chronic care cost upwards of $659 billion in 1990, including $425 billion in direct costs and $234 billion in indirect costs. On a local level, the cost per patient is striking when the disease is chronic, says Brent James, M.D., M.Stat., vice president for medical research at Intermountain. He estimates that the 20% of the health plan's enrollees who suffer from chronic ailments consume 50% to 60% of the system's resources.

Train Physicians to Look Beyond Diagnosis

Yet doctors typically treat the conditions the same way they would an acute problem. "We have this notion of illness that is bound and determined by acute perceptions," Mr. Hawley points out. "If I have a heart attack or an appendicitis attack, I rush to the hospital, there are all these interventions, and the whole goal is to solve the problem. With chronic disease and disability, it's important to recognize that there often is no solution to the problem."

Physicians are the first to admit that's easier said than done. "We're trained in medical school to make a diagnosis, understand the pathology, select the treatment and fix the problem," says Susan J. Denman, M.D., senior vice president for medical affairs at the Philadelphia Geriatric Center. "Physicians sometimes assume they just have to deal with the medical piece, and for most patients, that's okay. But people with chronic illnesses don't bounce back to a healthy, independent baseline. They force physicians to look beyond the medical problem."

That might mean probing a pregnant woman's past to learn why she is taking drugs, or exploring the environment of a frail, elderly man to determine that he doesn't eat because he's alone and depressed. Doctors "may resist collecting this information because they don't view this as doctor stuff," admits Dr. Denman.

10 STEPS TO SUCCESSFUL CHRONIC CARE MANAGEMENT

1. Define the population.
2. Develop a profile of the population.
3. Inventory existing prevention programs, both in the healthcare system and in the community.
4. Review the literature to learn from others' experiences.
5. Create protocols for treating populations with chronic diseases.
6. Intervene at key points to change behavior and prevent acute episodes.
7. Set targets for improvement and track outcomes.
8. Test the process before full-scale implementation.
9. Educate everyone involved, including medical staff and other caregivers, patients, family, friends and other providers.
10. Monitor progress and modify efforts if necessary.

Convincing doctors to spend more time collecting personal and lifestyle data from their patients can be a tough sell. "We have found that medical residents are more receptive when they can see a direct impact on a medical treatment. We need to reach physicians in training in order to improve the future care of individuals with chronic illnesses," says Dr. Denman. "You have to have people buy in to why these issues are important. It's a long process."

But she cautions that even the most carefully constructed plan for the recovery of a chronically ill patient after a hospitalization will fail if the doctor does not take personal and lifestyle concerns into consideration. Deborah Paone, vice president of the Bloomington, Minn.-based National Chronic Care Consortium, agrees: "Anyone who's spent some time with people with chronic disease would admit that a very big component of lifestyle and environment and socioeconomic issues affects them to the extent that they can or cannot follow a medical regimen," she says. "There's a medical, social, spiritual and emotional component that's very difficult to separate. You can't say, 'We're only going to do this one piece.'"

"People with chronic illnesses don't bounce back [from an acute episode] to a healthy, independent baseline. They force physicians to look beyond fixing the medical problem."

Susan J. Denman, M.D.
Senior Vice President
for Medical Affairs
Philadelphia Geriatric Center

Indeed, those advocating a population-based approach look not only at whole communities of people suffering from similar illnesses, but also at each person as a whole. "A holistic look at someone's life is essential, especially when that person becomes frail with chronic illnesses and functional decline and when they must rely on complex networks of psychosocial support," says Dr. Denman. "It's all intertwined. Medical problems cannot be effectively managed in isolation."

Steps to Success

Organizations that successfully use a population-based approach to managing chronic conditions usually follow a common path. Most steps are basic tenets of care — often overlooked and underappreciated, but critical, say these experts.

■ **Define the population.** For Intermountain Health Care, the population in which patients with diabetes were identified included employees of one of the health plan's clients. Healthcare systems that have their own health plans have their population readily identified for them: It includes the plan's enrollees, and data often can be collected from new enrollees who are asked to fill out extensive risk-assessment forms.

Others don't have it so easy. In their quest to identify patients with heart failure, administrators at Carondelet Health Network in Tucson, Ariz., quickly realized that "there is no one easy way to identify everyone with heart failure." In fact, the system identified three tiers of heart failure victims, ranging from the least severe patients with the most active lifestyles to the most severe victims with multiple chronic conditions. Gerri Lamb, Ph.D., senior corporate director and a registered nurse, urges others to "spend the necessary time to clearly identify the targeted population."

■ **Develop a profile of the population.** Aside from collecting demographic data, the provider should know the overall health status of the group, how often its members visit the doctor or hospital and how much those visits cost the system. In addition, clients should be polled as to their satisfaction with the healthcare system. "Anything that seems related to the kinds of changes you want to make or the eventual outcomes you want to achieve" should be gathered and recorded, advises Ms. Paone.

Many systems collect these data using a risk-screening tool each time the patient visits a doctor or hospital. At Philadelphia Geriatric Center, for instance, patients and their families are quizzed about the patient's functional status before the episode that led the person to seek inpatient care, where he or she lived, what kind of support system was in place, what the patient's cognitive status was, whether any medications cause allergies and how well nourished the patient is. "Regardless of why they're in the hospital," says Dr. Denman, "this information is important." Several systems are keeping this information updated in computerized patient registries, which not only list demographic information for each patient in a given population, but indicate whether the person is current on preventive checkups.

■ **Inventory existing prevention programs**, both in the healthcare system and in the community. Ms. Paone advises caregivers to form partnerships with local service providers, ranging from the public health department to the mayor's office. Sometimes an issue as decidedly nonmedical as a lack of transportation can prevent a patient from going to the drugstore for medicine. In that vein, David Bearman, M.D., deputy director for health policy and grants development at the Santa Barbara Regional Health Authority, says its doctors will be enlisting the aid of the California county's Head Start program to prevent youngsters from following in the footsteps of their drug-habituated parents. The effort is part of a comprehensive intervention effort held in conjunction with the county's Mental Health Department Multiple-agency Integrated System of Care program. The program's target population is mothers with a dual diagnosis (e.g., mental illness and substance abuse) receiving Temporary Assistance for Needy Families (formerly Aid for Dependent Children).

The prevention effort is based on a successful program in Chicago, run by Ira Chasnoff, M.D., which resulted in high-risk first graders (children whose mothers used cocaine while pregnant) testing with higher IQs than offspring of non-substance abusing mothers who lived in the same school district but were not participants in the program. Interventions included drug treatment and parenting skills training as well as educational stimulation programs for the children.

■ **Review the literature**. Find out what has worked for others, Ms. Paone says; it's quite possible that another organization has already tackled the problem at hand. Sometimes, the literature will provide clues for handling situations; other times, it will indicate that the ideas an organization is generating are unrealistic. "It's important to pick some interventions that have some research behind them," Ms. Paone says, "so that if the healthcare system is going to expend this effort, it should have some reasonable assurance that this is going to work."

"This step is absolutely critical, because population-based strategies must be based on what has been shown to work," says Edward Wagner, M.D., M.P.H., director of the Center for Health Studies and director of the W. A. MacCol Institute for Healthcare Innovation at Group Health Cooperative of Puget Sound in Seattle. "For example, the reason we go after patients to get their eyes examined is because we have

"A very big component of lifestyle and environment and socioeconomic issues affects the chronically ill to the extent that they can or cannot follow a medical regimen."

Deborah Paone, M.D.
Vice President
National Chronic Care Consortium

strong scientific evidence that laser treatment will prevent blindness. That's why we're doing it."

■ **Create protocols.** At Sisters of Providence Health System in Portland, doctors and administrators collaborate to create guidelines that physicians across the system can use to similarly treat populations with chronic diseases. A protocol for diabetes, for instance, calls for physicians to make sure that five things happen each year for each patient: an annual physical, an assessment of metabolic status, urine protein screening, cholesterol screening and retinal examination. Realizing that conducting these tests takes time, doctors are enticed to follow the regimen with bonus dollars for each patient who takes all five tests. Physicians can tap the $2 per-member-per-month incentive for following the protocols for other chronic illnesses as well.

Dr. Wagner says his system supports physicians to make sure it's easy for them to follow its protocols. The guidelines for diabetes, for instance, call for each patient to have a retinal examination every year. Instead of relying on the primary care physician's office to follow up with the patient, the computer flags delinquent patients and prompts the appropriate ophthalmologist's office to intervene. "We have little system interventions to help the practices stay in their guidelines," says Wagner.

SCREENING FOR PROBLEMS DURING PATIENT VISITS

Providers should spend time with each patient receiving acute care for a chronic condition to determine the patient's:

1. Functional status before the episode occurred.
2. Residential environment.
3. Support system in the community.
4. Cognitive status.
5. Prescribed medications.
6. Nourishment status.
7. Comorbid medical conditions.
8. Values and wishes regarding treatment decisions.

Source: Philadelphia Geriatric Center

■ **Intervene at key points.** This is the part of the process where the healthcare providers actively intervene in the patient's life. It might mean a caseworker phones a patient who has been flagged on a computer registry as being delinquent in having an annual exam. It could be a home visit by a social worker on the lookout for high-risk activity — or inactivity — in the patient's environment. Or, it could take the form of patient education, either one-on-one in a doctor's office, in small-group classes or via direct-mail literature that describes self-care procedures. "Take active steps," advises Dr. Wagner. "Go out there and make sure the services get to them."

■ **Set targets and track outcomes**. Sisters of Providence Health System in Seattle aims to reduce smoking among high-risk cardiac patients from 21% today to 15% by the year 2000. To that end, the system is offering stop-smoking classes, has published a handbook for smokers, is training primary care physicians and office staff how to counsel smokers to quit, has added nicotine replacement therapy to its health plan benefits and even lobbied Congress to hike cigarette taxes. The system's Oregon-based facilities are trying to make sure 75% of the plan's patients with diabetes receive all five screening tests every year as soon as possible, up from less than 50% last year. Ms. Paone advises providers to "set the expectations with some reasonableness."

■ Test the process. Before Intermountain Health Care assigns a care manager to every primary care physician's office — a strategy administrators there believe could be "wildly successful" in helping patients practice prevention, says Dr. Hoggard-Green — the system has been testing the theory for the past two years in a few clinics and expects to draw some conclusions as to its success later this year. "There is so little literature out there ... so we wanted to really understand the impact to the consumer, to health status and to physician, and what kind of ratios we need to have," she says. Before assigning care managers to the pilot sites, she adds, the system polled patients and physicians to get a baseline perception of each group's satisfaction, which can be measured against a similar survey taken at the end of the test.

Likewise, Carondelet Health Network put a good idea to the test when it recruited 60 patients with heart failure for a two-month pilot project that taught them the skills they need to self-manage their conditions. During the project, the system tracked the number of times each patient visited the hospital, how often they exercised and how well they understood their illnesses. Quality and cost outcomes improved, says Dr. Lamb, an indication the program was a success and should be more widely implemented.

■ Educate everyone involved. Typically, more than one person is involved in a successful intervention. Doctors, nurses, patients, family, friends, home health workers and other providers need to understand the problem and the agreed-upon solution. Some organizations offer small-group instruction for similarly afflicted patients; others send home care workers to work one-on-one with patients and their families. "It's a pretty big process, because we're talking about changing behavior," Ms. Paone says.

■ Monitor progress. Collecting data as the prevention progresses enables caregivers to determine whether changes to protocols and interventions are warranted. That can be difficult when the population is drawn from a pool of enrollees in a health plan, says Dr. Denman. "It's frustrating because people change plans and they change doctors," making it difficult to track the same population for an extended time. Mr. Fletcher agrees but adds: "This is kind of a TQM sort of thing. You're never there. You're constantly looking at your processes and trying to improve them."

Pay Now, Benefit Later

Adding care managers, spending time digging into a patient's environmental influences and creating computer registries, of course, cost money. And while the payoff may come down the road when prevention replaces more emergency care and surgeries, the bill for services rendered is due today.

"Let's face it," says Mr. Fletcher. "A health system doesn't get paid to go out and prevent smoking in the community at large." Ms. Paone concurs: "Organizations get paid when they do something — when they hospitalize somebody, inject somebody, cut somebody. That's how healthcare organizations have been reimbursed for decades."

"Organizations get paid when they do something — when they hospitalize somebody, inject somebody, cut somebody. That's how healthcare organizations have been reimbursed for decades."

Deborah Paone

> **"The further upstream you move, the more you can manage patients before you have to pay for them. They may never come into the hospital. And if you move further upstream, you find ways to prevent chronic heart disease."**
>
> Brent James, M.D.
> Intermountain Health Care

In fact, adds Ms. Paone, practitioners working in a fee-for-service environment are unlikely to embrace a population-based approach to any kind of healthcare because it doesn't pay for them to do so. Those who engage in population-based care management, admits Ms. Paone, "are very much receiving a hit on their bottom line, because not enough patients are paid for that way. It's a schizophrenic world doctors are living in."

And while most agree that managed care is more apt to reimburse a practice for keeping its population well, Ms. Paone says each payer reacts to population-based measures differently. "Just because a group may be capitated does not equal a population-based approach," says Ms. Paone, "because providers might not be paid in a population health approach. We've got to think outside the box of traditional healthcare. And if the payment rates were sufficient, then it would be a very good situation for the population and for the industry and for the employer and for everybody. But that's a lot of ifs."

Still, advocates of the population-based approach say providers will save enough money in the long run to pay for the interventions they use now. "When I do one of these things," admits Dr. James, "it will hurt me in this budget cycle. But at the end of the year ... it helps me get and keep contracts. It works as a long-term strategy, but as a short-term strategy, it looks like it's hurting you. You have to be able to deal with that organizationally."

If population-based care management is allowed to play out long-range, he adds, it will save a great deal not only for the practicing system but for the whole healthcare system.

"The further upstream you move, the more you can manage patients before you have to pay for them," says Dr. James. "They may never come into the hospital. And if you move further upstream, you find ways to prevent chronic heart disease."

Dr. Denman agrees: "If the number of hospitalizations and emergency room visits can be reduced, the resources saved could be redirected for community healthcare interventions." In fact, adds Dr. Lamb, Carondelet Health Network paid substantially less for its eight-week pilot intervention with each heart failure patient than it would for one hospital day.

A Complex Choreography

But payment problems aren't the only part of population-based care that requires extra effort on the part of its advocates. "It's hard work," admits Mr. Hawley. "Not only is it hard work, but it's new work."

Dr. Wagner agrees: "We underestimated in some respects how difficult this is." Doctors and other providers have their hands full as it is, he says. And while he says a healthier population eventually will reduce the amount of work caregivers have to do, primary care physicians in the meantime are hard-pressed to add the complex social and emotional pieces of a patient's care to the press of attending to their physical needs.

That's especially true because the fruits of population-based care are not immediately evident. In acute care situations, Dr. Wagner explains, "the payoff is fairly immediate. If the patient responds, you'll know in a couple of days. But if you prevent blindness in a patient because you got 100 patients to their eye exams, the practitioner will never see that unless we give it to them in the form of statistics.

"It's the age-old problem of prevention, in that it's very difficult to see the benefits of your preventive energies."

Still, Dr. Wagner and others say they'll stick with the strategy, even though there are few data so far to prove their efforts will pay off. "There's an enormous opportunity for this," argues Glenn Rodriguez, M.D., regional director of health improvement programs at Sisters of Providence Health System in Portland.

Dr. Lamb says weaving together the contributions of various caregivers, payers, family members, community leaders and patients is an important skill that advocates of population-based care are developing. "It's like choreographing a dance," she says. "Everybody needs to know their steps. They need to move in a specific sequence, according to what the individuals in the population need. If any parts of the sequence are not strong, or if there's any fragmentation, you're not going to have the same level of outcomes.

"But when it works, it's wonderful."

For more information ...

David Bearman, M.D.
Santa Barbara Regional Health Authority
Phone: (805)685-9525

Susan J. Denman, M.D.
Philadelphia Geriatric Center
Phone: (215)456-2092

John Fletcher
Providence Health System in Oregon
Phone: (503)216-2217
E-mail: john_fletcher@phsor.org

Chuck Hawley
Sisters of Providence Health System, Seattle
Phone: (206)464-4237
E-mail: cehawley@aol.com

Jill Hoggard-Green, R.N., Ph.D.
Intermountain Health Care
Phone: (801)442-3730
E-mail: cojgreen@ic.com

Brent James, M.D., M.Stat.
Intermountain Health Care
Phone: (801)442-3730
E-mail: bjames@ihc.com

Gerri Lamb, R.N., Ph.D.
Carondelet Health Network
Phone: (520)571-88744

Deborah Paone
National Chronic Care Consortium
Phone: (612)858-8999
Internet: dpaone@compuserve.com

Glenn Rodriguez, M.D.
Sisters of Providence Health System in Portland
Phone: (503)216-6020
E-mail: glenn_rodriguez@phsor.org

Edward H. Wagner, M.D., M.P.H.
Group Health Cooperative of Puget Sound
Phone: (206)287-2877
E-mail: wagner.e@ghc.org

Oregon Collaboration Standardizes Ambulatory Diabetes Care

A project led by the Oregon Health Division aims to improve consistency of diabetes care for Medicare and Medicaid patients through a single set of guidelines for providers statewide. Implementation of the guidelines is left to individual HMOs, but the state's quality improvement organization is collecting outcomes data to help health plans measure and improve physicians' compliance and patients' outcomes.

"Diabetes care is a key component of Medicare and Medicaid, and it was a priority at the HMOs, but the recommendations for care [made by each body] were not at all compatible," says Nancy Clarke, OHD managed care coordinator for chronic disease and health promotion.

The state's population, particularly Medicare and Medicaid patients, is heavily capitated, and about 98% of physicians in the state contract with at least one HMO, so the guidelines have the potential to affect the care of nearly every diabetic in the state, says Ruth Medak, M.D., principal clinical coordinator for OMPRO, the state HCFA-contracted quality improvement organization.

Immediate Interventions, Long-term Goals

In 1995, the department organized a working committee of 15 to 18 members, with representatives from the healthcare organizations, including five of the state's 20 HMOs. The group took an outcomes-oriented approach, creating both short-term and long-term measures, mostly for early detection and prevention of complications.

"Short-term measures might be to increase the annual testing rate for retinopathy within a certain time period. The long-term goal was to reduce diabetic retinopathy," says Cindy Klug, director of the Regional Chronic Care Program, Sisters of Providence Health System, Portland, one of the HMOs that participated.

Although the guidelines cover everything from flu vaccination to preconception counseling, they are not blanket recommendations for all diabetic patients, Medak says.

"They're not super-detailed, because you're not meant to have 100% compliance," she says. "Depending on the case mix, each HMO should determine its own right target percentage."

For example, the guidelines don't call for 100% screening for smoking or risk for end-stage renal disease because "if you have a patient who is of moderate age with type 2 diabetes and they haven't started smoking by age 35, they probably won't, so it would be too rigid to ask that at every visit," Medak says. By the same token, a patient with diabetes and terminal cancer is unlikely to benefit from the sorts of screenings that are intended to catch complications early and improve quality of life.

TARGETS FOR THE OREGON GUIDELINES

In the long term, the Oregon guidelines are expected to reduce incidence of:

- Cardiovascular disease;
- Myocardial infarction;
- Cerebrovascular accidents;
- Smoking-related diseases;
- Ketoacidosis;
- Severe hypoglycemia;
- End-stage renal disease;
- Blindness;
- Lower extremity amputations;
- Osteomyelitis;
- Infected lower extremity ulcers;
- Decayed, missing or filled teeth;
- Influenza; and
- Pneumococcal pneumonia.

HMOs Adapt Guidelines for Practice

The participating groups produced initial guidelines in fall 1995 and distributed them to their endocrinologists and primary care physicians for review. The final guidelines were mailed in spring 1997. Nearly all HMOs in the state have adopted the guidelines and distributed them in booklet form to physicians throughout the state who care for diabetes patients.

"It's up to the HMOs to design the tools to put the guidelines more concretely to work in practice," says Klug. Implementation still isn't consistent across the participating health plans, but Sisters of Providence, for example, has developed several tools for its providers:

- A flow sheet now accompanies patient records *(see p. 184)*. Much of the flow sheet can be filled out by the medical assistant or nurse.
- Practices with quality managers have set up prompts to remind physicians of steps in the guidelines that need to be followed.
- Patient education tools help clinicians remind patients that they must "do their part" to keep the condition under control, she adds.

Also in the works are companion guidelines for patients, so they expect the same full amount of care that physicians are encouraged to provide during office visits, Clark adds. The state also will be using the guidelines in collaborations with county health departments to develop community-based diabetes projects.

"Especially in the rural areas, some practices have a predominance of patients older than 80. In those cases, you don't expect screening for early impairment of the kidney. You focus on blood pressure and diabetes control."

Ruth Medak
OMPRO

Measuring Improvement

With the guidelines in use, OHD and OMPRO are working on specifications for data collection to help HMOs track improvements in diabetes care. OMPRO is analyzing baseline data collected from 1993 to 1995 and will compare them with 1997 data, including frequency of testing for glycosylated hemoglobin levels and eye and foot exams.

A project that targets rural practices will examine why physicians use or don't use the guidelines. Medak speculates that many physicians who appear to be noncompliant with the guidelines actually will be making choices based on their case mix: "Especially in the rural areas, some practices have a predominance of patients older than 80," she says. "In those cases, you don't expect screening for early impairment of the kidney. You focus on blood pressure and diabetes control."

The sample measurement for the main data collection, however, will use primarily younger patients who are more likely to benefit from the full range of screening recommended by the guidelines.

"Each HMO has its own quality improvement plan, and they didn't all address the same concerns initially," says Ruth Michels, OMPRO diabetes project coordinator. "We'll be providing them with data that will look at the results of their own QI projects, and the information on areas they didn't set out to improve initially will serve as the baseline for future improvements."

Oregon Diabetes Project — Draft Flow Sheet for Encounter Data Collection

Pt. Name_______________________________ Provider/Clinic name _______________________________
Sex _____________ DOB _____________ Address _______________________________
ID #_______________________________ Phone _______________________________
Diabetes type _____________ Onset date _____________ ID #(s) _______________________________
Optional Information: *Of childbearing age?* _____________ *(if yes, see educ. sheet)*
Insulin ________ *Oral agent* ________ *Diet only* ________ *Allergies* _______________________________
Pneumovax given _______________________________ *Co-morbid conditions* _______________________________

If indicator not assessed, leave results blank.

Preventive Screening Services	Date								
HbA1c Monitoring — Target ≤8.0% ❑ Type 1: min. semiannually ❑ Type 2: min. annually		❑ ≤8 ❑ >8	❑ ≤8 ❑ >8	❑ ≤8 ❑ >8	❑ ≤8 ❑ >8	❑ ≤8 ❑ >8	❑ ≤8 ❑ >8	❑ ≤8 ❑ >8	❑ ≤8 ❑ >8
Blood Pressure — Target: ≤130 syst/≤85 dias Type 1 or 2: min. semiannually		❑ ≤target ❑ >target	❑ ≤target ❑ >target	❑ ≤target ❑ >target	❑ ≤target ❑ >target	❑ ≤target ❑ >target	❑ ≤target ❑ >target	❑ ≤target ❑ >target	❑ ≤target ❑ >target
ACE or antihypertensive_______________									
Microalbuminuria — Target: neg. or <30mg/24 hr Type 1 (after 5 years) or 2: annually	❑ n/a	❑ <30 ❑ >30	❑ <30 ❑ >30	❑ <30 ❑ >30	❑ <30 ❑ >30	❑ <30 ❑ >30	❑ <30 ❑ >30	❑ <30 ❑ >30	❑ <30 ❑ >30
Visual Foot Inspection — See exam sheet Type 1 (after 5 years) or 2: each routine visit	❑ n/a	❑ yes	❑ yes	❑ yes	❑ yes	❑ yes	❑ yes	❑ yes	❑ yes
Complete Foot Exam — See exam sheet Type 1 (after 5 years) or 2: annually/new abnormality	❑ n/a	❑ yes	❑ yes	❑ yes	❑ yes	❑ yes	❑ yes	❑ yes	❑ yes
Dilated Eye Exam — Target: neg. for retinopathy Type 1 (after 5 years) or 2: annually	❑ n/a	❑ neg. ❑ pos.	❑ neg. ❑ pos.	❑ neg. ❑ pos.	❑ neg. ❑ pos.	❑ neg. ❑ pos.	❑ neg. ❑ pos.	❑ neg. ❑ pos.	❑ neg. ❑ pos.
Specialist referral _______________									
Lipid Screening — Target: LDL <130 mg/dL ❑ Type 1 or 2 and ≥18 years old: annually ❑ Type 1 or 2 with CAD: Per NCEP algorithms		❑ ≤100 ❑ <130 ❑ >130	❑ ≤100 ❑ <130 ❑ >130	❑ ≤100 ❑ <130 ❑ >130	❑ ≤100 ❑ <130 ❑ >130	❑ ≤100 ❑ <130 ❑ >130	❑ ≤100 ❑ <130 ❑ >130	❑ ≤100 ❑ <130 ❑ >130	❑ ≤100 ❑ <130 ❑ >130
Oral/Dental Screening — Target: neg. for prob. Type 1 or 2: annually		❑ neg. ❑ pos.	❑ neg. ❑ pos.	❑ neg. ❑ pos.	❑ neg. ❑ pos.	❑ neg. ❑ pos.	❑ neg. ❑ pos.	❑ neg. ❑ pos.	❑ neg. ❑ pos.
Referred to dentist _______________									
Influenza Immunization — Target: yes Type 1 or 2: annually	❑ n/a	❑ yes ❑ no	❑ yes ❑ no	❑ yes ❑ no	❑ yes ❑ no	❑ yes ❑ no	❑ yes ❑ no	❑ yes ❑ no	❑ yes ❑ no
ASA Prophy. — Target: low-dose ASA qtl/qod ___mg ❑ Type 1 or 2 > 40 years with risk factors ❑ Type 1 or 2 with CAD, CVD, PVD	❑ n/a	❑ yes ❑ no	❑ yes ❑ no	❑ yes ❑ no	❑ yes ❑ no	❑ yes ❑ no	❑ yes ❑ no	❑ yes ❑ no	❑ yes ❑ no
Patient Education — Target: as needed Per guidelines (see educ/counseling sheet)		❑ yes ❑ no	❑ yes ❑ no	❑ yes ❑ no	❑ yes ❑ no	❑ yes ❑ no	❑ yes ❑ no	❑ yes ❑ no	❑ yes ❑ no
Tobacco Use — Target: none ❑ Type 1 or 2 — nonuser: annually ❑ Type 1 or 2 — user: each visit (see educ./couns. sheet)		❑ none ❑ user	❑ none ❑ user	❑ none ❑ user	❑ none ❑ user	❑ none ❑ user	❑ none ❑ user	❑ none ❑ user	❑ none ❑ user
Record Next Visit Date — circle needed services ❑ Have pt. mark their health record for next visit.									

KEY to Recording Diabetes Preventive Care Service Results

(1.) always denotes desired target result

HbA1c Monitoring	(1.) ≤8.0% or write in actual value (2.) >8.0% orwrite in actual value
Blood Pressure	(1.) ≤130/85 (target) or write in actual value (2.) >130/85
Microalbuminuria	(1.) neg. or <30 (mg/24 hrs) (2.) >30 n/a (not appropriate for this patient — has known nephropathy, or has had Type 1 less than 5 years)
Visual Foot Inspection (record results/referral on separate form)	(1.) yes (inspection was performed) n/a (not appropriate for this patient — bilateral amputee, or has had Type 1 less than 5 years)
Complete Foot Exam and Assessment (record results/referral on separate form)	(1.) yes (exam was performed) n/a (not appropriate for this patient — bilateral amputee, or has had Type 1 less than 5 years)
Dilated Eye Exam (record referral and follow-up)	(1.) neg. (for retinopathy) (2.) pos. n/a (not appropriate for this patient — has known retinopathy, blindness, or has had Type 1 less than 5 years)
Lipid Screening (LDL)	(1.) ≤100 (mg/dL) or write in actual value (2.) <130 (3.) >130
Oral/Dental Screening (record referral and follow-up)	(1.) neg. (for tooth or soft tissue problems) (2.) pos.
Influenza Immunization	(1.) yes (vaccine given) (2.) no (vaccine offered but patient refused) n/a (not appropriate for this patient — has a medical contraindication)
Aspirin Prophylaxis (record dose and schedule)	(1.) yes (patient is taking as ordered) (2.) no (not taking as ordered) n/a (not appropriate for this patient)
Patient Education (record details on separate form)	(1.) yes (ordered or provided) (2.) no (assessed — not needed at this time)
Tobacco Use Assessment (if user: record counseling/referrals on separate form)	(1.) none (2.) user (uses any tobacco products)
Preconception Counseling	*(if appropriate, record details on separate form)*

If a Preventive Care Service is not assessed, leave the results section blank.

Health Plans, Providers Struggle With Quality in Alternative Medicine

Consumers are demanding access to alternative and complementary medicine, leaving health plans and providers to sort out appropriate quality indicators for such treatments without much rigorous scientific evidence to back them up.

Last fall Harvard Vanguard Medical Associates invited chiropractors, acupuncturists and massage therapists to practice in its Cambridge, Mass., office. HVMA physicians knew many of their patients were seeing alternative providers and not discussing it with their physicians. "Patients are already doing it, and there is evidence of clinical merit for some alternative modalities, so we believe the time for a more integrated approach has arrived," says Rick Weisblatt, Ph.D., site medical director for the HVMA medical offices in Cambridge and Watertown.

Today HVMA physicians discuss alternative treatment methods with their patients, and advise them on potential risks and benefits. Under the new arrangement, chiropractors, acupuncturists and massage therapists lease space in the Cambridge office and do their own billing, while the clinic provides administrative assistance and phone support. Patients still pay out-of-pocket for alternative treatments, though the health plan did negotiate a 20% discount for its members.

The most significant aspect of the program, according to Dr. Weisblatt, is the opportunity it offers for improved communication and coordination between conventional and alternative providers. "When we started we invited the alternative providers to do an in-service for our clinical staff, describing their training, what they do and the theoretical background of their practice," he recalls. "Since then we've had two case review sessions where the internist and alternative provider who both see the patient present the case together."

HVMA's new program has been popular; in six months the clinic has more than doubled its scheduled number of sessions with alternative providers, and HVMA offices in other parts of the Boston metro area plan to initiate similar programs. There have been occasional "miracle stories." One woman in her late 50s who'd experienced severe headaches for 20 years tried chiropractic treatment after discussing it with her internist. "She had an initial treatment about three months ago, and hasn't had a headache since then," Weisblatt says. "She had two follow-up visits and is essentially headache-free."

More often, the patients discussed during case review have shown improvement "but not as much as we would like to see," Weisblatt reports. During case review internists, chiropractors, acupuncturists and massage therapists sit side by side, all trying to envision the treatment that would help a particular patient reach better health.

Patients in other parts of the country are interested in alternative thera-

From *The Quality Letter for Healthcare Leaders*, Vol. 10:5, 1998

pies, too. In 1997, a nationwide survey commissioned by California-based Landmark Healthcare, a managed alternative healthcare provider, found 42% of respondents had used some form of alternative care during the past year. About 40% said their attitude toward alterative care had become more positive during the past five years, while only 2% said it had become more negative.

Because of this growing interest in alternative treatment methods, mainstream medical institutions are considering closer relationships with alternative providers. An increasing number of insurers offer reimbursement for complementary and alternative medicine (CAM); for example, chiropractic care is now covered to some extent by about half the nation's HMOs. Just over half of medical schools offer courses designed to increase physicians' familiarity with alternative treatments. Each year, at least 20 CAM educational programs, typically lasting four days or more, offer category-one continuing medical education credit for established physicians.

DEFINING ALTERNATIVE MEDICINE

The term "complementary and alternative medicine" (CAM) refers to medical interventions that are not taught widely in U.S. medical schools and are not generally available in U.S. hospitals. CAM modalities typically include chiropractic, acupuncture, massage, naturopathy and herbal medicines.

A seminal article published in 1993 by Harvard University Professor David M. Eisenberg, M.D. estimated 60 million Americans use unconventional therapies, spending about $14 billion a year, mostly out-of-pocket. At that time more than 70% of the patients who used alternative therapies did not discuss it with their physicians.

At the same time, many physicians are extremely skeptical about the value of treatment modalities based on unfamiliar and unverified concepts such as the flow of an energy called chi in invisible meridians, or the principle that like cures like, or that disease is a disruption in the body's innate intelligence. They are concerned that some patients may turn to unproven methods in place of allopathic methods known to be effective. In addition, at present there are no clear standards of appropriate practice for conventionally trained physicians who advise their patients about alternative medical therapies.

Complementary therapies clearly vary in effectiveness, and there are few definitive answers yet on which forms of CAM truly are effective for which conditions. While most CAM therapies are relatively safe, there have been reports of occasional problems, such as deaths caused by overdoses of the Chinese herb ma huang, which contains ephedrine.

As mainstream healthcare starts to integrate some forms of alternative medicine, care providers are taking a closer look at ways to apply quality principles to complementary therapies and to incorporate popular alternative medicine into consumer health plans without raising prices. Key issues that must be resolved include how to evaluate and credential CAM practitioners, and how to facilitate effective communication between physicians and alternative providers.

Shaped by the Market

Many healthcare organizations that use CAM say the market demands it. "We sit down with our marketing staff once a year," says Karen Reed, senior vice president of operations for 145,000-member New Hampshire-based Matthew Thornton Health Plan. "They told us employers were requesting these services. We did do a literature search, but the information we needed wasn't readily available, so our decision on exactly what to cover was based more on market research than on hard science." Last year the plan decided to offer its members several forms of alternative medicine, including chiropractic, acupuncture, homeopathy and naturopathy.

During its initial planning process, Matthew Thornton asked several focus groups about their attitudes toward CAM. "To our surprise, we learned that manufacturing organizations, which have a great deal of experience dealing with workers' compensation injuries, believe chiropractic will get people back to work faster than traditional medicine," says Reed. "We learned small employers believe access to complementary medicine will decrease drug costs. That's not a proven fact, but it is their perception."

When Mid-Columbia Medical Center, a rural health system based in The Dalles, Ore., considered adding alternative therapies, it conducted a community survey throughout its service area, looking at current usage patterns as well as residents' interests. "We reviewed the current scientific literature, especially the National Institutes of Health recommendations, and we also reviewed the top diagnoses in our community," recalls Jacque Scott, RN, vice president for clinical services. Inthe past two years, Mid-Columbia has opened a Center for Mind & Body Medicine and added an acupuncturist.

Alternative Medicine's Effectiveness

In recent years, there have been several attempts at the federal level to analyze which forms of alternative medicine are effective. For example, a multi-disciplinary panel convened by the Agency for Health Care Policy and Research drafted a clinical practice guideline for acute low back problems in adults, published in 1994. After reviewing a wide range of methods for assessment, patient education and symptom control for low back pain, the guideline summary states, "relief of discomfort can be accomplished most safely with nonprescription medicine and/or spinal manipulation."

In 1991, Congress created the Office of Alternative Medicine within the National Institutes of Health, to support research evaluating alternative therapies and promote public awareness of CAM research. Last November an NIH consensus development conference on acupuncture, co-sponsored by OAM and the Office of Medical Applications of Research, listed musculoskeletal pain and nausea as the conditions most successfully treated by acupuncture. The draft consensus statement said "the incidence of adverse effects is substantially lower than that of many drugs or other accepted medical procedures used for the same conditions."

However, the availability of the AHCPR guideline and the acupuncture consensus statement has certainly not resolved the debate over the effectiveness of chiropractic or acupuncture; the fact that these issues are under

INCORPORATING ALTERNATIVE MEDICINE INTO PRIMARY CARE

One of the strongest reasons for integrating alternative therapies into conventional medicine is that patients are already using it, and they need information about how to use it safely. They need access to recent, reliable information about the safety and relative efficacy of alternative treatments — and many patients will respect and trust that information most when it comes from their primary care physician.

However, some allopathic physicians understandably hesitate to take on this new role; they may lack the necessary training and expertise; they may fear possible liability if they discuss alternative treatments; or they may be opposed to the use of complementary and alternative medicine. In the July 1, 1997, issue of the *Annals of Internal Medicine*, David M.Eisenberg, M.D., Harvard Medical School, proposes a step-by-step strategy so that conventionally trained physicians can discuss the use or avoidance of alternative therapies with their patients. He recommends:

➤ When taking a history, physicians should routinely ask their patients whether they have used or thought about using "other kinds of therapy to find relief."

➤ Physicians should not engage in detailed discussions about alternative therapies until the patient has:

- received a complete conventional medical evaluation;
- been advised about conventional treatment options; and
- tried or exhausted conventional options.

serious consideration by the medical establishment appears to mark the beginning of a discussion, not a resolution. *(See Views on Acupuncture, page 194, and Views on Chiropractic, page 196)*

Robert B. Keller, M.D., executive director of the Maine Medical Assessment Foundation, which specializes in healthcare utilization analysis and outcomes research, notes there are marked variations in physician practice patterns even within generally accepted medical care. "Part of this variation is due to insufficient scientific evidence and clinical research," he says. "When we closely analyze the medical literature, we find many studies that are not well designed or analyzed. The accumulated literature of allopathic medical care is better than the literature of any other form of treatment — and it's not very good."

THE LANDMARK STUDY

In November 1997, Landmark Healthcare Inc. commissioned a random sample of households throughout the United States by Michigan-based InterActive Solutions. A total of 1,500 interviews were completed. Respondents were at least 18 years old and currently covered by some form of health insurance.

Use of specific types of alternative care in the past year

	Percent		Percent
Herbal Therapy	17	Acupuncture	2
Chiropractic	16	Biofeedback	2
Massage Therapy	14	Hypnotherapy	1
Vitamin Therapy	13	Naturopathy	1
Homeopathy	5		
Yoga	5		
Acupressure	5		

Change in visits to medical doctor or specialist since starting alternative care:

	Percent
No change	62
Decrease	30
Increase	3
Don't know	6

However, Keller is encouraged by the increasing sophistication of clinical research. "The quality of medical research has improved dramatically over the past 10 years, and continues to improve today." he says. "But it shouldn't surprise us, since we find poorly designed studies within the medical establishment, which tries so hard to be purely science-based, that we also find similar problems in research on alternative treatments."

Ideally, research on medications takes the form of a placebo-controlled, double-blind, randomized, replicable trial. However, CAM often relies on integrated, "whole-person" approaches that combine several modalities, such as diet, herbal medicines, exercises, guided imagery and counseling. Some alternative methods rely on difficult-to-evaluate — and impossible to blind — skills, such as the precise placement and manipulation of acupuncture needles. Many CAM proponents question whether those research techniques are the most appropriate way to evaluate alternative medicine.

In fact, there are many conventional procedures that similarly cannot be evaluated by double-blind, placebo-controlled trials, notes William Jarvis, Ph.D., professor of public health and preventive medicine at Loma Linda University, Calif., and a member of the advisory board of QuackWatch, a nonprofit corporation founded in 1969 to combat health-related fraud, fads and myths.

"To test the effectiveness of procedures, you have to actually do that procedure on one group of patients and then track them over time to see how they fare compared to similar patients who haven't had the procedure," he says. "This sort of prospective cohort study has been used to evaluate bypass surgery, for example, or to compare various forms of psychotherapy, and would be an appropriate research method to evaluate other forms of treatment."

Dr. Keller warns that complementary treatments — and many forms of conventional treatment — are often used for conditions that are self-limiting and/or poorly understood. "Today we tend to medicalize relatively benign conditions, where we don't understand the underlying biological mechanism." he says. "Many of these conditions are self-limiting.

A practitioner offers treatment; when in the course of time the patient gets better, both patient and practitioner feel it was due to the treatment. This applies to physicians as well as alternative practitioners, by the way." His solution: "We're all carrying a major burden; we all need to do better research before we disseminate and promulgate new treatments, whether 'alternative' or 'mainstream.'"

John Weeks, principal of Seattle-based Integration Strategies for Natural Healthcare, says there is more research supporting alternative interventions than the conventional medical community tends to acknowledge. "Unfortunately, here in the U.S. we've been living in a climate of substantial medical prejudice," he says. He notes that George Lundberg, editor of the *Journal of the American Medical Association*, has referred to the barrier between conventional and alternative medicine as "the bamboo curtain."

DEFINITIONS

Chiropractic: Developed by Daniel David Palmer in 1885 in the United States, chiropractic is based on the idea that spinal misalignment is a fundamental cause of disease, and manual manipulation can resolve this misalignment. The basic principles are that human beings have an innate healing potential, and accessing this "innate intelligence" should be the first goal of the healing arts. In 1993 there were more than 45,000 licensed chiropractors practicing in the United States.

Massage Therapy: The manipulation of soft body tissues is one of the oldest and most widely practiced methods of healing. Massage therapists use a variety of manual techniques to apply pressure to the body. They are licensed by 25 states and the District of Columbia; in most of these places candidates must have 500 or more educational hours from a recognized program, and pass a licensing exam. Methods include Swedish massage, deep-tissue massage, sports massage, neuromuscular massage and manual lymph drainage.

Naturopathy: Founded in the United States at the turn of the century by medical practitioners from several natural therapeutic disciplines, naturopathy emphasizes the body's ability to heal itself. The goal of naturopathy is to integrate traditional natural therapeutic methods (botanical medicine, nutrition, homeopathy, acupuncture, traditional oriental medicine, hydrotherapy and naturopathic manipulative therapy) with modern scientific medical diagnostic methods and standards of care. Naturopaths are licensed to practice in 12 states and the District of Columbia, and there are two accredited naturopathic medical schools in the United States.

Acupuncture: Based on the principles of Chinese medicine, which developed over several thousand years, acupuncture involves the insertion and manipulation of thin needles at key points to influence the flow of "chi," or internal energy, along certain channels within the body. The traditional training program for a practitioner is typically about five years. Acupuncturists are licensed, certified or registered in 30 states and the District of Columbia.

Homeopathy: Developed by Samuel Hahnemann, M.D., a German physician, during the late 1700s, homeopathy is based on the principle that "like cures like," and often uses highly diluted natural substances as remedies. Critics deny any possibility such extreme dilutions could have a real effect, but the *British Medical Journal*, after publishing a meta-analysis of the available literature, stated in an editorial that homeopathy does appear to be effective. Homeopathic remedies are made from naturally occurring plant, animal or mineral substances; they are regulated by the Food and Drug Administration and manufactured under strict guidelines.

Herbal medicines: Botanicals are widely used in the United States by alternative practitioners and also as part of traditional folk medicine. Many herbal medicines are undoubtedly biologically effective; about a quarter of the prescription drugs dispensed by local pharmacies in the United States contain at least one active ingredient derived from plant materials. Critics are concerned about the variable potency of natural herbal materials and possible contamination during an unregulated manufacturing and distribution process. For these reasons, the National Institutes of Mental Health/Office of Alternative Medicine/Office of Dietary Supplements clinical trial of St. Johnswort for depression will use a standardized botanical extract of the herb, which meets standards set by the U.S. Pharmacopoeia. In April 1998, the FDA issued guidelines to prevent herbal medicine manufacturers from making inaccurate claims about their products' properties. Such products can no longer be said to prevent or cure specific diseases; they can be said to facilitate general improvements in health, such as stimulating the immune system.

In the Nov. 25, 1997, issue of *USA Today*, Lundberg said, "the bamboo curtain is beginning to splinter."

Weeks, editor of the newsletter *Alternative Medicine Integration & Coverage: A Practical Resource for Payers and Providers*, notes that supporters of CAM methods often argue that they stimulate the self healing or placebo effect while limiting adverse side effects. However, "alternative providers tend to underestimate the role of the self-selecting, self-paying patient in generating the placebo effect," he says. "It is not clear how well these methods would work when someone who has no particular interest or belief in them is referred to them by their physician. Even with something as basic as improved nutrition, the patient must actually follow the recommended protocol for it to be effective."

There is only one point on which all observers agree: Additional, well-designed studies are needed — and this research is under way. The OAM has funded 11 specialty research centers in alternative medicine at institutions including Harvard Medical School, Columbia University College of Physicians and Surgeons, and Stanford University. The OAM also plans to fund CAM research in collaboration with other mainstream organizations. For example, a three-year, multi-center controlled clinical trial of the potential benefits and risks of hypericum perforatum (St. Johnswort) for the treatment of depression is being jointly funded by OAM, the National Institute of Mental Health and the Office of Dietary Supplements.

"The term 'alternative medicine' covers a broad range of modalities," notes James Dillard, M.D., medical director for alternative medicine for Oxford Health Plans, a Norwalk, Conn.-based health plan with more than 2.1 million members. "While some are effective, there are many things called 'alternative medicine' which do not in fact work. This is not a reason to blindly dismiss the entire field. It is a reason to conduct carefully designed research to discover which treatments work, for which specific conditions."

PLACEBO OR CURE?

One unanswered question is whether the fact that people independently choose and pay for alternative therapies might make them more effective. If and when complementary and alternative medicine is truly integrated into mainstream healthcare, it will reach a much larger array of patients. Will it still be equally effective if patients receiving such treatment don't necessarily believe in its efficacy?

David M. Eisenberg, M.D., of the Center for Alternative Medicine Research at Beth Israel Hospital Deaconess Medical Center/Harvard Medical School is spearheading a study designed to answer some of these questions. Patients with low back pain will be randomly assigned to either traditional treatment or "choice." These patients will make their own choice among traditional therapy or acupuncture, chiropractic and massage therapy. During an extensive follow-up period Eisenberg will record specific interventions, and track patient expectations and outcomes.

"This research will test whether patients who choose a treatment they believe in, and enter treatment with positive expectations, may in fact have better outcomes than other patients," notes Rick Weisblatt, Ph.D., medical director of Harvard Vanguard Medical Center, Cambridge, Mass.

Selecting, Communicating With Providers

One of the challenges health systems face as they add CAM is how to monitor and evaluate providers who are not practicing conventional medicine *(see Quality Agenda, pp 199-200)*.

The first step is to select modalities that are licensed or credentialed or certified in that state, and to do primary source verification of credentials similar to that used for any other provider. There should be a thorough review of educational background, work history, and possible malpractice actions, including queries to state licensing agencies and the National Practitioner Data Bank. Practitioners should maintain appropriate malpractice insurance.

Landmark Healthcare has a great deal of experience credentialing alternative providers; its networks total about 5,000 practitioners, serving 3 million to 3.5 million patients in 11 states. "We recognize the value of a license, but our credentialing criteria far exceed state requirements," says Marla Orth, president and CEO. "Out of more than 3,000 licensed acupuncturists in California, there are approximately 350 who meet our criteria." For example, Landmark looks for acupuncturists who speak and write English (an essential for communicating with allopathic physicians), use botanicals that meet stringent manufacturing standards and use disposable needles. Landmark conducts site visits to ensure the facility is accessible and professional.

Once a practitioner forms a relationship with the organization, the organization can use many of the same methods it would use to monitor any healthcare provider: careful records of patient complaints, untoward events and outcomes data; utilization review; and member satisfaction surveys. Landmark tracks utilization patterns relative to the appropriate scope of practice for each modality, and does a random chart review every two years when providers are recredentialed.

NIH OFFICE OF ALTERNATIVE MEDICINE RESEARCH CENTERS

Center for Addiction and Alternative Medicine Research
University of Minnesota Medical School, Minneapolis
Specialty: Addiction
www.winternet.com/~caamr/
Phone: (612)347-7670

Complementary and Alternative Medicine Program at Stanford
Stanford University, Palo Alto, Calif.
Specialty: Aging
scrdp.stanford.edu/camps.html
Phone: (650)725-5012

Center for Alternative Medicine Research in Asthma and Immunology
University of California, Davis
Specialties: Asthma, Allergy and Immunology
www-camra.ucdavis.edu/
Phone: (916)752-6575

Bastyr University AIDS Research Center
Bothell, Wash.
Specialty: HIV/AIDS
www.bastyr.edu/research/recruit.html
Phone: (206)823-1300

Consortial Center for Chiropractic Research/Palmer Center for Chiropractic Research
741 Brady St.
Davenport, Iowa 52803
Specialty: Chiropractic

Center for Alternative Medicine Research
Beth Israel Hospital/Deaconess Medical Center
Harvard Medical School
Specialty: General Medical Conditions
www.bidmc.harvard.edu/medicine/camr/,index.html
Phone: (617)667-4431

Center for Alternative Medicine Pain Research and Evaluation
University of Maryland School of Medicine, Baltimore
Division of Complementary Medicine
Specialty: Pain
http://207.123.250.14/
E-mail: vlieno@kernan2.umuc.ab.umd.edu

University of Texas Center for Alternative Medicine
Houston
Specialty: Cancer
www.sph.uth.tmc.edu/utcam/
E-mail: utcam@utsph.sph.uth.tmc.edu

Center for Research in Complementary and Alternative Medicine for Stroke and Neurological Disorders
Kessler Institute for Rehabilitation
West Orange, N.J.
www.umdnj.edu/altmdweb/web.html
Phone: (201)243-6972

Center for Complementary and Alternative Medicine Research in Women's Health
Columbia University
New York City
Specialty: Women's Health Issues
cpmcnet.columbia.edu/dept/rosenthal/
Phone: (212)543-9550

University of Virginia Center for the Study of Complementary and Alternative Therapies
Charlottesville
Specialty: Pain
www.med.Virginia.edu/nursing/centers/alt-ther.html
Phone: (804)924-0113

VIEWS ON ACUPUNCTURE

The [National Institutes of Health] conferees on acupuncture did not represent a broad consensus. All the people who made presentations were proponents, and people who were critical of acupuncture were not invited. It was unlike any other consensus conference NIH ever did.

Even if acupuncture does have value, which is questionable, most practitioners are not competent to make a diagnosis. While medical acupuncturists use endorphins and other secular mechanisms to explain what they do, the Traditional Chinese Medicine practitioners claim to be manipulating mystical energies that have no correspondence to reality. TCM practitioners examine the tongue and evaluate six aspects of the patient's pulse said to correlate with body organs and functions. One TCM practitioner whom I have consulted said I had "congestion of the blood," which I certainly do not have.

Stephen Barrett, M.D.
Chairman, Quackwatch Inc.
Allentown, Pa.

Every NIH consensus conference is a venue where experts get together and review the quality of the research in a particular area. The chair of the acupuncture evaluation panel was the president of the University of Maryland; to suggest the panel was biased is ridiculous on its face. There is a great deal of decent research which suggests that acupuncture is a reasonable treatment for some conditions, and the findings of the NIH panel were moderate and academically appropriate.

James Dillard, M.D.
Medical Director, Alternative Medicine, Oxford Health Plans
Medical Faculty, Columbia University College of Physicians and Surgeons, New York

Our patient care database goes back 12 years over 3 million members. The average cost of maintaining an asthma patient, in the literature, is $3,100 per year. We've found that for the majority of people who seek acupuncture treatment, the average cost including drugs is probably $700 to $1,000 per year, for an acute case. One study of acupuncture for patients with severe knee osteoarthritis found that 25% of patients responded positively, reversing earlier recommendations for surgical intervention, with an average cost of $9,000 per patient compared to knee replacement at $65,000.

Marla Orth
President and CEO
Landmark Healthcare

The Institute for Health and Healing, which includes a specialty patient care clinic employing conventional and complementary practices within San Francisco-based California Pacific Medical Center, holds regular chart reviews for difficult cases, according to William B. Stewart, M.D., medical director. "We're taking cues from the quality improvement efforts in other departments of the medical center, and holding ourselves to the same standards," he says.

Dual Leadership Criteria

A physician trained in allopathic medicine doesn't speak the same language as an alternate provider whose discipline may be based on a completely different view of the healing process. For this reason, people with experience in both alternative and conventional healthcare tend to take the lead in setting up and administering CAM programs within mainstream healthcare. For example, the Health and Healing Clinic at California Pacific is headed by two physicians with CAM training: One is a board-certified internist who also trained at University of California, Los Angeles in acupuncture and studied mindfulness meditation at the University of Massachusetts Medical School; the other is a board-certified pediatrician who is boarded in infectious disease, with a master's degree in public health, who is also trained in reiki (manipulations of the body's energies), nutrition, herbal medicine and guided imagery. Mid-Columbia Medical Center, which has just decided to add an acupuncturist, is relying on a registered nurse/acupuncturist to design the program and assist during the interview process.

Another way to ensure the effectiveness and reliability of CAM modalities is to select practitioners with standardized training in recognized "brand name" programs. When Mid-Columbia Medical Center decided to add meditation to its array of mind-body programs, it did not advertise in the local newspaper for meditation instructors; instead it sent 10 staffers (physicians, medical directors, nurses, social workers and respiratory therapists) to the East Coast to receive training at Harvard's Mind/Body Medical Institute.

Translating Among Disciplines

Oxford encourages written and phone communications between alternative providers and primary care physicians. One problem is that the underlying theory and language of allopathic medicine is strikingly different from that of many alternative modalities. "Often I feel like a translator," says Dillard, who is board certified in physical medicine and rehabilitation and is also a doctor of chiropractic and a certified acupuncturist.

"When an internist and acupuncturist get on the phone together, it forces both of them to think outside the box." says Dillard. "The acupuncturist can't talk about rising chi to the lungs or a blocked gall bladder meridian; he has to talk directly about the patient's symptoms. For the internist, even considering the possibility that sticking pins in someone could possibly improve their condition is thinking outside the box. Once they start to communicate, barriers are broken and the care process becomes patient-centered. We want to see that sort of cooperation and teamwork between providers, and that's what the future needs to hold for the sake of the patients."

> "When an internist and acupuncturist get on the phone together, it forces both of them to think outside the box. The acupuncturist can't talk about rising chi to the lungs or a blocked gall bladder meridian; he has to talk directly about the patient's symptoms. For the internist, even considering the possibility that sticking pins in someone could possibly improve their condition is thinking outside the box."
>
> James Dillard, M.D.
> Oxford Health Plans

Deciding Who Pays

Although Harvard Vanguard and Oxford are forming their own direct relationships with alternative providers, some organizations are choosing to offer CAM through a carve-out contract with a specialty providers such as Landmark and Alignis, an Atlanta-based specialty managed care company offering alternative care services to health plans and insurers. There is some risk that carve-out contracts will tend to limit communications between allopathic physicians and alternative providers, who are, after all, in two completely separate organizations while serving the same patients. To avoid this problem, Alignis encourages its providers to routinely send case reports to the primary care physician. It also has developed a secure intranet on which all providers can post chart notes and communicate with each other.

Landmark lets patients' primary care physicians know when they are being treated with alternative modalities. "In many plans, we send PCPs copies of the pre-treatment plans," notes Orth. "Our case managers, chiropractors or acupuncturists on our staff will get on the phone with the PCP to explain the course of treatment. We do this for continuity and coordination and also to educate physicians about CAM interventions."

Strong supporters of CAM argue that its preventive, integrated approach eventually will lead to lower healthcare costs. More cautious supporters say the general effect on costs can be discovered only empirically, over time. Opponents argue that because CAM providers routinely schedule numerous visits in response to vague symptoms, alternative therapies will end up costing more than conventional treatments.

"CAM costs can be controlled," says Rick Kunnes, M.D., national practice leader for medical management for Ernst & Young. "It's ridiculous to think of CAM as some unending invitation to steal from Fort Knox."

At present, there are four ways CAM coverage may be offered to patients:

- **Wellness Programs**. Widely used stress-management and mind body modalities are often integrated into a comprehensive wellness program, which also typically includes classes on disease management, nutrition, exercise and smoking cessation. These relatively low-cost group programs are offered to members at little or no cost.

- **Contracted Rate.** A managed care organization or insurer can negotiate with a network of CAM providers to offer their services to patients through contracted access, which may be lower than the rate charged the general public.

- **CAM Rider.** An insurer or managed care organization may offer CAM services as a rider on a standard contract, offering access to defined services for a specified extra fee. For example, the Oxford Health Plans rider offers direct access to chiropractors, acupuncturists and naturopathic physicians in states in which they are licensed. It is available only to group purchasers, not to individuals, and costs about 3% to 4% more than the standard premium.

- **Integrated CAM Services**. When an insurer or managed care organization is convinced specific CAM services are effective for a given condition, it may choose to cover those services as part of its standard benefit package. To this end, MCOs can push to integrate the treatment into a patient-centered model of care.

"When healthcare organizations start including CAM as part of their standard plan, they will be vulnerable to potential lawsuits about the scope of coverage," notes Grace Powers Monaco, J.D., vice president of Medical Care Management Corp., Bethesda, Md., and director of the Medical Care Ombudsman Program, a network of academic physicians who research whether particular patients can expect to benefit from high-tech or high-risk procedures, frequently in cases of coverage disputes with payers.

"If you start paying for something that is not demonstrated effective, you have to pay for everything that is not demonstrated effective. However, if they offer CAM as a separate rider then that stands on its own feet, and follows its own rules," she adds. "Even for a rider, the plan must define the range of practitioners and treatments that will be covered, and set guidelines for appropriate treatments. Once they have defined standards for the rider, they must follow them scrupulously and even-handedly."

Under a contracted rate, the cost of care remains the responsibility of the patient. When an insurer or MCO offers either a CAM rider or fully integrated CAM services, it must define and manage the benefit so that income covers costs. The same methods used to manage the cost of conventional therapies can be used to manage alternative therapies, including:

- set maximum number of covered visits per year;
- co-payments;

VIEWS ON CHIROPRACTIC

Last week I spoke to a consumer whose HMO gave her a list of chiropractors. The plan only covers 10 visits, but when she saw this chiropractor he told her she needed 56 treatments in order to get well. That sort of long-term chiropractic treatment is a scam.

— William Jarvis, Ph.D.
Professor of Public Health
and Preventive Medicine
Loma Linda University
California

In about 95% of the programs we offer, patients self-direct to the chiropractor or acupuncturist, and are automatically approved for their first visit. Then the practitioner develops a patient care plan, which we evaluate for medical necessity and appropriateness. The patient is authorized two, four, eight, or however many visits are appropriate for their particular medical condition.

We've tried to address consumer protection issues by building in quality checkpoints. The scope of practice for chiropractors as defined by the state of California allows them to do everything except surgery and prescribing drugs. However, we only cover chiropractic as a clinically appropriate intervention for neuro-musculoskeletal conditions. If chiropractors tell me they do routine gynecology or high colonic cocktails (a fancy word for enemas) or they are treating cancer, they don't get to participate in our system.

— Marla Orth, President and CEO
Landmark Healthcare

Spinal manipulation for low back pain in appropriately selected patients is probably cost effective if it involves only a few visits. However, chiropractors usually recommend more. Note that chiropractic is not the same as manipulation; chiropractic includes scores of other practices, many of which are wacky. For example, some chiropractors put substances in the patient's mouth and pull down on the patient's arm to determine supposed "allergies," a practice called applied kinesiology.

— Stephen Barrett, M.D.
Chairman, Quackwatch Inc.
Allentown, Pa.

- referral needed from primary care physician;
- treatment approved only for appropriate, clinically necessary care;
- treatment available only for specified conditions; and
- practice guidelines.

"There are hundreds of ways costs and utilization can be controlled, and these methods apply equally to all forms of treatment," says Kunnes. "If you're going to incorporate alternative therapies into your program, you treat them the same way you would any other therapy."

For example, Alignis has collected 20 years' worth of chiropractic practice patterns. When a patient presents with low back strain, the company develops a treatment plan based on symptoms, history, medications, co-morbidities — a total of 20 different factors. The patient's projected progress is compared to actual progress throughout the course of care, using indicators such as increase in range of motion, decrease in pain, and decrease in muscle spasm.

Alignis has similar protocols for acupuncture and massage therapy. "Even though an acupuncturist has a totally different way of diagnosing patients than a chiropractor or a physician, the functional outcomes we are seeking are the same," notes Alignis President Daniel Hollis.

Lovelace Health System, based in Albuquerque, N.M., is required by state regulation to include acupuncture and chiropractic care within its standard benefit. "We focus our use of chiropractic and acupuncture on areas where there is demonstrable efficacy," explains Michael Coyle, M.D., medical director and vice president of managed care for Lovelace Health Plan. "We routinely approve chiropractic care for acute and chronic lower back pain, with six to nine visits on the initial treatment plan. Historically we have restricted the use of acupuncture to chronic musculoskeletal and neurogenic pain, although since the recent NIH consensus panel, we've expanded that to hyperemesis associated with chemotherapy and pregnancy. We evaluate the need for acupuncture or chiropractic for other conditions on a case-by-case basis."

What Can We Expect in the Future?

The fact that alternative medicine is controversial should surprise no one. Conventional medicine has been marked by "turf wars" for as long as anyone can remember; conventional practitioners with differing skills frequently battle fiercely over who should offer which services.

What is surprising is how much the atmosphere has changed, how quickly. Ten years ago there were no respected voices within the healthcare establishment arguing in favor of CAM. In the past year, the Journal of the American Medical Association editorial board selected alternative medicine as one of the three top subjects to be covered in future issues, and issued a call for CAM research papers to be published this fall.

As Dr. Keller sums up, "We, the medical profession, can no longer say 'No methods work except ours.' On the other hand, alternative methods need to be tested, just as ours do."

PUBLICATIONS

Integrative Medicine: Integrating Allopathic, Alternative and Complementary Medicine
Andrew Weil, M.D., Editor-in-Chief
To order: (888)437-4636
www.elsevier.com/locate/intmed

The Scientific Review of Alternative Medicine
Wallace Sampson, M.D., Editor
To order: (716)636-7571

Alternative Medicine Integration & Coverage: A Practical Resource for Payers and Providers
John Weeks, Founding and Executive Editor
To order: (800)632-0123

Alternative & Complementary Therapies
To order: (914)834-3100

Alternative Therapies in Health and Medicine
To order: (800)345-8112

Complementary & Alternative Medicine at the NIH
To order: (888)644-6226
Current and past issues are posted at altmed.od.nih.gov

Fundamentals of Complementary and Alternative Medicine
Marc S. Micozzi, M.D., Ph.D., Editor
To order: (800)553-5426
www.churchillmed.com

Reader's Guide to Alternative Health Methods
By John F. Zwicky, Ph.D., Arthur W. Hafner, Ph.D., et al
To order: (800)621-8335, ask for #OP313792

Complementary and Alternative Medicine: Issues Impacting CoverageDecisions
Executive summary of conference sponsored by Office of Alternative Medicine
To order: (888)644-6226

Or as Weeks puts it, "we need to focus on building relationships and improving communications at the same time we measure the effectiveness of various methods. The most important thing is to stop this polarization between 'conventional' and 'alternative' medicine. We need to bring everybody to the table and ask, how can we bring all our various tools to the best service of the patient?"

"Right now most patients are paying a premium to access CAM. It is being used alongside conventional methods, basically as a marketing ploy," says consultant Peter Boland, president of California-based Boland Healthcare Inc. and publisher of *Making Managed Healthcare Work*.

"At some point, we will begin to focus on what actually helps the patient. We'll ask which methods are most cost-effective and produce the best outcomes. When we reach that point, we'll see an increasing use of high-touch methods instead of high tech. We'll see medical management and CAM replacing high-cost surgical interventions. When CAM begins to substitute for conventional therapies, that's when we'll really have integrated medicine."

Finding the Right Alternative Medicine Practitioners

When a clinic decided to add alternative medicine to its services, its selection committee began with recommendations from clinic staff. Licensing, credentials and a willingness to work closely with allopathic providers also were key criteria for selection.

When the Cambridge, Mass., office of Harvard Vanguard Medical Associates decided to forge a closer relationship with selected chiropractors, acupuncturists and massage therapists in 1997, it looked for partners who had not only strong skills in their own fields but the interest and ability to work in partnership with allopathic physicians.

Several HVMA physicians expressed a strong interest in complementary and alternative medicine, and they participated in the planning process for the project and interviewed candidates together with the project's administrative manager.

The practice's first step was to decide which CAM modalities were suitable for integration into the clinic. They chose treatments that:

- are currently utilized by the practice's patients. (One reason for forming relationships with CAM practitioners is to facilitate communication among all providers who are seeing the patient.)
- are licensed, certified or registered by Cambridge or the state. (Chiropractors and acupuncturists take a national exam before licensing by the state of Massachusetts; massage therapists register with the Cambridge Department of Health and Hospitals.)
- are supported by evidence of effectiveness in the scientific literature.

The HVMA planning committee decided to rely on personal recommendations to find providers who might be suitable candidates for this new relationship. It sent a questionnaire to all staffers working at the Cambridge center. It received recommendations for more than 50 alternative providers whom staff members either knew by reputation or had used themselves.

Clear Professional Standards

HVMA mailed a request for proposal to each person on its list of potential candidates, inviting them to supply the information needed to evaluate their professional standing for the new position, including:

- license;
- accreditation/certification;
- educational history;
- professional experience;

> “What we could evaluate ... was the person’s clinical manner, their attitudes toward medicine, how they would deal with patients, and their interest in coordinating and communicating with our own providers.”
>
> Rick Weisblatt, Ph.D.
> Harvard Vanguard Medical Associates

- professional recommendations;
- malpractice coverage; and
- review of work history.

Candidates also were asked to describe their attitudes and approach to traditional medicine and whether they would be able to work in close cooperation with other alternative practitioners as well as traditional medical staff.

In addition to formal evidence of professional qualifications and a strong sense of professional teamwork, candidates were evaluated on several factors relating to the particular needs of the Cambridge office:

- special skills in providing care for the elderly;
- sensitivity to gay and lesbian issues;
- ability to work on the clinic schedule, including Saturdays; and
- familiarity with quality assurance processes.

Interviews

HVMA physicians and the CAM program manager interviewed the candidates whose qualifications best matched the openings.

“A physician trained in allopathic medicine cannot evaluate the professional skills of a chiropractor or an acupuncturist,” says Rick Weisblatt, Ph.D., site medical director for the Harvard Vanguard medical offices in Cambridge and Watertown. “We had to rely on recommendations, training and accreditation for that. What we could evaluate during the interview process was the person’s clinical manner, their attitudes toward medicine, how they would deal with patients and their interest in coordinating and communicating with our own providers.”

The interviewers followed a standard set of guidelines, and probed for communication skills, motivation and adaptability. They also asked questions designed to elicit attitudes toward patient care in this unusual setting, covering subjects that included:

- philosophy of health and healing;
- ability to explore a range of treatment options (both traditional and alternative) with patients;
- willingness to refer to traditional practitioners;
- ability to handle patient dissatisfaction;
- analysis of conditions that are most likely and least likely to respond to their own form of treatment; and
- awareness of situations in which they should not treat a patient.

Before making a final decision on any of the candidates, HVMA conducted a thorough professional background check that included verifying professional and personal references, and researching malpractice history, Medicare/Medicaid sanctioning, professional sanction status and any complaints registered with the Better Business Bureau.

The alternative providers have a one-year renewable contract with HVMA. The program started out with two acupuncturists, two chiropractors and two massage therapists, each working two five-hour shifts per week. Since its inception, the program has more than doubled the scheduled number of sessions.

Identifying and Caring for Depressed Patients: Healthcare Organizations Try New Approaches

Evidence suggests that depressed patients are seriously undertreated. Healthcare organizations are responding with new models of care, treatment protocols, training and heavier reliance on primary care.

Depression — one of the most common illnesses in our society — affects as many as 15% of men and 24% of women at some point in their lives. At any given time, major depression occurs in 2% to 4% of people in the community and among 5% to 10% of primary care patients. It's an expensive illness — one of the 10 most costly in the United States — resulting in $12 billion in direct medical outlays each year and $31 billion in indirect costs resulting from premature death, job absenteeism and lost productivity. Pain, illness, work problems, family problems and usage of medical services all are higher among depressed patients. A recent study suggests that depressed primary care patients use double to triple the amount of healthcare services as their nondepressed counterparts. Patients with depression have greater mortality rates than average, and depression has been shown to increase the risk of developing such serious disorders as coronary heart disease and diabetes.

The good news about depression is that, if detected and treated properly, a complete remission occurs in 80% of cases. But much work still needs to be done to educate health professionals and the public and to develop cost-effective models of care that are geared to today's busy healthcare organizations.

There is strong evidence that people with depression are getting inadequate treatment — and sometimes no treatment at all. In January 1997, *The Journal of the American Medical Association* published a report from a consensus conference on the undertreatment of depression, organized by the National Depressive and Manic Depressive Association. People with depression are "seriously undertreated," the report says, citing such reasons as social stigma that prevents people from seeking care, limited access to services, poor provider education about depression, lack of time to evaluate and treat depression, and prescribing inadequate dosages of antidepressant medications for too short a time.

Healthcare Organizations Take Action

Across the country, healthcare organizations are working to do a better job of spotting depression and improving quality of care for depressed patients. In many organizations, primary care physicians — who deliver 50% of mental healthcare today — are being trained to detect depression and provide more effective treatments, including medication and behavioral therapy. Others emphasize early referral to mental health services when depression is suspected. And protocols and guidelines are being developed to help physicians and mental health providers make appropriate treatment choices.

From *The Quality Letter for Healthcare Leaders*, Vol. 9:7, 1997

Henry Ford Health System, which provides care to 2.5 million Michigan residents, started a new depression initiative in July 1997 as part of its quality improvement process. The initiative focused on enhancing primary care physicians' role in detection and treatment, and results after one year are cause for optimism. HFHS developed a clinical care pathway internally, and implemented it in a "stepwise fashion," according to C. Edward Coffey, M.D., vice president for behavioral services and chair of the department of psychiatry. "You could have as many different approaches to treating depression as you have doctors," he notes. "We decided to identify the best practice according to the scientific literature and then to articulate that practice in terms of a pathway." Dr. Coffey says HFHS's approach is based on evidence that "management of depression by primary care practitioners is suboptimal. They often fail to recognize it, and even when they do diagnose, treatment tends to be suboptimal."

STRATEGIES FOR IMPROVING DIAGNOSIS AND TREATMENT OF DEPRESSION

- Make mental health practitioners available to consult with and support primary care practitioners.
- Develop evidence-based, user-friendly treatment protocols.
- Involve patients in the diagnosis and treatment of their condition.
- Create an environment in which mental health providers are valued team members.

Dr. Coffey declined to give specific numbers, but said that the initiative has been "a great step." "In general, patients' recognition of their problems increase, antidepressent utilization has improved and compliance is up," he says.

Development of HFHS's depression pathway started at the end of 1996. Now, specially trained teams of behavioral health personnel — psychiatrists, psychologists and nurses — are taking the pathways to clinical sites and teaching primary care physicians how to use them. They are starting at sites of different sizes — one small, one medium and one large — "to get experience and iron out the kinks," Dr. Coffey explains. "Based on that experience, we'll be able to move more rapidly across the system."

At Group Health Cooperative of Puget Sound in Seattle, Wash. — the nation's largest consumer-governed HMO, with nearly 700,000 enrollees — depression is one of roughly two dozen disorders being addressed through its "road map" program of evidence-based clinical guideline development and systematic implementation. The depression guideline, which can be accessed at computer workstations on physicians' desks in primary care clinics, is "very popular," according to Neil Baker, M.D., chief of Group Health's Seattle-area Behavioral Mental Health Service. "Primary care physicians are really happy to have something that gives them guidance in approaching these patients."

Although the guideline, implemented in 1997, offers pointers on spotting depression, screening and detection are not areas in which Group Health is placing great emphasis; rather, it is focusing on improving treatment and outcomes. "Several studies in our setting have shown that primary care doctors are generally pretty good at identifying people who have significant depression," Dr. Baker notes. "We don't have resources to do everything, so our organizational decision was to go where evidence suggests we can do the most good."

In addition to the road map, Group Health developed the Integrated Care Program, a comprehensive model for treating depression that incorporates behavioral health into primary care. For primary care providers the ICP provides strategies for assessment, patient education, clinical management and drug therapy. It emphasizes problem-solving and coping skills to help patients manage their disease. It also outlines a consulting role for behavioral health specialists, in which they carry out interventions for sicker patients, conduct group therapy, train healthcare providers and assist with assessment.

Scripps Clinic, a network of nine medical centers throughout San Diego (Calif.) County, emphasizes early detection of depression and timely assessment by mental healthcare specialists. "We think it's better to make an intervention early, when symptomatology is in the mild to moderate range," says David Naimark, M.D., a staff psychiatrist. "That way we'll have a quicker and better response." Primary care physicians are encouraged to send all patients in whom they suspect depression to the Division of Mental Health for an evaluation; because it's an open-access system, patients can also come in without referral if they feel they need mental healthcare. Complicated cases are treated by mental health specialists, while simpler cases may be referred back to primary care physicians, many of whom are comfortable treating depression once a clear-cut diagnosis is made. "Our access is open because we view behavioral health as primary care," notes Mark Reade, Ph.D., head of the Division of Mental Health. "Mental health problems are closely linked with medical problems."

A PRIMER ON DIAGNOSTIC FEATURES OF SELECTED MOOD DISORDERS COMMONLY SEEN IN PRIMARY CARE

Depressive Disorder	Diagnostic Features
Adjustment disorder – with depressed mood – with mixed anxiety and depressed mood	A response to an identifiable psychosocial stressor Developed within three months of the stressor Characterized by marked distress or significant impairment in social role or functioning Resolves within six months of termination of the stressor
Major depressive disorder	Characterized by one or more major depressive episodes
Dysthymic disorder	Characterized by at least two years of depressed mood for more days than not Accompanied by additional depressive symptoms Does not meet criteria for a major depressive episode
Mood disorder due to a general medical condition	Characterized by a prominent, persistent disturbance in mood that is a direct physiological consequence of a general medical condition
Substance-induced mood disorder	Characterized by a prominent, persistent disturbance in mood that is a direct physiological consequence of alcohol abuse, a prescribed medication or exposure to toxins

Source: Robinson, P., C. Wischman and A. Del Vento. *Treating Depression in Primary Care: A Manual for Primary Care and Mental Health Providers.* Reno, Nev.: Context Press. Page 3, 1996. Reprinted with permission.

The mental health practitioners in Scripps' managed care plans focus mostly on short-term, solution-focused work that emphasizes "hitting the ground running," Dr. Reade says. The average length of therapy is four visits, but when patients need care of longer duration — even more than their health plan specifies — they will continue to be seen. "We're flexible that way because it makes a lot of sense," says Dr. Reade. "If a person has a severe psychiatric problem and you cut things off at their 20 visits or whatever, they'll go right back to their primary care doctor, who will be calling us to ask: 'What do I do?'" Scripps' treatment is decided on a case-by-case basis, and, although it is in keeping with general guidelines, it is medical necessity — not arbitrary limitation of insurance benefits — that determines the level and extent of treatment.

The Value of Addressing Depression

Unlike Scripps, however, some HMOs would like to ignore mental health problems because they see them as unnecessary expenses, says Jeff Mitchell, M.D., chairman of the Department of Psychiatry at Lovelace Health System in Albuquerque, N.M. "So we set out to demonstrate the economic value of diagnosing depression in our medical care system," he notes.

In a recent unpublished study, researchers looked at 2,079 patients who had been diagnosed by their primary care providers as having depression. After examining data about their utilization of medical care in the year before and the year after diagnosis, it was found that those patients accounted for a $2.1 million reduction in the use of medical services. "We don't have data on what happened to those people or how they were treated," Dr. Mitchell explains. "All this really says is that there is economic value in detecting depression in the primary care system."

"Only advanced coronary artery disease has been found to result in more bed/disability days than depression, and only arthritis causes more chronic pain."

"The Economic Burden of Depression in 1990"
Journal of Clinical Psychiatry

Lovelace's physicians received special instruction to help them detect depression, including practice guidelines adapted from those released in 1993 by the U.S. Agency for Health Care Policy and Research and training in administering the Zung Self-Rating Depression Scale, which was selected for its ease of use. Physicians were taught to watch for clues such as frequent use of medical services or complaints with no organic cause, such as pain and body aches, low energy, fatigue, apathy, irritability or sexual complaints, and to administer the Zung scale when depression is suspected. "We found that 37% of our heavy utilizers had Zung scores above the cutoff point for depression," Dr. Mitchell notes.

"The Economic Burden of Depression in 1990," a report published in the Journal of Clinical Psychiatry in 1993, points out that accurately treating and diagnosing depression would not only lower the indirect costs of depression related to decreased productivity but also lower the costs associated with other physical and mental disorders that often occur in conjunction with depression. Furthermore, better detection and treatment would have a positive impact on quality of life, which declines significantly with depression. "Only advanced coronary artery disease has been found to result in more bed/disability days than depression, and only arthritis causes more chronic pain," the authors state. They note that depression tends to be more debilitating than diabetes, arthritis, gastrointestinal problems and hypertension. Employers are highly concerned about depression because of its steep cost: roughly $4,200 per depressed worker, which equals $250 per employee.

The 1997 consensus report from the National Depressive and Manic Depressive Association notes that although appropriate care for depression may increase total costs of care, it improves the cost-effectiveness — or value — of care because each dollar spent on care provides "more health benefits."

Patient compliance with therapy is another important economic issue, Dr. Mitchell points out. Data suggest that 20% to 59% of primary care patients stop taking prescribed medication for depression within three weeks of the initial prescription. "There are studies that show over and over again that when patients comply with their medication or whatever their treatment is, that's when you save money," says Dr. Mitchell. "And the better you train your physicians to educate patients, the better their compliance." Lovelace's primary care physicians go through a two-hour training session on patient education plus half-hour refresher courses every six months to reinforce key points, such as the importance of explaining a diagnosis of depression to the patient. "In the old days, physicians would prescribe antidepressants without telling patients why," Dr. Mitchell notes. Other information physicians are urged to provide includes exactly how to take the medication, the importance of not missing doses or stopping even if symptoms disappear, when the medication will start taking effect, possible side effects and how to reach the doctor if the patient has problems or questions.

Economics, however, should not drive health systems' interest in recognizing and treating depression, Dr. Mitchell asserts. "You should do it because it's the right thing to do, not because you want to save money. Even if you find it costs more to treat this illness, so what — would you not treat diabetes because it costs money?"

"The payoff is that the person will feel better, require fewer visits, and in the long run use less of your time and resources that could be used for other patients."

C. Edward Coffey, M.D.
Vice President
Behavioral Services
Henry Ford Health System

Primary Care, Specialty Care?

Views are mixed on exactly who is best equipped to handle the diagnosis and treatment of depression. Because primary care practitioners are most patients' entry point into the healthcare system, it makes sense for them to be involved in depression care. A big problem, however, is lack of time, as Dr. Coffey of Henry Ford Health System points out. "Primary care practitioners have their patient encounter down to a fine art — about 15 minutes a visit. How can you add screening for a very common condition and not add work and extra time to what the doctor is already doing?" Include treatment — especially behavioral therapy or patient education — and the minutes add up. Convincing primary care practitioners of the value of detecting and addressing depression — even if it takes more time during an individual visit — means emphasizing positive outcomes, he suggests. At HFHS, training sessions on using protocols and managing depression include facts from the literature about results the physicians' efforts are likely to bring about. "The payoff is that the person will feel better, require fewer visits, and in the long run use less of your time and resources that could be used for other patients," says Dr. Coffey.

Dr. Naimark, who specializes in geriatric psychiatry, says that Scripps' mental health professionals definitely spend more time with each patient than primary care practitioners can — 60 minutes for an initial evaluation and 20 to 40 minutes for follow-up. He believes that because primary care doctors have less time to assess symptoms, they may be less likely to make an accurate diagnosis of depression. Alan Savitz, M.D., president of PacifiCare Behavioral Health in Laguna Hills, Calif., feels that although some primary care practitioners are "terrific" at diagnosing and treating depression, many others are not interested in getting involved in mental

GOOD INFORMATION IMPROVES COMPLIANCE

Whether a patient sticks with prescribed treatment depends strongly on how well the patient understands his or her illness, the rationale for taking a medication and the instructions for use, according to Debra Roter, Dr.P.H., of the Johns Hopkins School of Public Health. Dr. Roter, who has spent her career studying physician-patient communication, stresses that "the rationale is very important, because many patients are actually ill-disposed toward drugs. They don't want to take them unless they're convinced there's a really good reason."

It's also critical for physicians to anticipate barriers to compliance, such as being unable to afford the drug. "Belief" barriers can be identified by asking whether the patient has any misgivings or fears about the drug regimen, Dr. Roter notes. "Once negative beliefs are on the table, the physician can deal with them and correct misconceptions." Physicians should be sure to monitor compliance regularly in a nonjudgmental way with such questions as, "Lots of people have problems taking their medications, have you?" Or, "Did you stop taking your medications at any time because you felt worse or better?" "If you pose your question in a way that allows a negative answer," she says, "you're much more likely to get a truthful response."

Detailed information on improving communication in medical visits appears in *Doctors Talking With Patients/Patients Talking With Doctors* by Debra L. Roter and Judith A. Hall, published in 1992 by Auburn House, 88 Post Rd. West, Westport, CT 06881.

healthcare and simply cannot fit it into their heavy workload. "I think you have to accept the limitations of primary care physicians' practices and make sure that health systems allow patients direct access to behavioral healthcare when they want it." Some patients, however, fearful of the stigma of "mental illness," prefer to have primary care doctors treat them for depression and are unlikely to see a behavioral health specialist, especially if it is up to them to initiate the visit.

Patricia Robinson, Ph.D., a psychologist and researcher with Group Health Cooperative of Puget Sound, believes that primary care physicians play an important role in managing depression. But she and her colleagues found in one study a tendency for physicians to diagnose major depression — and to treat it with medication — when in fact a patient is suffering from minor depression, a condition that often responds well to education and supportive counseling. "If you give medication to a person with minor depression, they'll probably feel better in a month, but they would have felt better anyway," she notes.

The clinicians interviewed for this article stress the importance of having mental health practitioners available to consult with and support primary care physicians in the detection and treatment of depression. When possible, it is useful to have a psychiatrist or psychologist assigned to the same office or clinic, at least for certain hours each week. At Scripps, mental health clinicians are found in several sites where primary care physicians practice, so "there's a lot of interaction, consultation and in-service education," Dr. Reade says.

In 1997, Dr. Robinson helped conduct a four-year study funded by the National Institute of Mental Health that tested two "integrated" models of care, in which mental health professionals joined forces with primary care practitioners. It found that having primary care doctors refer depressed patients to a psychologist for a very structured intervention that lasted 2.5 hours to 3.5 hours (broken into visits of about a half hour each) brought about improved clinical outcomes. The findings were particularly strong for major depression, but the interventions worked for minor depression as well. Other key outcomes included greater patient and provider satisfaction, better adherence to pharmacologic treatment and more consistent use by patients of behavioral coping strategies targeted in the intervention. To keep primary care doctors "in the loop," the psychologists provided them with brief summaries after every patient visit. The patients developed written relapse prevention plans, which were placed in their chart so the physician could review them with patients during medical visits. After the acute phase of treatment, the psychologists initiated four telephone follow-up calls to patients over six months to help prevent or identify relapse. In the other model, which was less successful, primary care physicians counseled depressed patients, who also saw a psychiatrist twice, on average, for medication consultations.

Dr. Robinson emphasizes that collaborative arrangements are the most desirable way to manage depressed patients. For integrated models to work well, the basic structure of healthcare in the primary care setting must change so that mental health providers become valued, long-term members of the team. Barriers to be overcome include differences between mental health and primary care providers in training, theoretical paradigms, professional languages and working styles.

Approaches to improving the quality of care for depressed patients and efforts to define the functions of primary care are, for the most part, in their infancy. The jury is still out on what works best, but there's no question that both primary care providers and mental health specialists have key roles to play.

Overcoming Barriers

During a 1997 talk at the National Managed Health Care Conference in Washington, D.C., Dr. Robinson spoke of barriers to delivering timely, cost-effective care to patients suffering from depression. Healthcare organizations are overcoming these barriers in various ways:

Incomplete or inaccurate diagnosis. Dr. Robinson believes that this can be improved with better education and accessibility of tools. Self-report inventories are quick, easy ways for practitioners to assess the severity of a suspected problem. Some popular ones are the Beck Depression Inventory–Short Form, the Center for Epidemiological Studies' Depression Scale and the Zung Self-Rating Depression Scale. The Geriatric Depression Scale uses language that may increase the accuracy of diagnosis in older patients. Dr. Reade of Scripps recommends diagnosing depression according to criteria in *DSM IV* (the *Diagnostic and Statistical Manual of Mental Disorders, 4th edition*, published by the American Psychiatric Association) and having a quality assurance committee that systematically reviews records for completeness and accuracy of diagnosis. Dr. Baker says that Group Health is training primary care doctors in using DSM IV, but he admits that accuracy of diagnosis is a dilemma. "The primary care doctors really like having [DSM IV] as a guide, but only experience will say how well it works. I don't think there's a simple tool that's going to consistently pull out an accurate diagnosis of major depression — there's no laboratory test. Because of the potential inaccuracies, in our system we plan to follow up with all patients who have a diagnosis of major or minor depression to

For more information ...

Group Health Cooperative of Puget Sound
Contact: Neil Baker, M.D.
E-mail: baker.n@ghc.org
or
Contact: Patricia Robinson, Ph.D.
Phone: (206)287-2589
E-mail: robinson.p@ghc.org

Henry Ford Health System
Contact: C. Edward Coffey, M.D.
Phone: (313)874-6887
E-mail: ecoffey1@smtpgw.is.hfh.edu

Lovelace Health System
Contact: Jeff Mitchell, M.D.
Phone: (505)856-8400

PacifiCare Behavioral Health
Contact: Alan Savitz, M.D.
Phone: (714)206-5240

Scripps Clinic
Contact: David Naimark, M.D.
Phone: (619)622-0394
or
Contact: Mark Reade, Ph.D.
Phone: (619)622-0394

ADDITIONAL RESOURCES FOR MANAGING PATIENTS WITH DEPRESSION

Federal Guidelines Available for Detecting, Diagnosing and Treating Depression in Primary Care

In 1993, the U.S. Agency for Health Care Policy and Research released a comprehensive set of guidelines to help practitioners address depression in the primary care setting. Many health systems have used them as helpful resources as they build their own approaches to improving depression outcomes. *Depression in Primary Care: Detection, Diagnosis and Treatment* describes symptoms, provides algorithms to assist in diagnosing specific mood disorders, and reviews treatments, medications, side effects and follow-up. The guidelines are available by calling (800)358-9295 or directly from the agency's Web site at www.ahcpr.gov/.

Drug Treatment Protocols

Computerized psychopharmacology algorithms for depression, expected to be available over the Web, are now under development by David Osser, M.D., of Taunton State Hospital in Massachusetts and Robert Patterson, M.D., of Mental Health Connections Inc. in Lexington, Mass. "We're trying to produce an expert system that accounts for as many variables as we can think of and that we can update constantly," Dr. Osser explains. "The trouble with current [algorithms] is that they're often out of date the day they appear in print." For more information, contact Mental Health Connections Inc., 21 Blossom St., Lexington, MA 02173, (800)788-4743, www.mhc.com.

The American Pharmaceutical Association offers sample drug treatment algorithms for depression that can be adapted for individual health systems' use. These tools are part of a comprehensive program called *The APhA Guide to Drug Treatment Protocols.* For more information, contact the APhA, 2215 Constitution Ave., NW, Washington, DC 20037, (202)429-7517, www.aphanet.org.

determine the course of their symptoms and to rediagnose patients who are deteriorating."

Unclear clinical management protocols. "Give primary care physicians a good protocol to work with, and they'll use it," Dr. Robinson notes. "But right now, ours are unclear. It's who's talked to them lately that they're most influenced by — who came by and gave a continuing medical education course." She adds that simplicity and user-friendliness are characteristics that greatly enhance protocol usage. Dr. Coffey of the Henry Ford Health System emphasizes that protocols should be based on a thorough review of the literature, as well as on recommendations from other health systems that have identified effective approaches. "But developing pathways is really quite easy to do compared with the implementation — making them come alive in the primary care setting," he says. It's important to design something that can fit comfortably into the "15-minute hour" and to get doctors to commit to using the protocol even if it takes a bit longer. Implementation must involve training and ongoing support from mental health specialists, he notes. "You can't just knock on the door, give the doctor a book containing a pathway, wish them good luck and be on your way. There's a lot of cultivating to do."

Overprescribed medications. Primary care physicians write 80% of antidepressant prescriptions in the United States — but how many of them are unnecessary? In the study described earlier, in which Dr. Robinson and colleagues found primary care physicians prescribing medication for minor depression, 56% of the patients diagnosed with major depression actually had minor depression. Solving this problem requires better protocols, education and support to help primary care physicians distinguish different forms of depression and understand appropriate treatments. Dr. Baker points out that another reason for overprescribing is widespread belief that selective serotonin reuptake inhibitors, such as fluoxetine (Prozac), are benign. "Personally, I don't think we know yet. And certainly SSRIs do cause side effects. There is tremendous advertising pressure around these medications for both patients and doctors. Ads do not create an accurate impression of the world of depression, which is a continuum; at some places along that continuum medication may be called for, but at others, alternative forms of therapy are appropriate." Follow-up is an important factor in addressing overprescribing and improper use of medications, Dr. Baker says. "How many patients in our busy primary care system end up getting placed on antidepressants, and they're not seen again within three or four months? This is not a criticism of primary care providers. They see 30 to 40 patients a day and have two million bits of information to remember. How in the world are you going to keep track of these people unless you get help from the clinical delivery system?" Healthcare organizations need clinical information systems to support physicians, he notes.

Among other problems Dr. Robinson cited are not recognizing when patients are ready for their medication to be tapered and not recognizing when to end treatment. "Physicians need support in how to talk to patients about discontinuing medication. It's often a difficult subject to bring up, because patients fear relapse." Additional factors are inconsistent development of behavioral health plans, which help patients pinpoint strategies for coping and bringing enjoyment into their lives, and a scarcity of good educational materials to use with patients. "We've found that if you can have a whole clinic using the same materials, there's a culture that starts to develop, with the same critical messages being repeated again and again," Dr. Robinson says.

Much Work Ahead

Despite the high incidence of depression, many myths persist. A survey of 1,166 adult Americans by the National Mental Health Association found that 54% think depression is a personal or emotional weakness and 48% think it is a normal part of aging. One in four would try to tough it out themselves without seeking help, and 54% would seek treatment from someone other than a health professional. Even physicians have wrong notions about depression. According to Dr. Jeff Mitchell of Lovelace Health System, "It's still fairly common to hear a physician say: 'Well, if I had a heart attack or cancer, I'd be depressed, too.' You have to tell them: 'There are a lot of people with that same problem who aren't depressed.' Treating the depression really makes a difference in the quality of life and the outcome."

It's important for healthcare organizations to recognize the pervasiveness of depression, the increased morbidity and mortality it causes and the benefits that addressing it can bring, suggests Dr. Coffey of Henry Ford Health System. "We're lucky," he notes, "that our system has the vision to recognize the importance of this illness in the medical setting."

Improving Care for Adults With Asthma Across the Continuum

Despite the publication of guidelines by the National Institutes of Health and interest from many specialty groups, the delivery of asthma care has not substantially changed. A group of health care providers with an integrated delivery system in Illinois wanted to effect a change in its care of asthma patients, and found that such a multi-site project can be effective when each location establishes its own leadership for change but is supported by centralized services such as education and production of patient materials.

Before launching an adult asthma improvement team, the health care providers wanted to understand the needs of the primary service area communities surrounding eight system hospitals. Because hospital admissions are regarded as an indication of poorly controlled asthma, researchers obtained the total number of hospitalizations at any Illinois hospital from the Illinois Hospital and Health Systems Association. Healthy People 2000 set as a goal hospital admissions of 160 per 100,000. Hospital admissions were used for the numerator, and total population in the primary service area constituted the denominator. Tremendous variation exists within the eight hospital areas in the state: The hospitals located within the city tend to have higher hospitalization rates for asthma; they also tend to have lower socio-economic status, a greater proportion of African Americans and increased barriers to access to health care.

To identify care provided within the hospitals, researchers examined the number of Emergency Department visits and hospitalizations, using ICD-9 (International Classification of Diseases-9th revision) codes for data analysis. In 1994, over 2,000 emergency department visits occurred for asthma in the survey hospital area. The same year, 900 adult patients were hospitalized with asthma as the principal diagnosis, and total charges for inpatient care exceeded $5.6 million. In 1995, 832 hospitalizations and 2,111 emergency department visits occurred. In 1996, 857 adults were admitted for asthma and 2,310 were seen in the emergency department.

In addition, practice patterns of 46 physicians surveyed prior to beginning the asthma initiative revealed considerable variation, including inpatient care (use and frequency of nebulized medications; use of

ASTHMA'S IMPACT ON U.S. HEALTHCARE

In the United States, the total prevalence of asthma has increased substantially, affecting 14.6 million individuals in 1994. Nationally, the overall costs for asthma in 1990 exceeded $6.2 billion. Most patients have reversible symptoms that respond well to outpatient management. Annually, however, asthma accounts for nearly 2 million emergency department visits and more than 450,000 hospitalizations with an average length of stay of five days. The number of physician office visits for asthma has also increased rapidly since 1990.

Based on data from the Centers for Disease Control and Prevention, prevalence rates of self-reported asthma increased 42% from 1982 through 1992, from 34.7 per 1,000 to 49.4 per 1,000. The overall death rate due to asthma increased 62 percent from 1982 through 1991, from 3,154 deaths to 5,106 deaths. A disproportionate increase has occurred in the African-American population. A study conducted in Chicago noted that between 1968 and 1991, asthma mortality did not significantly change for whites but increased 337% among African Americans. Age-adjusted death rates for asthma are three times higher in black males than in white males and nearly three times higher in black females than in white females.

From *Journal of Nursing Care Quality*, Vol. 12:6, 1998

Doctor's Name ____________________

Doctor's Phone Number ____________

Asthma Zones

My personal best peak flow

Zone	My Peak Flow Range
GREEN (Over 80%)	____________
YELLOW (50-80%)	____________
RED (Below 50%)	____________

My medicines:

Name	How Much	How Often

Courtesy of Advocate Health Care, Oak Brook, Illinois.

- If you are having any of your symptoms of asthma use your peak flow meter to check your peak flow number.
- Write your number down and note if you are in the Green, Yellow or Red zone.
- Take 2 puffs of your short-acting beta-agonist inhaler ________ (insert name of short-acting beta-agonist here).
- Follow the instructions below.

If You Are In the RED Zone:

- **Call your doctor immediately.** Tell your doctor you are in the Red Zone.
- Your doctor will tell you where to go to be treated.
- Take another 2-4 puffs of (insert name of short-acting beta-agonist).
- Recheck your peak flow.
- **If your peak flow is still below 50%, go to the Emergency Room.**

And begin________ / _______ mg (your corticosteriod medicine)

If You Are In The YELLOW Zone:

- Take 2-4 puffs of ____________ (insert name of short-acting beta-agonist) every 20 minutes for 2 doses.
- Recheck your peak flow after each treatment.
- Take 4 puffs of ______________(insert name of beta-agonist) every hour.

Begin____________ / _______mg (your corticosteroid medicine)

- Call your doctor if your symptoms and peak flow do not improve in 2 hours.

steroids) and outpatient care (use of peak flow monitoring and classification of asthma).

Based on these findings, the health system believed that there were opportunities to improve patient care. The Adult Asthma Clinical Improvement Team was established to address these needs. The interdisciplinary team included individuals from medicine (including specialists in allergy and immunology, emergency medicine, family practice, internal medicine, and pulmonology), nursing, pharmacy, respiratory care and administration. Drawing heavily upon the national and international asthma guidelines, the team identified four major goals:

1. Improve management of adult asthma patients in outpatient settings, including physician prescribing practices.

2. Enhance partnership between patients and health care providers to improve patients self-management skills and use of medical resources.

3. Improve identification and care of the most severe asthma patients.

4. Adopt and implement system-wide inpatient and emergency department care pathways.

Outpatient Management

A variety of clinical products was developed including Algorithms for Home Management of Acute Exacerbation of Asthma in Adults, Diagnosis of Asthma by Primary Care Physicians and Exercise-Induced Asthma; an Asthma Severity Classification; and an Environmental Assessment for Primary Care. Specialist referral criteria were developed to address the identification and referral of patients with the most severe asthma.

Hospital Management

Emergency department and inpatient care pathways were developed to further improve hospital-based care. These pathways standardized patient care and included medical management and education.

Patient Education

The team identified the need to establish a partnership between patients and health care providers. To accomplish this goal, patients needed to be empowered through education to take a more active role in their care. The team first identified components to be included in patient education materials and surveyed existing materials. Because no single educational piece met the needs identified, the team developed patient education materials using two formats: a patient education brochure and a wallet card.

The brochure provided general goals for controlling asthma. It then elaborated on three aspects of asthma management: an everyday treatment, medications and how to handle an acute asthma episode. The brochure included checklists (lists of asthma triggers, early asthma symptoms) and write-in sections (personal best peak flow, medications).

A wallet card summarized critical information contained in the brochure and made that information immediately accessible to patients. The card includes information about medications and peak flows as well as a treatment plan for managing asthma symptoms.

The team identified three pilot sites to test both the products and the process of implementation. Implementation teams were formed at each site. These teams planned and delivered the site rollout, including communication, physician and staff education, and implementation of the protocol.

Measurement Plan

The adult asthma team developed a measurement plan including four primary areas: clinical outcomes, functional status, patient satisfaction and resource utilization. When possible, the team used data that were retrievable from existing databases rather than creating additional data collection tools. Unfortunately, physician offices tended to be less automated than hospitals. To measure functional status, patient satisfaction and the important process variables of medication use and peak flow meter access, a patient questionnaire was developed. The team decided to administer the questionnaire to adult patients with asthma when they were seen in the physician's office for any reason.

As part of the evaluation, data were collected from patients, physicians and other clinicians. In addition, patient functional status was measured. Physicians and other clinicians were very pleased with the protocol. A formal evaluation revealed that physicians were most appreciative of the patient education materials. Other clinicians also found the patient education materials to be helpful.

Patients completed a quality of life survey at the time they were seen by the physician. Preliminary results reveal a population greatly affected by their disease. Patients will be asked to complete the survey three and 12 months after their initial treatment.

Lessons Learned

Talented clinicians, including physicians and other associates, were willing to participate in this clinical process improvement project without financial compensation. The team has learned a great deal together.

Patti Ludwig-Beymer, RN, PhD, is director of care management at Advocate Health Care, Oak Brook, Ill.; Sue Peterson, RN, BS, is team leader, quality assurance, Trinity Hospital, Chicago; Colleen Gorman, RN, MA, is associate administrator, Advocate Medical Group, Park Ridge, Ill.

Each site needed to have autonomy to make the program work in its environment. For example, in some settings, respiratory care practitioners took the lead in providing education to physician office staff and patients. In other sites, registered nurses took ownership of this activity. In some emergency departments, the physician initiated the pathway. In others, the nurse initiated the pathway. In all situations, however, the need for collaboration in the delivery of care was emphasized.

However, some functions were better centralized. For example, pharmaceutical companies were eager to partner with the health system in clinical improvement projects. Rather than negotiate with pharmaceutical companies at individual sites, this was handled centrally. Successful partnerships resulted in the funding of Food for Learning at lunches, honorariums for physician educators, peak flow meters and placebo inhalers for training, and an unrestricted educational grant for the printing of materials and implementation of the measurement plan. In addition, ongoing support for the clinical improvement teams, including coaching, facilitation, database management, data analysis, and project management, was provided centrally.

Another important lesson learned from this project surrounds the challenges of implementing clinical improvements across the continuum. To truly improve care, clinical improvement activities must take place in all clinical settings, not only in hospitals. The hospitals within the system had a history of using continuous quality improvement techniques since 1990. This groundwork, along with the ability to communicate centrally, made effecting change within hospitals easy compared with implementing change in physician offices. Implementation in physician offices, on the other hand, required extensive resources. In addition, many primary care physician offices were not designed with space and personnel to provide in-depth education to patients with chronic diseases such as asthma. This is an issue that requires a long-term approach for resolution.

Asthma product	**Number and % who have used the product**	**Number and % who found the product helpful (of those who used the product)**	**Number and % who found this to be the most helpful product**
Patient education brochure	13 (81%)	11 (85%)	6 (38%)
Wallet card	11 (69%)	7 (64%)	5 (31%)
Asthma diagnosis algorithm	10 (63%)	7 (70%)	
Asthma classification scale	13 (81%)	10 (77%)	1 (6%)
Environmental assessment	9 (56%)	8 (89%)	
Exercise-induced algorithm	8 (50%)	7 (88%)	
Chronic mild algorithm	11 (69%)	9 (82%)	
Medication algorithm	10 (63%)	8 (80%)	
Referral criteria	5 (31%)	4 (80%)	
Asthma flow sheet	12 (75%)	11 (92%)	2 (13%)
Acute exacerbation algorithm	10 (63%)	9 (90%)	1 (6%)

Number and % of physicians who report using guidelines has changed the way they care for patients: 8 (50%)

Reported ways in which care has changed (open-ended question)

- Use peak flows more often
- Take a more standardized approach
- Earlier use of home management and patient initiated PO steroids
- Spend more time teaching

Improving Care at the End of Life

Healthcare providers need to address not only dying patients' pain and comfort needs but also the way in which services are organized and delivered.

Americans' longer lives, and longer deaths, are combining with cost and quality concerns to force healthcare providers to face inadequacies in end-of-life care. Most quality improvement projects in the field are relatively new, but experts already have mapped priorities and goals to help providers move forward.

Demography drives some of this attention. When the century opened, Americans' life expectancy at birth was 50 years. Now, 73% of deaths are among people at least 65 years old, and 24% of deaths are among those at least 85 years old, according to an end-of-life committee of the Institute of Medicine. Modern medicine not only has granted more people an old age, but it also has slowed the process of dying. "Medical treatments can control pneumonia, kidney failure and other immediate causes of death that accompany cancer, heart disease and other 'slow killers,'" which are the leading causes of death, the IOM panel notes. The "end of life" may last several years. Some experts say end-of-life care initiatives not only should reach patients in their final few months, but also should concern anyone with a progressive, incurable, fatal illness.

Trajectories of Dying for Colon Cancer and Congestive Heart Failure

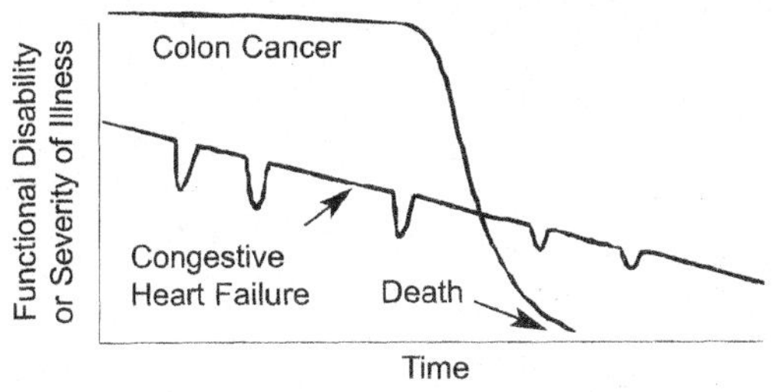

Source: Center to Improve Care of the Dying

As baby boomers and their parents age, problems in end-of-life care are increasingly well documented, from undertreated pain to unwanted or futile treatments to prolong life. "One of the few large studies to look at a range of diagnoses ... in seriously ill hospitalized patients found severe pain reported by about 40% of family members of conscious patients," reports the IOM committee. At the same time, anywhere from 10% to 50% of various patient populations receive care that violates their preferences, often in the form of costly emergency room visits or intensive care.

More hospice referrals are not a perfect solution. For most end-of-life patients, a mix of curative and comfort care, rather than palliative care alone, is most effective for controlling symptoms and maintaining patients' spirits. To receive Medicare's hospice benefit, a patient must be expected to die within six months, and the patient must forgo curative therapies. Most deaths are in hospitals — 57% in 1992 — and hospices served only 17% of those who died in 1995.

Thus providers have turned to other projects — case management, home care, support services and pain control — to minimize patients' discomfort when curative steps alone no longer are appropriate.

From *The Quality Letter for Healthcare Leaders*, Vol. 10:10, 1998

“Dying does not have to be agonizing. Physical suffering can *always* be alleviated. People need not die alone,” palliative care expert Ira Byock, M.D., writes in his book *Dying Well.* “When people are relatively comfortable and know that they are not going to be abandoned, they frequently find ways to strengthen bonds with people they love and to create profound meaning in their final passage.”

“Dying does not have to be agonizing. Physical suffering can *always* be alleviated. People need not die alone.”

Ira Byock, M.D.
Dying Well

Planning Improvement Projects

Providers can make rapid improvement in several areas of end-of-life care, including pain and symptom relief; advance care planning; support of patient and family efforts to make the end of life meaningful; and, perhaps more difficult, continuity among a patient’s care providers.

The Institute for Healthcare Improvement, a Boston-based nonprofit organization, outlined best practices and improvement goals in those four areas. For example, IHI teams pushed providers to reduce by 50% the number of patients who report pain greater than 5 on a 0-to-10 scale. The institute’s QI team recommended the use of advance care planning so that CPR is attempted at death for no more than 3% of patients known to be in their last phase of life. *(See charts, p. 226-27.)*

Institutionalizing systems for high-quality end-of-life care demands changes not only in practices but also in provider and patient attitudes toward pain and dying. That may require “a 10-year plan,” says Marjorie Ginsburg, executive director of Sacramento (Calif.) Healthcare Decisions, a nonprofit organization that led a community collaborative project called “Extreme Care, Humane Options.” Making smaller changes that improve some aspects of care, on the other hand, can be done immediately.

Controlling Symptoms

Undertreatment of pain is a problem of attitudes, not pharmacology, says Joanne Lynn, M.D., director of the Center to Improve Care of the Dying at The George Washington University Medical Center, Washington, D.C., and president of Americans for Better Care of the Dying, a not-for-profit advocacy group. Clinicians and patients often assume agony is inevitable near death or consider it unimportant while they pursue a cure. Misplaced caution about opioid addiction leaves many patients in too much pain to seek closure as they die. By educating clinicians and patients and instituting protocols for routine pain assessment and treatment, providers can vastly improve care, and at a low cost.

“If you treat pain quickly, it is much less likely to escalate out of control. If you leave it, it may escalate to the point that it will damage the nervous system and lead to intractable pain,” notes Frank D. Ferris, M.D., coordinator of inpatient and research services at the Temmy Latner Centre for Palliative Care at Toronto’s Mount Sinai Hospital. Ferris leads the development of Canada’s national palliative care standard through the Ottawa-based Canadian Palliative Care Association.

The first step is to add pain assessment to the list of vital signs regularly tracked. Attention to pain can yield results fast: In Madison, Wis., St. Mary's Hospital asked nurses on a medical-surgical unit to measure all patients' pain levels and kept the project in the forefront with written information, staff meetings and posted reminders. Within 16 weeks, the percentage of patients who were asked whether their pain level was acceptable rose from 5% to 50%, and the percentage who had their pain treated promptly rose from 60% to 100%.

Franciscan Health Systems, Tacoma, Wash., has trained volunteers to call patients in its end-of-life care program every few weeks. The calls find some patients with pain that they had not planned to report. The project coordinator notifies primary care physicians, who can prescribe additional medication. The portion of patients rating their pain control as excellent rose from 50% of those monitored to 80%.

Some providers give outpatients the tools to prevent break-through pain. In Fort Myers, Fla., Hope Hospice pre-prescribes "comfort care kits" with single doses of drugs for pain or dyspnea *(see contents at right)*. When patients are in distress, they or their family members call the hospice for coaching on administering the appropriate medication; a nurse follows up immediately with a visit. Most patients don't use the kits, but they use fewer emergency services in part because they feel better knowing the drugs are available, says Samira Beckwith, Hope's CEO.

Beyond pain, other undertreated symptoms include shortness of breath, loss of appetite, nausea, bowel problems, pressure sores, itching, swelling, fatigue, confusion, anxiety, depression and unresolved psychological problems.

In Wilkes-Barre, Pa., Wyoming Valley Health System reduced dyspnea and anxiety along with pain. Its end-of-life team developed standing physician orders and instructions for certain medications corresponding to specific patient-reported pain levels, shortness of breath and anxiety. Clinicians also tracked dosing around the clock to minimize break-through pain. The project reduced patients' average time in pain from 53 minutes to 12 minutes; the average time in dyspnea from 48 minutes to 33 minutes; and the average duration of anxiety from 46 minutes to 28 minutes. The number of pain events dropped from about seven per patient to one. Dyspnea events dropped from five to four; anxiety from five to three.

Palliative care should complement all other care, whenever it is needed — "even before we know the diagnosis," adds Ferris, a faculty scholar with the Open Society Institute's Project on Death in America. Clinicians and payers have drawn "a line in the sand" between cure and comfort. "We need to move ... [toward] mixed management," he says. Palliative care can even boost curative therapies by fostering the

COMFORT CARE AT HOME

Hope Hospice, Fort Meyers, Fla., includes the following single-dose items in its comfort care kits for patients with cardiac disease:

- Nitroglycerin 0.4 mg (1 bottle)
- Morphine 10mg/5cc UD (2)
- Morphine inject 10 mg (2)
- Lasix 40 mg (4)
- Lasix 100 mg IV (2)
- Lorazepam 0.5 mg (5)

Other items, less frequently used, include naproxen, sucralfate, compazine and pentobarbital suppositories. The drugs are packed in a sealed bag. Hope is able to reuse unopened bags for other patients, but not all states allow drugs to be reused.

patient's energy and will, Ferris notes. "Pain and stress may themselves shorten people's lives and interfere with [curative] therapy."

Supporting the Patient and Family in Transition

Comprehensive palliative care does more than treat symptoms. By controlling pain and symptoms, healthcare providers let the patient attend to other dimensions of dying, Byock notes. Providers should support patients, and their families, in this work.

"Palliative care refers to the comprehensive management of the physical, psychological, social, spiritual and existential needs of patients," say the "Precepts of Palliative Care" developed through the Last Acts Campaign of the Robert Wood Johnson Foundation, Princeton, N.J., a major funder of end-of-life care improvement projects. "Palliative care ... helps the dying patient who wishes to address issues of life completion and life closure."

A palliative care index adopted by the Veterans Administration requires depression screening and treatment, and it directs hospital staff to offer psychosocial support or guidance to the patient and family or caregivers.

Ferris says palliative care providers should offer support with economic and housing issues; advance directives, living wills and other legal issues; and spiritual closure: Patients may want help to arrange rituals, resolve family issues, pass on gifts or explore feelings about dying and meaning.

In palliative care, the unit of care is the patient plus loved ones and caregivers. Providers should offer bereavement support, respite care and other help to the families, both before and after their loved one dies, says Joan Teno, M.D., associate professor of community health at Brown University's Center for Gerontology in Health Care Research, Providence, R.I. Like the physician, family members provide important components of care, Teno says. "We need to address their concerns."

PRECEPTS OF PALLIATIVE CARE

Excerpts from Last Acts Campaign of the Robert Wood Johnson Foundation

Palliative care refers to the comprehensive management of the physical, psychological, social, spiritual and existential needs of patients. ...

The goal of palliative care is to achieve the best possible quality of life through relief of suffering, control of symptoms and restoration of functional capacity while remaining sensitive to personal, cultural and religious values, beliefs and practices.

Palliative care can be complementary to other therapies that are available and appropriate to the identified goals of care. The intensity and range of palliative interventions may increase as illness progresses.

Palliative care ... helps the dying patient who wishes to address issues of life completion and life closure.

Palliative care has become an area of special expertise within medicine, nursing, social work, pharmacy, chaplaincy and other disciplines. However, advances in palliative care have not yet been integrated effectively into standard clinical practice.

The Precepts of Palliative Care set qualitative standards in five areas:

- Respecting patient goals, preferences and choices;
- Comprehensive caring;
- Utilizing the strengths of interdisciplinary resources;
- Acknowledging and addressing caregiver concerns; and
- Building systems and mechanisms of support.

Excerpt from the policy of Community Memorial Hospital, Menomonee Falls, Wis.

Palliative care affirms life and regards dying as a normal process. It neither hastens nor postpones death, but provides support and comfort to both terminally ill patients and their family ... By integrating psychological and spiritual aspects of patient care, it offers a support system to help patients live as actively as possible until death. It is focused on maintaining the personal dignity and self respect of the patient based on the person's own goals.

Psychosocial support that treats death as more than a medical event need not be exotic or expensive. It may be as simple as staying in touch with a network of community religious leaders or finding other ways to bring people together. Mercy Health Partners' hospital in Wilkes-Barre, Pa., uses volunteers to improve support for dying patients who have few family members nearby. Mercy's pastoral and hospice staff teaches volunteers about the dying process and train them in listening and communicating about spiritual needs. Every month, the volunteers make about 130 visits to 25 or so patients identified by hospital staff. They may simply deliver a glass of water or give a family member time to go home for a shower, but feedback from patients and families has been uniformly favorable, says Joanne Ennis, director of pastoral care. "We saw a need to bring in people who aren't in a hurry and can talk to patients, listen, pray with them or sit quietly. Their job is not to do for but to be with."

Managed care may have advantages for providing psychosocial support, says Rick Levine, president of Levine Healthcare, Boulder, Colo., a managed care consulting firm. At Kaiser Permanente of Colorado, a clinic brings enrollees older than 65 together in groups of 15 or 20 for a monthly, 90-minute meeting with their primary physician and other clinicians to discuss topics such as making advance directives, maintaining health or managing medications. Doctors can provide more information than in individual patient sessions, although one-on-one time is offered too, says Kathleen Bohland, spokesperson for the Denver-based plan. Discussion time "allows patients to learn more about their doctor and the doctor to learn more about the patients' personal lives," she notes. "It is a social thing for seniors because a lot of them live alone and don't have [much] social interaction," Bohland notes. Adds Levine, "In a fee-for-service system, no one would ever coordinate that."

Physicians can identify patients for whom advance care planning — along with the gamut of palliative services — is appropriate by asking themselves, "Would I be surprised if this patient died in the next year?"

Advance Care Planning

By some definitions, palliative care also includes making advance plans for care during foreseeable medical crises. Ironically, advance care planning usually begins too late. By the time a doctor can predict accurately how much time is left, patients usually are too close to death to attend to postponed wishes. Physicians can identify patients for whom advance care planning is appropriate — along with the gamut of palliative services — by asking themselves, "Would I be surprised if this patient died in the next year?" Caregivers can use crises that patients survive to introduce advance care planning discussions, perhaps saying, "It went well this time, but if things didn't go so well at some point in the future, what would be important to you?"

Again, advance care planning takes time because it concerns attitudes and expectations, says Susan Fox Buchanan, executive director of Colorado Collective for Medical Decisions, Denver. The collective initiated an educational dialogue among providers, payers and the public about end-of-life priorities and drafted guidelines to reflect community and professional values.

"Choosing palliative care as a treatment goal does not mean that the patient is going to be abandoned or neglected, or that we're going to give up caring," Buchanan says. "Even when it's not possible to cure, palliative care combines aggressive care with the emotional, comfort-oriented dimension. That can relieve a huge amount of stress for the patient and family and let them think about things like closure.

"Administering CPR to a frail, elderly, demented patient just so the patient has to die again of the same mortal disease is not sharing the breath of life," she adds. "A lot is done out of medical momentum, legal defensiveness, emotional discomfort" and fear of judgment.

Advance directives such as living wills and "do not resuscitate" orders — or, equally, the patient's refusal of a DNR order — may be products of advance care planning, but they are the tip of the iceberg. Good advance care planning helps patients to understand their prognoses and options, and it gives patients and families opportunities to formulate and reflect on important goals and plans. It also encompasses contingency planning to ensure that the patient's preferences are honored.

"If someone with chronic lung disease says, 'I do not want to go on a ventilator,' we'll write that on a chart," Teno says. That is a start, but it is not planning. The patient and family need to know what to do if respiratory distress strikes at home in the middle of the night. "If you don't have a plan in place, the patient is at risk of [enduring] terrible symptoms or calling 911" when planning, family education and available drugs could allow the patient to be treated at home. Planning includes documenting discussions and making sure those documents will be accessible during emergencies.

Fear of unwanted life-prolonging treatment, along with fear of untreated pain, underlies support for assisted suicide. In Oregon, where these suicides are legal, providers have engaged in various initiatives to reduce the demand by improving advance care planning and palliation.

VA ADDS ACCOUNTABILITIES FOR PALLIATIVE CARE

In 1997, the Department of Veterans Affairs incorporated a palliative care index in the performance agreements of its regional directors. Within three months, the portion of patients whose charts met the standard had risen from 52% to 67%. The VA cautions that the baseline data reflect only about 2,000 charts, but the agency's initiative already won recognition from Americans for Better Care of the Dying. The VA initiative began in late 1997 with patients with various cancers, congestive heart failure and chronic obstructive pulmonary disease. If dying patients are not enrolled in hospice or home-based care programs, their charts are reviewed in light of seven questions:

- Did care providers discuss the patient's or family's preferences regarding resuscitation?
- Have needs for nutrition and hydration been assessed?
- Did appropriate staff — such as the attending physician, a psychiatrist, social worker, nurse or chaplain — offer psychosocial support or guidance to the patient, family and other caregivers?
- For those discharged to their homes, were both patient and caregivers given instruction in post-hospital care and information about respite care and other support?
- Was the patient assessed for pain and, where needed, a plan for pain management made?
- Was the patient assessed for shortness of breath and, where needed, a treatment plan made?
- Was the patient assessed for depression and, where needed, a treatment plan made?

"We figured that if we did all those things well, we would have made a hell of a dent," says Debby Walder, performance improvement facilitator in the VA's Office of Performance and Quality. At a minimum, the network directors' negotiated performance agreements aim for 95% success, or at least good progress toward that threshold. While the VA would like to include more diagnostic groups and patients still receiving curative care, "you have to start somewhere," Walder says.

Oregon boasts the nation's lowest rate of deaths in hospitals. In 1996, only 31% of Oregonian deaths occurred in acute-care hospitals. Hospice referrals are rising, and 29% of Oregonians die with hospice support, compared with 17% nationally. Oregon leads in annual per capita use of morphine, and prescriptions rose by 70% from 1994 through 1996.

A tool that has helped in Oregon is the Physician Orders for Life-Sustaining Treatment, a uniform advance care planning tool that is familiar to everyone from EMS drivers to nursing home staff to hospital personnel. The form was developed and tested over five years by a task force convened by the Center for Ethics in Health Care, Oregon Health Sciences University, Portland, which distributes the forms to physicians. A bright pink wallet card notifies emergency medical personnel of the existence of the POLST and summarizes the patient's preferences on resuscitation, antibiotics, provision of fluids and nutrition and other interventions.

Preliminary data show the POLST is rarely ignored, says Susan W. Tolle, M.D., director of the university ethics center. While the form spares patients unwanted treatments, it is not a barrier to palliation. "It appears that physicians who consider the POLST make a comfort care plan," Tolle says.

Nuance in communication is crucial to advance care planning. Patients may cling to the hope of treatments they don't really want unless they hear options that are consistent with their values. For example, rather than asking, "Do you want everything done?" physicians might ask, "Do you want everything done to try to get you home?" or "What is most important to you at this time?"

"We need a new definition of what 'doing something' means," Colorado's Buchanan says. "Doing something may mean an action that is oriented toward spiritual healing as a person is dying. If we become more attuned to the healing that happens in the course of dying we might be less fearful and less driven."

The thought is seconded by Gail Gazelle, M.D., who chairs the end-of-life care initiative at Boston's Harvard Vanguard Medical Associates, a large group practice within Harvard Pilgrim Health Care. "We're taught to cure and not take away hope, [but] I think physicians get confused about what 'hope' means in dying," Gazelle says. At life's end, "hope means death with dignity, living life to the fullest, spending

HELPING PATIENTS SET PRIORITIES

Gundersen Lutheran, a medical center in LaCrosse, Wis., uses the following questions as part of its holistic healthcare planning process. The questions, usually asked in a conversation between a patient and a social worker or other care planner, typically take about half an hour.

1. Maintaining or fulfilling what activities or experiences are most important for you to feel your life has quality or for you to live well? (What makes you happy?)

2. What fears or worries do you have about your illness or medical care?

3. If you have to choose between living longer and quality of life, how would you approach this balance?

4. Are there any special events/activities that you are looking forward to?

5. What needs or services would you like to discuss?

6. Do you want information about anything related to your present or future care?

7. What sustains you when you face serious challenges in life?

8. Do you have any religious or spiritual beliefs that are important to you?

9. In what way do you feel you could make this time especially meaningful to you?

10. What do you hope most for those closest to you?

time with loved ones, resolving conflicts, finishing the business of life—without undue suffering."

Continuity of Care

Advance care planning facilitates continuity of care among providers. It can prevent disorienting transfers into the care of unfamiliar providers, especially in the last days of life. For St. Thomas Hospital, Nashville, Tenn., the $500 extra per day it costs to keep patients in intensive care is worthwhile if it improves care for the patient and family: The hospital mandates that no ICU patient who is expected to die within 48 hours be moved out of the unit.

Continuity of care means that, when patients have a crisis, "whatever time of day it is, whatever happens, there will be someone on the other end of the line who knows about them and understands what is happening," says Byock, who heads the Missoula (Mont.) Demonstration Project, The Quality of Life's End. "If as a system we can't provide that level of confidence and a crisis plan that is responsive to people's needs, we've failed in the mission of serving patients and families." Not only is the standard reasonable, he adds, but it is the norm for postoperative patients who are expected to recover.

"If you sit down with a woman who is newly diagnosed as pregnant, you can say, 'We know how to deal with this. You will be monitored well; we'll customize some aspects of care.' We need to be able to have that kind of conversation with someone who is dying."

Joanne Lynn, M.D.
Center to Improve Care of the

Varied sectors of healthcare — nursing homes, hospices, skilled nursing facilities and hospitals — "don't have to be fully integrated to develop a set of protocols and formal and informal agreements to create a system that is seamless from the patient and family's point of view," Byock maintains.

Integrated managed care organizations have an advantage. "It's our own hospital, our own medical group, home health agency and hospice," says Richard D. Della Penna, M.D., Kaiser Permanente Southern California's coordinator of home health, continuing care and hospice services. "That allows better coordination of services and potentially better communications and a more cohesive philosophy of care. If you're networking and contracting with 160 agencies and hospitals, it's hard to have a common purpose."

Throughout Kaiser San Diego, Della Penna says, pain is assessed as a fifth vital sign. The organization's hospice benefit includes physician home visits every few weeks and medicines to treat secondary diagnoses. Patients within two or three days of death may remain in the hospital if they wish rather than being transferred to hospice care or a nursing home.

Assessing Quality of Care

Many crucial aspects of end-of-life care lend themselves to measurement, including patients' pain levels, sites of death, transfers shortly before death and rates of advance care planning. After-death surrogate surveys can gather open-ended suggestions for further improvement, and they can be used to check on the status and needs of bereaved family members.

When Harvard Pilgrim Health Care conducted focus groups of family members who had experienced a recent death, staff feared the study would upset family members. "We found just the opposite," says Susan Block, M.D., an internist and psychiatrist in the managed care organization. "They welcomed the opportunity to talk even though it was hard and sad. They appreciated that the organization wanted to use their experience to improve care. There was a generosity among these family members that was really moving. We ought to take advantage of their willingness to be partners with us."

Costs and Benefits

The budgetary impact of end-of-life care quality improvements is unclear, both systemwide and for single institutions. Few initiatives have gone far enough to measure financial benefits or tradeoffs. Experts say savings is not the point, however. Comprehensive palliative care advance planning and coordination are good medicine. It is easy to improve patient satisfaction in this area, and quality initiatives pay off, too, in professional morale and longevity.

"Staff time and [sympathy for the] anguish of patients are also a resource," says Buchanan, of the Colorado collective. "Staff time can be translated into money, but there is [also] a substantial ripple effect in terms of burnout, [low] morale and neglect of other patients."

Charted Territory

As modern healthcare takes more people into extreme old age, the challenges of extended end-of-life care will test almost every sector of healthcare. The current surge of interest in the field is producing replicable guidelines and tools that providers can use without waiting for further research. Above all, improving end-of-life care requires "a decision not to tolerate the usual ways," says Lynn.

Several other branches of medicine offer models. Tomorrow's goals in end-of-life care are today's norms in obstetrics and gynecology, Lynn says. "If you sit down with a woman who is newly diagnosed as pregnant, you can say, 'We know how to deal with this. You will be monitored well; we'll customize some aspects of care.'" Providers will include the whole family and address psychosocial features of what is not just a medical event but a major life transition. "We need to be able to have that kind of conversation with someone who is dying."

Byock agrees. He cites the National Hospice Organization's framework of treating symptoms, preventing foreseeable problems, and promoting opportunities for the individual and family to grow — that is, to grow in their sense of self, relationships, perception of meaning and readiness to die. "People say, that's more than medicine," Byock says. "I say, it is not: It's exactly what medicine is. It's just not the current internal medicine approach. But it's [typical] in pediatrics."

Pediatrics treats the individual and family as the unit of care. In pedi-

For more information...

Susan Fox Buchanan
Colorado Collective for Medical Decisions
ccmdco@aol.com

Center to Improve Care of the Dying
(202)467-2222
www.gwu.edu/~cicd/

Joanne Ennis
Mercy Hospital
(717)826-3634

Frank Ferris, M.D.
University of Toronto
(416)586-4800 ext 6772
frank.ferris@utoronto.ca

Marjorie Ginsburg
Sacramento Healthcare Decisions
(916)484-2485, shd@quiknet.com
www.ahd.org/SHD

Gail Gazelle, M.D.
Harvard Vanguard Medical Associates
ggazelle1@bics.bwh.harvard.edu

Institute for Healthcare Improvement
(617)754-4800, www.ihi.org

Rick Levine
Levine Healthcare Inc.
rhlevine@aol.com

Missoula Demonstration Project, The Quality of Life's End
(406)728-1613

Oregon Health Sciences University
Center for Ethics in Health Care
(503)494-4466,
www.ohsu.edu/ethics

Robert Wood Johnson Foundation
Last Acts Campaign
(609)452-8701, www.lastacts.org
Promoting Excellence in End-of-Life Care
www.dyingwell.org
Community/State Partnerships to Improve End-of-Life Care
(816)842-7110, www.midbio.org

Joan Teno, M.D.
Brown University
joan_teno@brown.edu

Debby Walder
Department of Veterans Affairs
debby.walder@mail.va.gov

atrics, "robust screening and anticipatory guidance" are routine, Byock notes. And like cutting-edge end-of-life care, pediatrics attends to the quality of the patient's significant relationships and personal development in what is a "turbulent but rich time of life." End-of-life care can do the same.

"This isn't rocket science," adds Ginsburg, of Sacramento. "It doesn't take a genius. It does take the commitment and involvement of the key leaders. Just take it one step at time, and don't be discouraged by the length of time it takes to begin seeing real changes. And really celebrate any change that does occur."

Targeting Best Practices in End-of-Life Care

To accelerate improvement in care for dying patients, the Institute for Healthcare Improvement convened a faculty of experts to sort out best practices and clearly chart the practical changes likely to have the greatest immediate impact on care.

For the collaborative project that ended in July 1998, IHI outlined standards and progress goals in four areas: pain and symptom relief; advance care planning; support for patient and family efforts to make the end of life meaningful; and continuity of care. These best practices and target measures appear on pages 226-227.

The chart of improvements relies on existing knowledge and emphasizes changes that will show a measurable impact quickly. It is not a compendium of everything that should happen in end-of-life care, notes Andrea Kabcenell, director of the collaborative and a senior research associate at Cornell College of Human Ecology, Ithaca, N.Y. Achieving goals set on the IHI chart may well require changes in institutional culture, Kabcenell says. Maintaining improvements certainly will. The most successful projects in the 1997-98 collaborative were those with the most specific goals, she adds.

IHI enrolled 47 hospitals, hospices and managed care organizations in the first collaborative, including for-profit and nonprofit institutions, public and private hospitals, big and small hospices, and a home care agency.

For more information, contact Andrea Kabcenell, R.N., M.P.H., at aik2@cornell.edu, or the Institute for Healthcare Improvement, (617)754-4800.

Measuring Patients' Pain Levels

Improving pain control starts with assessing patients' levels of discomfort. Healthcare providers in the Institute for Healthcare Improvement's end-of-life collaborative use numerical, descriptive or color-based charts to capture patients' perceptions of their pain *(below left)*. Several collaborative participants noted that patients have begun using the 1-to-10 scale on their own to assess their dyspnea, nausea and overall mood.

Hampered by some demented patients' inability to communicate and by the stoicism with which many cancer patients accepted their pain, On Lok Senior Health Services, San Francisco, developed a non-verbal cue assessment tool to help staff estimate patients' pain *(below right)*. There is no criteria for care to be given based on point totals, but values give staff a better idea of patients' overall comfort level.

Patients' Pain Intensity Scales

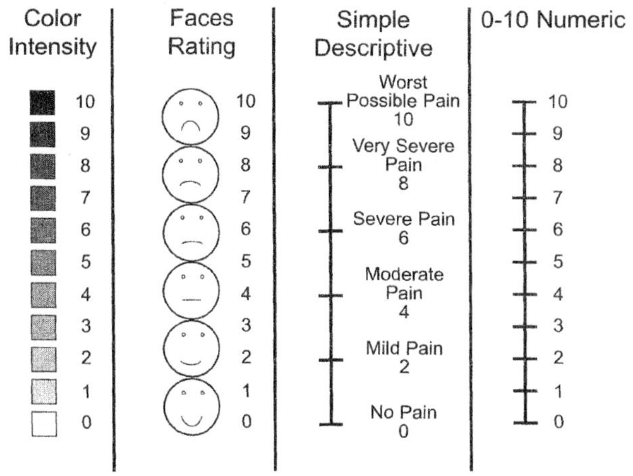

Staff Assessment Tool

Observation	Criteria	Points
Emotion	Smiling	0
	Anxious/Irritable	1
	Almost in tears	2
Movement	None	0
	Restless, slow decreased movement	1
	Immobile, afraid to move	2
Verbal Cues	States no pain	0
	Whining, whimpering, moaning	1
	Screaming, crying out	2
Facial Cues	Relaxed, calm expression	0
	Drawn around mouth and eyes	1
	Facial frowning, wincing	2
Positioning/Guarding	Relaxed body	0
	Guarding/Tense	1
	Fetal position, jumped when touched	2

Support of Family and of Meaningfulness

Current	Best Practices	Optimum Practice	Proposed Targets (for your population)
• Families are excluded or ignored, granted only the role of veto in care planning. • Families do not know prognosis, uncertainties, desirable timing of behaviors, who to turn to for counsel, or what is reasonably expected of them. • Many opportunities to complete relationships (human or transcendent) are not taken. • Many patients or families do not have an opportunity to attend to religious/spiritual issues or meaningful rituals. • Most families have no follow-up in bereavement by staff. • Many dissatisfied or guilt-ridden families are never heard, and some have lives blighted by their experience. • Families and patients have little practice at leave-taking.	• Care in hospice routinely includes family and spiritual concerns. • Hospice and home care agencies sometimes provide brochures and counseling about what to expect and how one might respond. • Hospice and some individual programs routinely follow families in bereavement, providing or referring to services as appropriate. • Some care providers insist upon enabling family cohesion and rearrangement, spiritual search for meaning and culturally meaningful rituals. • Some care settings help patients and families "rehearse" for dying by practicing leave-taking and imagining the time after.	• Center the experience in terms of spirituality and meaning, rather than medical and physiological issues. • Make human relationships and spiritual issues the central concern and, thus, professional caregiver habits are always subservient. • Use episodes of serious illness as "dress rehearsals" for eventual death. • Create rituals that mark stages and ensure reassurance. • Always follow up with family — explain, reassure, counsel. • Learn how to provide care that is death-accepting/enhancing, life-prolonging and physiology-restoring.	1. Have >90% of families report that they would want to be cared for in this way if ever they were similarly sick. 2. Have >90% of families report that they cannot recall: • a time when they were kept "in the dark" • a cruel or uncaring remark from a caregiver • a "put down" of their beliefs, practices or views. 3. All bereaved families get at least one follow-up call from a doctor or nurse who can answer "medical" questions and check for seriously dysfunctional grief. 4. Double the rate at which patients and families agree that "the last few weeks or months were especially meangful." 5. For chronic organ system failure, develop a care pattern in which 80% of staff and of patients/families feel that staff are pleased and supportive of survival and also supportive of a good dying. 6. Have >90% of families report that: • their loved one was given tender care • their emotional state was noticed and responded to • caregiver said or did something especially meaningful.

Advance Care Planning

Current	Best Practices	aOptimum Practice	Proposed Targets (for your population)
• Very little attention is paid to overall future course — not discussed, articulated, planned for. • Most people are not even asked to name a surrogate, even when it is quite unclear. • Among persons who have very little chance of surviving CPR and substantial chances of cardiopulmonary arrest, few have discussions about DNR, even when put at special risk by being in a hospital. • Most legal advance directives are too non-specific, unavailable or inapplicable to direct care, yet patients think they have solved their problems by filling them out. • Almost no care planning deals with specific drugs, skills or procedures needed to allow the patient's preferences to be effected. • Some specific documented patient preferences are thoughtlessly abrogated.	• Regularly offering formal written planning opportunities • Area-wide advance planning • Emergency kit of drugs and other paraphernalia at home, appropriate to family training and professional availability. • Emergency response team to go to home for pain, dyspnea, seizures, family crisis, etc. • Formatted advance planning discussions	• Likely course, including urgent complications and major decision points, is articulated for all chronically ill patients. • "Last phase of life" is noted, negotiated and shared — among providers, patient and family — for >80% of dying. • Plans are written and discussed for likely "urgent complications" and for prolonged incompetence for every "last phase of life" patient. • Plans made in one setting or by one set of providers working with the patient and family are honored and confirmed, as appropriate, throughout the care system. • Plans for urgent complications are translated into specific service needs (ie. drugs, oxygen, etc.), and these are put in place in the appropriate settings. • CPR is allowed with strong patient/family preference, but is very rare. • Patients and families are not browbeaten into acquiescence with caregivers, nor are they brutalized by having to review painful decision too often.	1. CPR is attempted at death for <3% of patients who are known to be in the last phase of life. 2. Decrease unplanned admission by 50%. 3. A written care plan documents priorities and plans for >80% of "last phase of life" patients. 4. An appropriate surrogate is known (and documented if necessary) for 80% of those in the last phase of life. 5. 90% of those who die in the system of chronic disease are identified as dying two months earlier, and half are identified one year before death. 6. Patients and families are aware of the eventual fatal nature of disease for >75% of those so identified. 7. >80% of patients in families know what to do for worsening pain, dyspnea, or for cardiac arrest and know the signs of impending death and what to do. 8. Plans for after death (who should come to share that time, funeral, burial, family support) are made and documented for >50%. 9. ER and 911 use declines by 50% in a target population. 10. 80% of "last phase of life" patients at home have plans documented to shape 911/EMS response appropriately.

Pain/Symptoms

Current	Best Practices	Optimum Practice	Proposed Targets (for your population)
• Most often not assessed/monitored. • Routinely treated with predictably inadequate treatment (e.e., drugs and dosages). • Usually treated only after established, rather than preventively. • Gaps and delays in treatment are agonizing and commonplace. • Major symptoms are treatable: pain, dyspnea, depression, anxiety (also nausea, itching, insomnia). • No one held accountable for shortcomings. • Patients and families expect severe symptoms.	• 100% assessment on regular, recurrent basis, e.g., "5th vital sign" or item in nursing home quarterly review. • WHO/APS/AHCPR guidelines for cancer pain. • Low rate of use of opioids for breakthrough pain: all opioids on regular dosing. • Patients or families in control of dose timing. • Coverage doses travel with patient during transfers. • Serious symptoms considered appropriate for emergency response (stat page, rapid home visit, calling on back-up provider). • Performance routinely reviewed and shortcomings addressed. • Patients and families expect comfort.	• 100% assessment of pain, depression, dyspnea and anxiety on appropriate schedule (admission, change in status, and periodically). • Use of all appropriate modalities, often on time-limited trials — including opioids, biofeedback, hypnosis, steriods, neuroablative procedures, stimulants, etc. Severe symptoms always have appropriately aggressive response. • Ready availability of skilled consultants in all settings (including ICU, hospital, nursing home and home). • Patient and family expect competence, control and comfort, and are enabled to be active participants in deciding and providing. • Patient never left suffering due to relocation. • Emergency response "on call" for serious symptoms in any setting. • Routine care review and routine system feedback for quality improvement, public education and accreditation.	1. 100% compliance with recurrent assessment protocol. 2. Guarantee initial assessment of serious pain or dyspnea within 5 minutes in hospital, 15 minutes in nursing home or at home, and initial intervention within 15 minutes in hospital and 1 hour in nursing home or at home. 3. All patients have pain <5 (of 10) in last two days of life (by patient or family report). 4. Reduce by 50% the number of patients who report pain >5 (of 10) in any time period or episode of care. 5. All cancer patient with pain >5 (of 10) on appropriate opioids, and all patients with >5 (of 10) are on appropriate analgesics. 6. All patients at risk of severe dyspnea have "stand by" plans and needed skills/supplies in place. 7. Resource people with proven skills in chronic pain management and in managing neuropsychiatric complications of serious illness (depression, psychosis, delirium, anxiety, seizures) are readily available to every patient regardless of setting or insurance. 8. Eliminate times when patient or family reports pain being overwhelming or out of control. 9. Reduce "prn" for breakthrough pain to less than 20% of opioid use. 10. All patients/families understand the patient's symptoms and management and can adjust medications within agreed range. 11. All patients with depression have a trial of drug treatment. 12. Individual and regular shortcomings are noted and reviewed in incident reports, QI committee and credentials review.

Continuity/Transfers

Current	Best Practices	Optimum Practice	Proposed Targets (for your population)
• Seriously ill persons have no one who stays with them throughout. • Transfers between settings are dictated mostly by utilization and financing issues for the care system, not patient or family preferences. • Transfers among professionals are dictated by professional convenience. • Most patients change settings and/or caregivers multiple times in the last few weeks of life. • The fact and the expectation of discontinuity precludes intimacy, empathy, promise-making and trust. • Many transfers lose settled care plans, treatment schedules and understanding. • Frequent transfers mean no one is held accountable for the overall course — or even for there being a standard for a good course. • Transfer to hospice or nursing home is especially discontinuous, and transfer by EMS is routinely maximally life-extending.	• Hospice usually ensures continuity in all settings, once enrolled. • Some nursing homes have developed capacity to care for seriously ill resident on-site, including a "hospice-like" mode. • Some special "advanced illness" programs coordinate all care out of one office and keep one nurse/social worker/physician in charge of care throughout. • Some programs have coordinated records available at all sites electronically, or by having the patient carry the record, or both. • Some nursing homes or home care agencies have arranged for special direct hospital or hospice admission to avoid trauma in ambulances and ERs. • Some states and regions have developed accord on orders that reshape EMS services.	• People dying with cancer, advanced old age or dementia virtually always die where they live. Services should be mobilized to these settings. • People dying with strokes and organ system failures die at home (or nursing home) or in a hospital, but in either case under the care of those who know them and with appropriate services. • Utilization-induced transfer should almost never hapen in the last two days of life. • Switching key personnel while a patient is in any one setting should be uncommon and viewed as unfortunate, and should be the subject of careful planning to support patient and family. • Patients dying in ICU, ER or busy ward settings should have available more family attentive settings for temporary use.	1. For cancer patients >50% are in hospice >4 weeks and <20% are in hospice for <2 weeks. 2. >60% of those living at home with established fatal disease should die there, with good care. 3. <10% of deaths change setting in last two days. 4. 90% of families can name the one or two care providers who (together) were constant over the period when their family member was very ill. 5. 80% of those living in nursing homes should die there, with good care. 6. >80% of dying persons who have available an integrated care system should get all services from that system. 7. 50% of deaths from CHF, COPD, cirrhosis, and stroke have >4 weeks in hospice or another special end-of-life program. 8. Serious errors in transfer yield adverse events for all participants: review, payment penalty, QI. 9. DNR orders established in one setting are transferred to another (and confirmed when appropriate) all of the time. 10. <10% of deaths have change of physician in last two days. 11. Written care plan moves with or ahead of patient for every change of care setting. 12. 90% of families feel that they knew who was "in charge" and how to reach that person at all times.

Books, Guidelines and References

Editor's note: This list of books and guidelines on end-of-life care is not comprehensive and does not represent an endorsement of the products listed below.

• **American Academy of Hospice and Palliative Medicine** series of self-study booklets for physicians. (703)787-7718, www.aahpm.org

• ***Approaching Death: Improving Care at the End of Life,*** by the Committee on Care at the End of Life, Institute of Medicine, Marilyn J. Field and Christine K. Cassel, editors. Comprehensive overview of demographic, medical, financial, legal, educational, research, and cultural issues, challenges and recommendations. Includes extensive bibliographic and organizational resource lists, sample clinical assessment tools, and other resources. (800)624-6242, www.nap.edu

• ***Caring for the Dying: Identification and Promotion of Physician Competency*** (new ed. 1998), by American Board of Internal Medicine, (800)441-2246, www.abim.org

• **"Colorado Collective for Medical Decisions Draft Guidelines,"** 8 pages, outlines a framework and details 12 guidelines; includes substantial attention to neonatal end-of life care, no fee for up to 10 copies, nominal fee for bulk requests. CCMD, 777 Grant St., Suite 206, Denver, Colo. 80203, ccmdco@aol.com.

• **"Community Recommendations for Appropriate, Humane Medical Care for Dying or Irreversibly Ill Patients,"** 19 pages, $2. Outlines indicators for offering comfort care, strategies for acute care facilities, roles of key healthcare providers. Extreme Care, Human Options project of Sacramento Healthcare Decisions, 4747 Engle Rd., Carmichael, Calif. 95608.

• ***Dying Well: Peace and Possibilities at the End of Life***, Ira Byock, M.D., Putnam/Riverhead, $24.95 hard cover (ISBN 1573220515) and $14 soft cover (ISBN 573226572). For medical professionals as well as those who are dying and their loved ones.

• ***Handbook for Mortals***, from the Center to Improve Care of the Dying, to be printed by Oxford University Press this year. Pictures, poetry, role plays, stories and text on end-of-life care.

• **"Meeting the Challenge: Improving End-of-Life Care in Managed Care: 12 Recommendations for Access, Accountability and Cost."** A report of the national task force on end-of-life care in managed care, prepared under a grant from the Robert Wood Johnson Foundation by the Center for Applied Ethics and Professional Practice, Education Development Center Inc., 55 Chapel St. Newton Mass. 02158; www.edc.org/CAE. Free.

• ***The Oregon Death With Dignity Act: A Guidebook for Health Care Providers***, developed by the Task Force to Improve the Care of Terminally-Ill Oregonians, available for $15 from the Center for Ethics in Health Care, Oregon Health Sciences University, L101, 3181 Southwest Sam Jackson Park Rd., Portland, Ore. 97201

• ***The Oxford Textbook of Palliative Medicine,*** Second edition, for physicians and nurses.

• ***Palliative Care: Towards a Consensus in Standardized Principles of Practice***, by the Canadian Palliative Care Association, 286-43 BruyÀre St., Ottawa, Ontario KlN 5C8 Canada; (613)241-3663 or (800)668-2785; fax (613)562-4226. Outlines Canada's national standards process and includes model guidelines and information to help leaders in all practice settings and program models to develop and implement their own standards of practice. Available for $20 per copy, but U.S. and other international orders add $10 for shipping.

• ***A Pathway for Patients and Families Facing Terminal Illness***, by the National Hospice Organization, Arlington, Va., 1997. ISBN 0-931207-51-7. Presents in detail a comprehensive model for treating the dying and their families. (800)646-6460, www.nho.org

• **"Peaceful Death: Recommended Competencies and Curricular Guidelines for End-of-Life Nursing Care."** Guidelines for preservice nursing education that are applicable to inservice education by the American Association of Colleges of Nursing, 1 Dupont Circle, NW, Suite 530, Washington, D.C. 20036-1120, (202)463-6930, www.aacn.nche.edu

• ***Sourcebook on Dying for Health Care Managers***, by Center to Improve Care of the Dying, March 1999 from Oxford University Press.

• **"State Initiatives in End-of-Life Care: Policy Guide for State Legislators."** Produced by the National Council of State Legislatures and the Center to Improve Care of the Dying. (303)830-2200,

Dispensing by non-proprietary name is authorized if not checked in this column.

DATE	HOUR	Routine Admit Orders for Palliative Care Service		Nurse's Notation

Respiratory Therapy:

Yes ____ No ____ O_2 to maintain patient comfort

Other specific respiratory treatment: ________________________

IV Fluid orders: ________________________

Medications - Check if requested:

PAIN CONTROL GUIDELINES

Pain level (0-10) assessed by protocol.

A. For Pain Level 1-4

____ Ibuprofen 400 mg q 4 hrs

____ Acetaminophen 650 mg q 4 hrs

B. For Pain Level 5-10

____ Oxycodone 5 mg q 4 hrs & one 5 mg tablet q 4 hrs - breakthrough pain

____ Hydrocodone/acetaminophen 1-2 tablets q 4 hrs

____ Other ________________________

____

If pain not controlled after above measures, continue with the following:

____ Start immediate release concentrated morphone 20 mg/cc at 0.5cc q 3 hrs PRN for pain

____ For severe unrelenting pain, IV morphine 2-10 mg q 2 hrs PRN

____ Evaluate post 24 hrs and add long acting opiate PO, if appropriate

____ Sustained release morphine 30 mg q 12 hrs

____ Sustained release oxycodone 20 mg q 12 hrs

(continued on page 230)

Dispensing by non-proprietary name is authorized if not checked in this column.

DATE	HOUR	Routine Admit Orders for Palliative Care Service		Nurse's Notation

Bowel Regimen

_____ Senna/docusate 2 po hs and titrate doubling dose qd for stool q 24 hrs
_____ MOM 30 cc qd PRN
_____ Bisacodyl suppository qd PRN
_____ Lactulose 30 cc po q 6 hrs until stool, if no stool after 48 hrs

Anxiety/Agitation

_____ Lorazepam 0.5 - 1.0 mg po or IV q 4 hrs PRN

Severe Dyspnea

_____ Oxycodone 5 or 10 mg q 4 hrs PRN in the opiate naive patient
_____ Morphine Concentrate (20 mg/cc) 0.5 - 1.0 cc q 3 hrs PRN

Nausea and Emesis

_____ Prochlorperazine spansules 15 mg tab q 12 hrs PRN
_____ Metoclopramide 10 mg tab q 4 hrs PRN
_____ Prochlorperazine 10 mg po or IV q 6 hrs
_____ Haloperidol 1 mg po hrs PRN
_____ Lorazepam 1 mg po or IV q 6 hrs PRN

Severe Anorexia

_____ Trial of Megestrol 40 mg/20cc, 20 cc qd
_____ Trial of Prednisone, 20 mg po qd

Depression

_____ Trial of antidepressant, Sertraline 50 mg qd
_____ Consultation with psychologist

Oral Care

_____ Nystatin 5 cc swish and swallow for oral candidates qid

Other Orders:

Reprinted with permission of North Kansas City Hospital

Organizations and Information Sources

The following organizations are among those that offer information or other resources related to end-of-life care.

Agency for Health Care Policy and Research
Clinical guidelines, including pain management
www.ahcpr.gov/clinic
American Academy of Hospice and Palliative Medicine
(352)377-8900

American Association of Colleges of Nursing
(202)463-6930
www.aacn.nche.edu

American Board of Internal Medicine,
Project to Improve End-of-Life Patient Care
(215)446-3500
www.abim.org

American Geriatrics Society
(212)308-1414
www.americangeriatrics.org

American Medical Association's Education for Physicians on End-of-Life Care project
(312)464-5944
www.ama-assn.org/EPEC

Americans for Better Care of the Dying
(202)530-9864
www.abcd-caring.com

Center for Ethics In Healthcare Oregon Health Sciences University
ethics@oshu.edu
www.ohsu.edu/ethics

Center to Improve Care of the Dying
George Washington University
(202)467-2222
www.gwu.edu/~cicd

Growth House (Web resource)
www.growthhouse.org

Hospice Association of America
(202)546-4759

Hospice Foundation of America
(202)638-5419
www.hospicefoundation.org

Hospice Nurses Association
(412)361-2470

Institute for Healthcare Improvement
(617)754-4800
www.ihi.org

Institute of Medicine
(1997 report, *Approaching Death*)
www.nap.edu/readingroom

National Hospice Organization
(703)243-5900
www.nho.org

Project on Death in America
(212)887-0150
www.soros.org/death.html

Robert Wood Johnson Foundation
Last Acts Project
(816)842-7110, ext. 239
www.rwjf.org
Promoting Excellence in End-of-Life Care
www.dyingwell.com
State/Community Partnerships to Improve End-of-Life Care
Midwest Bioethics Center
(816)842-7110, www.midbio.org

Funding Resources

The following is a sampling of philanthropic organizations and federal agencies that have funded healthcare projects and research related to palliative care, pain management, bereavement and other end-of-life issues.

Emily Davie & Joseph S. Kornfeld Foundation

Funds: Projects related to medical ethics, care of the dying and relief of pain, primarily in New York and Virginia.

Contact: Fenella Rouse, Executive Director, 30 Rockefeller Plaza, 55th Fl., New York, N.Y. 10112, (212)649-5800, fdncenter.org/grantmaker/kornfeld/index.html

Meyer Memorial Trust

Funds: Projects on health, including aging, in Oregon and other Northwest states.

Contact: Charles Rooks, Executive Director, 1515 SW 5th Ave, Suite 500, Portland Ore. 97201, (503)228-5512

Charles Culpeper Foundation Inc.

Funds: Organizations in the United States conducting research on social, ethical and other issues in human health and disease.

Contact: Mary Ellen Bucci, Financial Centre, 695 E. Main St., Suite 300, Stamford, Conn. 06901, (203)975-1240, www.culpeper.org

Nathan Cummings Foundation Inc.

Funds: Care that improves quality of life at the end of life

Contact: Charles Halpern, 1926 Broadway, Suite 600, New York, N.Y. 10023, (212)787-7300, www.ncf.org

Dorothy Rider Pool Health Care Trust

Funds: Lehigh Valley, Pa.-area development of health leadership in areas such as end-of-life ethics.

Contact: Edward Meehan, 1050 Cedar Crest Blvd., Suite 202, Allentown, Pa. 18103, (610)770-9346

Mayday Fund

Funds: U.S. research on better pain control, including the reduction of its psychological and physican consequences.

Contact: Fenella Rouse, 30 Rockefeller Plaza, 55th Fl. , New York, N.Y. 10112, (212)649-5800, fdncenter.org/grantmaker/maydaty/index.html

Robert Wood Johnson Foundation

Funds: U.S. healthcare projects related to access, drug and alcohol abuse, chronic health conditions and cost containment.

Contact: Edward Robbins, P.O. Box 2316, Princeton, N.J. 08543, (609)452-8701 www.rwjf.org, www.lastacts.org

Open Society Institute

Funds: The Project on Death in America is launching a new humanities and arts fund to more broadly portray the experience of illness, suffering, death and dying.

Contact: 400 W 59th St., New York, N.Y. 10019, www.soros.org/ death/rfa.html

National Institutes of Health

For these institutes, issues such as palliative care, pain management and improved quality of care for elderly patients are of critical and continuing concern:
National Cancer Institute
National Institute on Aging
National Institute of Nursing Research
National Institute of Neurological Disorders and Stroke
National Center for Nursing Research

See www.nih.gov/grants/funding/funding.htm for general NIH

Expanding Pharmacy's Role to Reduce Drug-Related Problems

Quality goes up and costs go down when pharmacists are part of the healthcare team, monitoring use of medications for potential problems and recommending better choices for treating the patient.

Health systems looking for greater efficiency may be overlooking a valuable resource — their pharmacists. Expanding pharmacists' role beyond drug dispensing, involving them in direct patient care as part of a multidisciplinary team, is helping systems such as Kaiser Permanente and Lee Memorial Hospital in Ft. Lauderdale, Fla., save thousands of dollars by preventing drug-related illness and encouraging use of cost-effective medications.

Medication use crosses all disciplines and, given the burgeoning number of drugs available to treat diseases and the increased potency of those drugs, opportunities for problems related to medication misuse have escalated. Today, drug-related problems are a major cause of hospitalization and illness throughout the nation. According to a 1995 report in the *Archives of Internal Medicine*, illness and death related to medication use cost an estimated $76.6 billion annually in the United States. This figure, which applies only to drug-related problems in ambulatory patients and does not include those stricken while hospitalized, amounts to approximately $300 per man, woman and child in the country every year. These costs relate to direct outlays for hospitalization, physician care and emergency department visits; indirect costs to society from loss of work and productivity were not considered. Problems the study takes into account range from getting the wrong drug or taking a drug that's not needed, to having a deadly reaction — problems that, in many cases, could be avoided *(see Quality Agenda, pp 243-244)*.

"Pharmacists can play a major role in preventing and resolving drug-related problems and minimizing their overall economic impact," says Lyle Bootman, Ph.D., dean of the University of Arizona College of Pharmacy and co-author of the study. "This is what they're trained to do, but in many environments they aren't being used to potential."

The Pharmaceutical Care Model

Dr. Bootman, like other pharmacy leaders and a growing number of healthcare experts, advocates an approach called "pharmaceutical care," in which pharmacists work with physicians, nurses, other providers and patients to prevent, identify and resolve drug-related problems. In this model of care, pharmacists have key responsibility for:

- recommending effective medications;
- ensuring that patients receive the correct drugs and dosage;

From *The Quality Letter for Healthcare Leaders*, Vol. 8:10, 1996

- counseling patients so they understand how to take their medications and can recognize potential problems;
- monitoring patients to ensure that drugs are working as intended; and
- educating other providers about appropriate drug therapy.

They assist with patient care in a proactive way, going far beyond the stereotypical "counting, pouring, licking and sticking." Their activities not only help ensure quality care but also save money by catching problems before they escalate and by allowing higher-paid physicians to concentrate a larger share of their efforts on complex cases.

> **"Drugs are front-line medical treatments. In medical circles we call them 'noninvasive,' but in actual fact you are inserting potentially dangerous chemicals into the body."**
>
> **Henri Manasse, Ph.D.**
> **American Society of Health-System Pharmacists**

Pharmacists at University Medical Center in Jacksonville, Fla., work alongside physicians and nurses in outpatient clinics on rheumatology, hypertension, diabetes and other diseases to recommend the safest, most effective drug therapies and ensure that patients are getting the expected benefit. Pharmacists help physicians work more efficiently by meeting with patients first, before the physician examines them, to take a medication history and pinpoint medication-related problems.

Pharmacists at the center also manage five clinics — asthma, sumatriptan treatment for migraine, lipid management, anticoagulation therapy and prescription refills — to assess the effectiveness of therapy and identify problems. Pharmacists' efforts are aimed not only at improving patient outcomes but also at cutting down on hospital admissions. Their services are in such demand that they have to prioritize carefully, focusing on the sickest patients.

Group Health Cooperative of Puget Sound, in the Seattle area, assigns pharmacists to patient-care areas to counsel patients and consult with physicians. For example, in a family practice site that trains medical residents, the physician typically examines the patient, makes a diagnosis and then confers with the pharmacist to determine the best medication based on effectiveness and cost. The pharmacist, who has complete access to the patient's chart and lab findings, looks for drug interactions or allergies and verifies that the dosage and regimen are correct before entering the prescription into a computer. The pharmacist then meets with the patient in a counseling area to discuss proper use of the medication and to answer questions.

Pharmacists at Group Health also evaluate new therapies and advise clinicians on their use; serve on steering committees for targeted disease management areas such as heart disease and diabetes; and play a leading role in anticoagulation clinics, smoking cessation programs and other areas where patient compliance is a major issue.

At Lee Memorial Hospital in Ft. Myers, Fla., each unit has a pharmacist liaison who works cooperatively with other caregivers to avoid drug-related problems and to educate nurses and physicians about options, such as using lower-cost oral tablets rather than intravenous formulations in patients who are able to swallow. Pharmacists focus on use of drugs with a narrow therapeutic index — those drugs for which the amount needed to treat disease is close to the toxic level — checking the lab findings to see if any patients show elevated levels of the drug and, if so, figure out why. They review lab data on kidney function daily to see if some patients could be having problems eliminating drugs from their system; they monitor culture and sensitivity data to be sure the best and most cost-effective antibiotics are prescribed; and they collect information to help the patient care team respond to trends such as increasing numbers of adverse effects or rising costs associated with particular medication therapies. For example, after noticing several adverse drug reactions in patients taking theophylline, the pharmacists presented an educational seminar for physicians about alternative therapies for asthma patients; subsequently the use of theophylline dropped sharply.

Lee Memorial pharmacists also participate in multidisciplinary teams that formulate care paths for patients with specific disorders such as stroke or chronic obstructive pulmonary disease.

"People often think of pharmacy as the department down in the bowels of the hospital that sends up things. Here pharmacists perform clinical monitoring and are an advocate for the patient."

Bill Johnson
Chief Operating Officer
Lee Memorial Hospital

Looking at the Big Picture

"When I started out in pharmacy practice in the mid-1960s, only something in the neighborhood of 650 drugs were licensed in the U.S.," notes Henri Manasse, Ph.D., of the American Society of Health-System Pharmacists. "Today we have almost 10,000 drugs and dosage forms in the marketplace. Drugs are front-line medical treatments. In medical circles we call them 'noninvasive,' but in actual fact you are inserting potentially dangerous chemicals into the body. That's why we've got to work in a team fashion with prescribers, patients and other health professionals to use medications effectively and minimize errors and adverse effects."

Dr. Manasse notes that pharmacy schools have expanded their curriculums to six years to accommodate in-depth coursework on pharmacology, pharmacokinetics, problem solving and case management. Pharmacists are trained to look for interactions, contraindications and errors in prescriptions; to educate patients on proper medication use and side effects; to monitor chronic conditions and assess patients for signs of overdose or lack of drug effectiveness; and to find acceptable alternatives when a certain drug has too many side effects, is too hard for the patient to take or costs too much — all good reasons why pharmacists are well equipped to help healthcare systems provide optimal care.

"It's difficult for nurses and physicians to stay as up-to-date with the vast world of pharmacology as they need to be, so they call on pharmacists for assistance," says Bill Johnson, chief operating officer at Lee Memorial. "Our pharmacists are well accepted on the healthcare team because there's a high level of trust, an understanding of each other's roles and a sense that everybody is working toward the same goal — better patient outcomes."

But even administrators who know of pharmacists' wide-ranging skills may not make the most of them because they do not look at the big picture or are not convinced that spending more to involve pharmacists in drug monitoring and patient care will cut costs in other areas, such as hospitalization. Cynthia Griffin, Pharm.D., head of pharmacy ambulatory care at Jacksonville's University Medical Center, notes that "hiring a pharmacist at $50,000 to $60,000 per year to do anticoagulation monitoring will save that much in a week if his or her efforts prevent one patient from an intracranial hemorrhage and intensive care. But the sticky issue is, you don't often know when you've prevented a serious adverse effect."

Marie Kelley, senior vice president for acute care and operations at Our Lady of the Lake Regional Medical Center in Baton Rouge, La.,

INITIATIVE TO REDUCE MEDICATION ERRORS UNDER WAY

Finding ways to reduce adverse drug events in healthcare facilities is the focus of a major collaborative effort, the Breakthrough Series Collaborative on Reducing Adverse Drug Events and Medical Errors, initiated by Boston-based Institute for Healthcare Improvement.

"We've focused on implementing changes in all phases of medication use, from medication ordering to dispensing by pharmacists and administration by nurses," says Lucian Leape, M.D., adjunct professor of health policy, Department of Health Policy and Management of Harvard School of Public Health and chairman of the Collaborative.

Forty healthcare organizations — including 50 hospitals — have implemented changes based on principles learned from human factors research. Looking for ways to standardize medication handling, they focus on the basics — procedures and processes that should be in place in hospitals to reduce the likelihood of errors:

1. Enforce standardized prescription writing — for example, use no abbreviations; eliminate the use of "u."
2. Work on handwriting problems.
3. Standardize the information presented on prescription orders.
4. Follow protocols for use of problematic drugs like insulin, heparin and warfarin.
5. Use unit dosing and error-prevention packaging.
6. Ensure that allergy information is accurately and prominently displayed.
7. Check computerized databases for potential problems in the drug profile.
8. Provide 24-hour availability of medications.

The breakthrough series effort is twofold: it is *multidisciplinary*, including pharmacists, nurses, quality assurance staff and physicians; and it is *collaborative*, emphasizing the exchange of information, with monthly conference calls and e-mail, says Dr. Leape.

Different groups are tackling different problems. For example, one group is working to standardize the chemotherapy process.

"The emphasis of the breakthrough series is to take unused information on proven techniques for improving systems and find ways to get it to the people," says Dr. Leape. Healthcare organizations involved make some real changes, tackle obstacles and find ways to overcome them.

"Each project has its own bag of worms," he says. "These groups have shown a great deal of innovation in dealing with problems."

One question that comes up with any change is how to measure improvements. "With drug use, there is no automatic measure like we see with reducing cesarean sections — you can count the number of C-sections that you do, and you know why you do them," says Dr. Leape. "So we were looking for measures. It's hard to show the teams have dropped the rate of errors, but they know certain types of errors should not happen again."

Fairview Health System has worked on this project since it began in October 1995, says pharmacist Steve Meisel, PharmD. "We've had pharmacists in the nursing units for years," he notes. "And any given month we can show data on pharmacists' involvement. For instance, we know that in October, pharmacists clarified 913 orders and intervened in 623 — and one-third of the interventions were categorized as potential adverse drug events."

firmly believes that pharmacists play an important clinical role. "But it's hard to quantify that spending extra on pharmacists saves money somewhere else," she says. "I feel I need to be cautious." Her 685-bed hospital employs five clinical pharmacists who consult with medical staff on the treatment of pediatric, oncology, geriatric and critical care patients; handle pharmacokinetics to be sure drugs are administered at the most effective level and are not toxic to the patient; calculate and recommend dosages; help develop clinical pathways in collaboration with other health professionals; and serve on clinical pathway teams to ensure that proper therapies are administered according to predetermined standards of care. She projects that in the current fiscal year, eight specific clinical pharmacy programs will save the hospital $600,000.

"Some of these savings will come about by changing from expensive to less costly medications, but some are what I call 'soft' savings — identifying a drug interaction or toxic drug level and preventing an extended length of stay," she says. "Soft savings are nice, but I have a tendency to want to see that my costs for expensive drugs like aminoglycosides or cephalosporins are down this year compared with last."

"Some savings will come about by changing from expensive to less costly medications, but some are ... soft savings — identifying a drug interaction or toxic drug level and preventing an extended length of stay."

Marie Kelley
Senior Vice President, Acute Care and Operations
Our Lady of the Lake Regional Medical Center

Improving Outcomes and Saving Money

Stories from pharmacists help paint a picture of the impact they have in patient care. Dr. Griffin of the University Medical Center says that a patient who recently complained of heartburn was taking her heart medicine only once a day instead of three times as prescribed. "She said it made her heart 'beat too fast,'" Dr. Griffin notes. The patient was switched to a once-a-day medication that did not increase her heart rate, and her pain — most likely angina — was resolved. Without pharmacist involvement, the problem could easily have gone undetected and landed the patient in the emergency room. "Physicians don't have the time to go over every detail with patients," Dr. Griffin says. "We ask the patients whether they take their drugs, whether the drugs are working and what problems they're having. We get everything from 'I can't afford them,' to 'My medicine makes me feel bad.' Many times we can find an alternative that costs less or avoids unpleasant or harmful side effects."

Nancy Louie Lee, director of pharmacy clinical services for Kaiser Permanente's Northwest Division in Portland, Ore., notes that when pharmacists stepped in to handle dosing and monitoring for niacin — the institution's lipid-lowering agent of choice — the percentage of patients sticking with the drug rose from 20% to 80%. "Because niacin can cause bothersome side effects, like flushing and gastrointestinal problems, it requires proper dosing and a lot of patient education." The program has reduced lipid levels and drug costs — niacin costs much less than the other lipid-lowering drugs — without increasing costs in other areas, and surveys show it brings about high patient satisfaction.

A second report, published in October 1997 by Dr. Bootman suggests that implementing pharmaceutical care in the ambulatory setting would save U.S. healthcare $30.9 billion annually, reducing the cost of medication-related illness and death to roughly $45 billion. His research used a probability pathway model in which pharmacists estimated the likelihood of drug-related problems and determined the probable result (hospitalization, office visit, etc.) in a typical group of 100 clinic patients.

A study by pharmacy professor David Bates and colleagues, published in the Jan. 22-29,1997, *Journal of the American Medical Association,* found that the cost of drug-related problems in patients hospitalized at two Boston-based hosptials — Brigham and Women's Hospital and Massachussetts General Hospital — totaled $5.6 million. Preventable adverse effects accounted for fully half that number.

SEVEN STEPS FOR STARTING A PHARMACEUTICAL CARE PROGRAM

1. Start where the biggest gains are likely to be realized.
2. Prioritize pharmacists' use by assigning them to work in areas with the most pressing needs.
3. Document all efforts and results to win organizational support.
4. Emphasize a multidisciplinary approach.
5. Build trust and rapport among caregivers.
6. Promote good communication skills among patient care team members.
7. Put effective systems in place for work flow, documentation and other procedures.

Pharmacists should check reports of adverse drug events and medication errors routinely to determine ways to prevent problems, Prof. Schneider notes. For example, when they saw a high rate of adverse reactions in patients known to be allergic to penicillin, they discovered that often the provider didn't know the product prescribed contained penicillin. Because of this, they recommended that drugs that can cause allergic reactions not be kept as floor stock. Nurses are now required to have the drugs dispensed through the pharmacy so their appropriateness can be checked first. "Without data like these, you might have conflicts between nurses and pharmacists," he points out, "but when we show that a strategy reduces allergic reactions by 50% compared with the previous year, everyone sees it's the best course of action. If someone says, 'We can't afford the pharmacists' time to do this,' you can counter with hard data on how much money you're saving by preventing adverse reactions."

MedOutcomes, a pharmaceutical care consulting firm in Richmond, Va., that trains pharmacists to tackle drug therapy problems for specific chronic diseases, completed a two-year study of nearly 200 patients in 1996 to determine what savings, based on insurance claims, are realized when community pharmacists take part in patient care. Community pharmacists in a retail chain provided ongoing patient education about a number of medical conditions (diabetes, asthma, hypertension and hypercholesterolemia), did limited assessments such as blood pressure and cholesterol readings, monitored drug therapy, formulated and followed up on therapeutic plans and maintained contact with patients' physicians. Average monthly costs were $206.17 lower per patient per month than costs for a control group that did not receive these pharmacy services. "The money saved is cold, hard cash for hospitalization, diagnostics and emergency room visits," says Wendy Munroe, PharmD, the firm's president. As for clinical impact, blood pressure was reduced an average of 2% in the first six months and 4% in the second six months; total cholesterol was reduced an average of 11.6 mg/dL compared to baseline.

Donald Berwick, M.D., a practicing pediatrician and president of the Institute for Healthcare Improvement, a nonprofit education and research organization, believes that making pharmacists an active part of the healthcare team, along with physicians, nurses and administrators, is an important step to reduce drug-related problems and errors. "Among things that we know help reduce errors are pharmacists going on rounds with clinical teams, face-to-face communication between physicians and pharmacists, and physicians taking more care to inform pharmacists not only of the drug they're ordering, but also of the reasons for the order," he says.

Dr. Manasse believes that quality management personnel could use a wake-up call about pharmacists' value. "Most probably don't have much contact with pharmacy, but they need to, because the issue of drug-related problems has risk management and legal implications for an institution, and has direct bearing on the quality of care." Anything that goes wrong in the prescribing, dispensing, administration or management of medications could harm the patient and open up the health system to lawsuits, he says. Making the most of pharmacists' skills helps reduce errors and adverse effects, which lessens risk.

NINE OBSTACLES TO PHARMACEUTICAL CARE

1. Healthcare administrators with narrow views of what pharmacists can do.
2. Lack of access to medical charts, lab reports and other patient information.
3. Expecting too much too soon.
4. Laws that restrict the use of pharmacy technicians for dispensing tasks.
5. The need to break old habits and accept new roles.
6. The need to update the knowledge and skills of older pharmacists.
7. A general lack of awareness that medication errors and adverse drug events are serious problems.
8. Turf battles.
9. Competition for resources in the healthcare system.

How to Get Started

Healthcare system leaders should incorporate the following seven steps when seeking to maximize pharmacists' contributions to patient care:

1. Start where the biggest gains are likely to be realized. Areas like oncology, where drug regimens are complex and potentially lethal; pediatrics, where dosing is not clearcut; and psychiatric care, in which the drugs used can have serious side effects, are good places to start. Targeting vulnerable groups, such as the elderly who often take many drugs at once, and chronic conditions that carry big price tags but respond well to early intervention and intensive monitoring, such as diabetes, asthma, and heart disease, is also a good idea. Kaiser Permanente's Nancy Louie Lee advises starting with a "win-win" situation, where everyone benefits. "Don't start with a difficult area that's very sensitive."

2. Prioritize. It's hard to launch pharmaceutical care throughout a healthcare organization in one fell swoop. Look at your patient population and try to meet the most pressing needs first or test the approach in one discrete area. Lee Memorial initially tried the concept in its orthopedics unit, which was reorganized several years ago according to a patient-centered care model, and had such a high level of success that pharmacists were gradually added to other units throughout the system.

3. Document all efforts and results. Data garnered from these records can be crucial in winning organizational support. For example, Lee Memorial can show that $22,622 was saved in 1995 because of pharmacists' recommendations on antibiotics. Outcomes must be documented, too; cost is not always the best indicator of success. Drug costs go up when patients are put on lipid therapy or asthma medication, says Donna Beall, Pharm.D., primary care clinical pharmacy services administrator at Kaiser Permanente's Rocky Mountain Division, but the result is fewer hospital admissions. Since March 1996, patients have been treated on an outpatient basis with low-molecular-weight heparin for deep-vein thrombosis — an approach that requires careful monitoring and counseling by clinical pharmacy specialists, but avoids a three- to five-day hospital stay.

> **"It would be a mistake just to say to pharmacists 'Go out and solve drug-related problems' without having defined their roles and practice area."**
>
> **Bill Baluch**
> **Director, Medication Use Management**
> **Group Health Cooperative of Puget Sound**

4. **Emphasize a multidisciplinary approach**. Pharmacists can't improve drug therapy alone; they must work on a team with other healthcare providers. Physicians must understand that pharmacists are not trying to practice medicine — that they are simply enhancing services for better patient care. Pharmacists, on their end, need to work cooperatively and keep other providers in the information loop. To promote multidisciplinary work, it's helpful to station pharmacists in patient care units so they are visible and accessible.

5. **Build trust and rapport**. Because pharmacists are moving into new territory, other healthcare providers may not know what pharmacists can do. The best way they can win another clinician's confidence is by demonstrating professional skill. "Once physicians see you perform a task reliably, they'll release it to you," says Connie Hogrefe, pharmacy clinical specialist at Lee Memorial. "Physicians are kind of like parents — they don't want to leave their child with a babysitter until they know that person is knowledgeable and trustworthy."

6. **Promote good communication skills**. For pharmacists' communications with physicians to be effective, they must be focused, direct and nonconfrontational. Some pharmacists may need additional training to learn how to make recommendations in an assertive but nonthreatening way. One savvy technique Ms. Hogrefe advocates is having pharmacists phrase recommendations as questions, such as "Would you consider...?" It's also helpful to formulate ahead of time standard phraseology — familiar to all providers — for all pharmacists to use.

7. **Put effective systems in place** for work flow, documentation and other procedures. Healthcare organizations with sophisticated online capability for storing patient data and recording interventions have an advantage because they allow pharmacists easy access to important information. A number of pharmaceutical care consulting firms have sprung up in the past few years to help facilities reengineer their pharmacy services and permit greater pharmacist/patient interaction.

Obstacles to Pharmaceutical Care

Dr. Manasse admits that certain hurdles must be surmounted before pharmaceutical care becomes widespread — some institutional, some personal, some endemic to the healthcare system. Near the top of the list, he says, are "healthcare administrators with narrow views of what pharmacists can do." Other obstacles include:

■ **Lack of access to medical charts, lab reports and other patient information**. In some settings, especially community pharmacies, pharmacists are getting around this problem by compiling health and medication histories from patient-supplied information and by performing limited assessments such as blood pressure readings and cholesterol measurements. A growing number of healthcare systems such as Kaiser Permanente give pharmacists full access to pertinent patient information.

■ **Expecting too much too soon.** If pharmaceutical care is not started in a small, well-defined area, if the proper systems are not in place for documentation and work flow and if a team approach is not emphasized, efforts may fall apart. Bill Baluch, director of medication use management at Group Health Cooperative of Puget Sound, cautions against underestimating the time and effort needed to move pharmacists into patient care and defining pharmacists' roles.

■ **Laws that restrict the use of pharmacy technicians**. These laws are changing, but right now some states make it tough for pharmacists to turn over the bulk of their dispensing-related tasks to technicians to free their time for pharmaceutical care.

■ **The need to break old habits and accept new roles**. Pharmacists have focused on the distribution end of medications for so long that some find it difficult to shift their thinking and actions to accommodate pharmaceutical care. "We've relinquished a lot of responsibility for dispensing to our technicians," notes Dr. Griffin, "but sometimes we forget and do things we don't have to do anymore." And some pharmacists simply do not want to change.

■ **The need to update the knowledge and skills of older pharmacists**. Those who graduated more than 15 years ago may not have been clinically trained. "The paradigm of pharmaceutical care represents a significant change over a short time," points out Lucinda Maine, senior vice-president for professional affairs at the American Pharmaceutical Association. "Back in the '60s, pharmacists weren't even supposed to talk to patients, let alone counsel them about their therapy or monitor their progress."

Other problems Dr. Manasse cites are a general lack of awareness that medication errors and adverse drug events are serious problems, turf battles and competition for resources in healthcare systems. Despite these obstacles, a growing number of health systems are turning to pharmaceutical care and finding it worthwhile. Dr. Beall notes that when she joined Kaiser Permanente's Rocky Mountain Division staff five years ago, there were only three clinical pharmacy specialists, but clinical demand for their services expanded so fast that more than 25 now work throughout the organization.

Lee Memorial's Bill Johnson laughs when asked what he would say to health system leaders skeptical about the value of expanding pharmacy's role. "Try it, you'll like it," he says. "Pharmacists are an untapped resource; we all underestimate their knowledge and capability. I feel certain that bringing them onto the patient care team pays dividends."

QUALITY agenda

Drug Therapy Assessment: Areas of Focus

Drug-related illness can result from many factors, including the patient's condition or lifestyle, the combination of medications prescribed and inappropriate medications or dosages. Because the reason for medication problems can be complex, a systematic method for solving clinical problems — called the "Clinical Skills Program: Advancing Pharmaceutical Care" — was developed by the American Society of Health-System Pharmacists. The program includes five modules that teach skills in designing, assessing, recommending, monitoring and evaluating patient-specific pharmacotherapy.

For assessing a patient's current drug therapy and identifying problems, the following checklist is recommended:

Assessing Drug Therapy

Correlation Between Drug Therapy and Medical Problems

YES NO

___ ___ Is the patient taking any drugs without a medical indication?

___ ___ Are any drugs unidentified or unlabeled?

___ ___ Are there any untreated medical conditions requiring drug therapy?

Appropriate Drug Selection

YES NO

___ ___ What is the comparative efficacy of the chosen medications?

___ ___ What is the relative safety?

___ ___ Has therapy been tailored to this individual patient?

Drug Regimen

YES NO

___ ___ Are the prescribed dose and dosing frequency appropriate for the condition?

___ ___ Are the route, dosage form and mode of administration appropriate in light of efficacy, safety, convenience, patient limitations and cost?

___ ___ Are the doses scheduled to maximize therapeutic effect and compliance, and to minimize adverse effects, drug interactions and complexity of the regimen?

Therapeutic Duplication

YES NO

___ ___ Are there any therapeutic duplications?

Drug Allergy or Intolerance

YES NO

___ ___ Is the patient allergic to or intolerant of any medicines or chemical agents being taken?

___ ___ Is the patient using any method to alert healthcare providers of the problem?

Adverse Drug Events

YES NO

___ ___ Does the patient have any symptoms or medical problems that may be drug induced? What is the likelihood they are drug related?

Interactions

YES NO

___ ___ Are there any drug-drug, drug-nutrient or drug-laboratory test interactions? Are they clinically significant?

___ ___ Are any drugs contraindicated given patient characteristics and current or past diseases?

Recreational Drug Use

YES NO

___ ___ Is the patient's use of social drugs problematic?

___ ___ Could the sudden decrease or discontinuation of social drugs be related to the patient's symptoms (such as withdrawal)?

Failure to Receive Therapy

YES NO

___ ___ Has the patient failed to receive therapy due to a system error or noncompliance?

___ ___ Are there any factors hindering therapeutic efficacy?

Financial Impact

YES NO

___ ___ Are the chosen medications cost-effective?

___ ___ Is the cost of drug therapy a financial hardship for the patient?

Additional Resources

Additional Resources

For a sample copy of the publications referenced in this book, call Aspen Publishers' customer service department at (800)234-1660 and use the following product codes:

The Quality Letter for Healthcare Leaders (#TQL)

The Quality Letter is the most authoritative resource available devoted to healthcare quality improvement, providing practical tips on the latest proven strategies. Detailed case studies highlight successful ways to apply continuous improvement principles and tools to increase efficiency, boost service and improve clinic outcomes. Get practical tips to improve HCO processes and increase profits while maintaining quality patient care. See how lower costs result from doing things better rather than simply cheaper. Before it's on the agenda of your Quality Council or QI committee, you'll have read about it in *The Quality Letter for Healthcare Leaders.*

Russ Coile's Health Trends (#HSR)

Use this extraordinary resource to discover the latest innovative, results-oriented approaches that facilities are using to compete and thrive in the increasingly competitive health care environment: what to do, how to do it and how to increase revenues and leverage the resources available. You'll find creative strategies and tactics in marketing, law, management, finance and planning. This newsletter offers insight into the rapidly changing health care environment, focusing on alternative delivery systems, after-care diversification strategies, new revenue sources, creative financing and new business.

Quality Management in Health Care (#QMHC)

This peer-reviewed quarterly journal provides a forum to explore the theoretical, technical and strategic elements of total quality management in health care. Each issue of *Quality Management in Health Care* features a timely symposium that addresses a critical issue in health care quality management. Also included in each issue is an in-depth interview with a key individual in health care quality management, an educational tutorial on basic quality management tools and processes, an information clearinghouse to encourage informal communication between those involved in the field of health care quality management, and a reference center that reviews books, journal articles, seminars and videos of interest. *QMHC* is indexed in Hospital and Health Administration Index, Health Planning and Administration Database, SilverPlatter Information, and UP-TO-DATE Library/Health Services Management.

QRC Advisor (#QRC)

This outstanding monthly newsletter offers sound, authoritative advice for effectively handling your quality assurance, risk management and cost control issues. Twelve times a year, *QRC Advisor* brings you 12 full pages of practical, stimulating, contemporary articles describing the latest developments in your field. Contains sound advice on how to get more from your quality assurance programs, insiders topics on meeting new Joint Commission standards, and updates on legislative and regulatory body rulings. Each information-packed issue is brimming with the valuable insights of seasoned professionals, experts in the field.

Journal of Nursing Care Quality (#633)

Now the *Journal of Nursing Care Quality* brings the future of information technology to your desktop! To help you meet new quality demands in a changing health care system, *JNCQ* has been extensively re-vamped and expanded. Now a three-part, full-service information package, *JNCQ* includes: six issues per year; an eight-page newsletter, *Pat Schroeder's Performance Improvement, Ideas & Innovations* (PI3), bound into every issue. With more proven strategies for improving health care quality, accountability, outcomes and performance, *JNCQ* is practical, comprehensive and timely.

9 780834 216075

Printed by Amazon Italia Logistica S.r.l.
Torrazza Piemonte (TO), Italy

10649741R00145